P9-CKT-742

Twayne's English Authors Series

Sylvia E. Bowman, *Editor*

INDIANA UNIVERSITY

Sir James Barrie

Sir James Barrie

By HARRY M. GEDULD
Indiana University

Twayne Publishers, Inc. :: New York

Copyright © 1971 by Twayne Publishers, Inc.
All Rights Reserved

Library of Congress Catalog Card Number: 77-120524

PR
4077
.G4

MANUFACTURED IN THE UNITED STATES OF AMERICA

66772

For Carolyn

Acknowledgments

To Charles Scribner's Sons for permission to quote from *Margaret Ogilvy* by James Barrie (Charles Scribner's Sons, 1896) and to quote the verse on p. 95 of Barrie's *Peter Pan* (The Scribner Library of Books for Young Readers, SL84, Charles Scribner's Sons, 1950).

Preface

The decline of Barrie's reputation is an outstanding example of the fickleness of literary fashion. After achieving great popular success as a journalist and novelist, he turned to the theater and rapidly earned acclaim on both sides of the Atlantic as an innovator in the drama. R. L. Stevenson and Bernard Shaw were among the many notable writers who echoed the plaudits of his contemporaries. His plays attracted some of the greatest acting talent of the age. His fiction reaped a fortune. He was lionized by the British and American public, and honored by distinctions conferred on him by his sovereign. But in the decade before his death in 1937, Barrie's plays became démodé; his novels, already regarded as quaintly Victorian, were mostly out of print; and Barrie himself was being bypassed by a new generation who had outgrown his and Mary Pickford's sentimentality.

Since the age of the flapper, only *Peter Pan,* and to a lesser extent, *The Admirable Crichton,* have continued to keep Barrie's name before the public. Like Swift and Defoe, but with far more justification, he has been popularly relegated to the nursery. Occasional revivals and film and television adaptations of some of his works have failed to reawaken widespread public interest in Barrie. And serious critical interest in his novels and plays has recently been hostile, when it has not been negligible or nonexistent. Thus, David Daiches, in the second volume of his *A Critical History of English Literature* (New York, 1960), dismisses Barrie as a writer whose work shows

> "How far technical theatrical skill could combine with a truly cunning exploitation of the sentimental tradition to achieve popularity in the age of Shaw . . . Barrie was quite out of touch with the new literary movements of his time, but exploited with determination and professional assurance the emotions, whimsies and sentimentalities implicit in the Scottish kailyard tradition and in so much Victorian and Edwardian and middle-class feeling. . . ."

But even in his heyday Barrie was never particularly "well-served" by his critics—though, typically, their "disservice" was in overpraising him rather than in providing unsympathetic criticism of his work. As a sentimentalist and the creator of charmingly attractive theatrical fantasies, Barrie stood apart, uniquely, from the contemporary intellectual drama of Shaw and Granville Barker and the "objective" social-conscience theater of Galsworthy. And, curiously, this uniqueness seems to have paralyzed the faculties of the earlier critics who had no hesitation in denouncing sentimentality when they came upon it in the work of Charles Lamb and Charles Dickens. By contrast, more recent critics have often accepted Barrie's sentimentality as a justification for cursory deprecation of his work or for completely ignoring it. Neither approach is satisfactory as a basis for reassessing Barrie's literary reputation.

This book provides, it is hoped, the new and deeper understanding of Barrie that is long overdue. It is concerned primarily with Barrie as a writer of sentimental fantasies, and its aim is to show Barrie's sentimentality as the outcome of a failure to transcend his own fantasies, to break through them and find beyond himself, new and viable subjects for creative treatment. The recurrent fantasies, motifs, and themes in his work are traced to their origins in certain "prototypic" autobiographical and psychological experiences, most of which are recounted by Barrie himself in his book, *Margaret Ogilvy*, a memoir of his mother. All of Barrie's significant, non-journalistic works are discussed as distortions of the prototypic material in order to expose the true nature of the sentimentalist "deceptions" that many critics have recognized in Barrie's work. Analysis of the relations of the prototypic material to the works discussed is assisted by the provision of elaborate plot summaries containing built-in commentaries; where necessary, these synopses also serve as a basis for discussion of unusual structural aspects of Barrie's works.

The book surveys, in six chapters, Barrie's early journalistic work and his connection with the Scottish Kailyard movement; all of his novels; *Peter Pan* in all its forms; the numerous one-act plays; and the major plays from *Walker, London* (1892) to *The Boy David* (1936). However, little reference is made to Barrie's correspondence, his speeches, literary associations, and personality—all of which have been elaborately surveyed by many of the commentators whose books are listed in the bibliography. These topics are not central to the discussion here. Barrie's active journalistic career and the theatrical history of his plays are treated only in outline—for thorough consideration of these subjects would require a separate volume. Barrie's dramaturgy and novelistic techniques, which have been extensively analyzed by his critics, also receive only cursory treatment. Even Barrie's most antipathetic critics have usually acknowledged his technical skill. But, curiously, his sentimentality, which has become the focus of most of the reaction against his work, has never been adequately explored.

Though no apologia for Barrie, this study, which examines the wellsprings of his sentimentality, the fantasies with which Barrie endeavored to disguise or repress fundamental truths about himself and his family relationships, reveals, we believe, for the first time, what Barrie was really writing about.

Indiana University
Bloomington, Indiana

HARRY M. GEDULD

Contents

Chronology

The main sources for this section are the entry on Barrie in the *Dictionary of National Biography*, Denis Mackail's biography, *Barrie: The Story of J.M.B.* (New York, 1941), and B. D. Cutler's *Sir James Barrie: A Bibliography* (New York, 1931).

1860 May 9—James Matthew Barrie born in Kirriemuir, Forfarshire, Scotland; ninth child and third and youngest son of David Barrie, a hand-loom weaver, and his wife, Margaret, daughter of Alexander Ogilvy, a stonemason. James received part of his early education at Glasgow Academy where his eldest brother, Alexander, taught classics.

1867 January—sudden death of Barrie's brother David (aged thirteen) from a fall on the ice; a crucial event in James's life.

1873-1878 Attended Dumfries Academy.

1878 Matriculated at Edinburgh University.

1882 Master of Arts at Edinburgh University.

1883 January—appointed leader-writer and sub-editor on the *Nottingham Journal;* also wrote anonymously and pseudonymously for many other journals.

1885 March—moved to London where he began an active journalistic career in Fleet Street.

1887 November—publication of *Better Dead,* his first book.

1888 Publication of *Auld Licht Idylls* and *When A Man's Single.*

1889 Publication of *A Window in Thrums.*

1891 April 16—Barrie's first play, *Richard Savage* (written in collaboration with H. B. Marriott Watson) presented in a special matinée at the Criterion Theatre, London; publication of *The Little Minister* (novel).

1892 February 25—first night of *Walker, London* at Toole's Theatre, London. The play ran for 511 performances and was Barrie's first commercial success in the theater. May 9—accidental death of Reverend James Winter, Barrie's friend and the fiancé of his sister Maggie. Two years later, Maggie married Winter's brother William. Both events leave their mark on Barrie's work.

1894 June 25—*The Professor's Love Story* opened at the Comedy Theatre, London, for 144 performances. July 9—married Mary, daughter of George Ansell, a licensed victualler. Mary Ansell, an actress, had played in *Walker, London.* After honeymooning in Switzerland, the couple settled in Gloucester Road, London, near Kensington Gardens. Their marriage was childless.

1895 September 1–sudden death of Barrie's spinster sister, Jane Ann; followed two days later by the death of his mother. Double shock profoundly affects Barrie.

1896 Publication of *Sentimental Tommy* and *Margaret Ogilvy.*

1897 November 6–*The Little Minister* opened at the Haymarket Theatre, London, for 320 performances.

1898 March–received an honorary LL.D. degree from St. Andrews University, Scotland.

1900 September 27–*The Wedding Guest* opened at the Garrick Theatre, London, for 100 performances. *Tommy and Grizel* published.

1902 September 17–*Quality Street* opened at the Vaudeville Theatre, London, for 459 performances. November 4–*The Admirable Crichton* opened at the Duke of York's Theatre, London, for 328 performances. *The Little White Bird* published.

1903 September 24–*Little Mary* opened at the Wyndham's Theatre, London, for 208 performances.

1904 December 27–*Peter Pan, Or The Boy Who Would Not Grow Up* opened at the Duke of York's Theatre, London, for 145 performances.

1905 April 5–*Alice Sit-By-the-Fire* opened at the Duke of York's Theatre, London, for 115 performances.

1906 Publication of *Peter Pan in Kensington Gardens.*

1908 September 3–*What Every Woman Knows* opened at the Duke of York's Theatre, London, for 384 performances.

1909 April 2–received an honorary LL.D. degree from Edinburgh University. October 13–divorced his wife who had been having an affair with Gilbert Cannan. She subsequently married her lover. Barrie never remarried. November–moved into an apartment in Adelphi Terrace, London, where one of his neighbors was Bernard Shaw.

1911 May–Sir George Frampton's statue of Peter Pan erected in Kensington Gardens. This was Barrie's idea and it was undertaken at his expense.

1913 Created a baronet by George V.

1916 March 16–*A Kiss for Cinderella* opened at the Wyndham's Theatre, London, for 156 performances; several revivals.

1917 October 17–*Dear Brutus* opened at the Wyndham's Theatre, London, for 365 performances.

1918 Four one-act plays published as *Echoes of the War.*

1919 November 1–elected Rector of St. Andrews University. Publication of *The Young Visiters* by Daisy Ashford (a nine-year-old authoress), with a Preface by Barrie who has often, mistakenly, been credited with having written the story.

1920 April 22—*Mary Rose* opened at the Haymarket Theatre, London, for 399 performances.

1921 May 27—*Shall We Join the Ladies?* first performed in celebration of the opening of the Royal Academy of Dramatic Art. The cast was probably the most distinguished ever assembled for a one-act play, and included Sybil Thorndike, Irene Vanbrugh, Lady Tree, Lillah McCarthy, Sir Johnston Forbes-Robertson, Gerald du Maurier, and Dion Boucicault. When the playlet was revived at the St. Martin's Theatre in 1923, it ran for 407 performances.

1922 Appointed to the Order of Merit.

1926 June 23—received an honorary D.Litt. from Oxford.

1930 June 5—received an honoray LL.D. from Cambridge. October 25—installed as Chancellor of Edinburgh University.

1936 November 21—*The Boy David* opened at the King's Theatre, Edinburgh; on December 14 continued its run at His Majesty's Theatre, London. There were 55 performances.

1937 June 19—Barrie died at the age of seventy-seven. His ex-wife was present at his deathbed. In accordance with his wishes, he was buried beside his parents and his brother, David, in Kirriemuir cemetery.

CHAPTER 1

From Journalism to the Kailyard

I *Journalism*

IT is difficult to find any support in the work of J. M. Barrie for Bernard Shaw's assertion in the preface to *The Sanity of Art* that the highest literature is journalism. If Barrie had found his métier through any discipline other than journalism, it is unlikely that he would have achieved popular success as promptly as he did; but it is quite probable that he would have been a greater novelist.

Barrie left Edinburgh University in 1884, spent the next two years as leader-writer for a Nottingham newspaper, and then two more years as a freelance journalist in London before publishing his first books of prose fiction: *Better Dead* (1887) and *Auld Licht Idylls* (1888). The four years of journalistic activity were not in the regular sense a period of literary apprenticeship. Nottingham and Fleet Street had nothing to teach Barrie about fluency and facility; he could write with consummate ease before he left Edinburgh. And, as a journalist, he immediately proved himself capable of writing at any length upon any subject.

But this period was one of discovery for him in so far as he was to learn, in a most lucrative fashion, the saleability of the superficial. Barrie found his journalistic formula—an attractive recipe of charm, whimsicality, and puckish wit—and he exploited it with the thoroughness and efficiency of a miner working a heavy vein of gold. The danger in finding just what the public wants lies in the temptation to go on giving it nothing else. Barrie's gifts as a writer were, as we shall see, considerable. His shortcomings as a novelist—and the basis for today's general neglect of his fiction—are, however, directly traceable to his journalistic concessions to the tastes of the reading public.

During the 1980's, the literary vignette became fashionable as a journalistic commodity. Barrie wrote and published extensively in this form before he realized that one kind of vignette—the essay of Scottish parochial life—was attracting more attention than the rest of his journalism. A revised collection of short pieces in this vein was to form the material for his first substantial book, *Auld Licht Idylls* (1888). An uneven array of twelve studies of Scots parochial life in the earlier half of the nineteenth century, most of the essays in this volume had appeared previously in the pages of two periodicals, *The St. James's Gazette* and *The British Weekly*; but several pieces, in which Scots dialect is used extensively, had been rejected by editors of every journal to which they had been submitted.

Unexpectedly, the first appearance of the essays in book form was to inspire a host of imitators and to give a new lease of life to the subgenre of Scots dialect fiction that had been popularized earlier in the century by Barrie's literary master, Robert Louis Stevenson. But, whereas the use of dialect in Stevenson is integral to the characterization and to the texture of the prose, it usually appears in Barrie's work as a quaint curiosity for the sophisticated reader. Barrie's Scots is not the language of his own age but a pseudo-dialect intended to recall the Scotland of his mother's childhood. *Auld Licht Idylls* was as quaint to the Scotsmen who first read it as it seemed to the Sassenachs over the border. Similarly, its pictures of provincial Scottish life referred to an age as remote from Barrie's contemporaries as we are today from the romanticized, self-sufficient small-town life of Mrs. Elizabeth Gaskell's Cranford.

The Auld Lichts of Barrie's title refers to members of the Auld Licht Kirk in the town of Thrums, Barrie's nickname for Kirriemuir, his birthplace in Forfarshire.[1] This particular kirk had been founded in 1833, when four ministers of the established Protestant Church of Scotland seceded from it over the issue of a congregation's right to nominate its own minister. It was one of many acts of secession provoked by the authorization in 1832 of an act which assigned nomination rights to a select body of kirk elders. The four secessionist ministers established a new church which quickly encountered a major problem in the attitude of its members to the National Covenants. Acceptance of the Covenants, as approved by the Established Church, was interpreted as countenancing state interference in kirk affairs. Because one group in the seceded kirk was prepared to submit to state intervention, it became known as the Old Lights (Auld Lichts). Another group, unwilling to brook any state interference, was the New Lights. Barrie's interest focused on the Auld Lichts, the more conservative of the two groups, who had separated from the New Light faction to establish their own kirk.

Numerous examples of the rigid Auld Licht adherence to traditions are to be found scattered through Barrie's stories of Thrums and its people. An amusing anecdote in the third chapter of *Auld Licht Idylls* describes quite typically how Mistress Tibbie McQuatty almost created a schism among the Auld Lichts by her refusal to tolerate the new minister's innovation of "run line"—a method of singing the whole psalm after first reading it in its entirety, in contrast to the traditional Auld Licht way of alternating the reading and singing of each line.

There is no evidence that Barrie had any close personal connections with the Auld Licht Kirk or any of its members. His own family belonged to the South Free Church, which had seceded from the Established Kirk later than the Auld Lichts. All that Barrie wrote about Thrums and the Auld Licht community was based on stories his mother had told him about the Kirriemuir of her childhood, or on what she remembered of her father's recollections of the town in the period before the Industrial Revolution had suppressed the local handloom weaving occupation. Hence, in Barrie's stories Kirriemuir is nicknamed "Thrums"—an archaic term for the fringe of threads remaining on a handloom when the web is removed.

Oddly enough, Barrie's journalistic instinct for conveying a seemingly authentic, detailed picture of Thrums prevented him from observing the Auld Licht community with the genuinely sympathetic eye of an insider. We turn away from his sketches of small-town life without the impression that a scalpel has been at work, for no souls have been bared. Barrie has evidently piled on the details, explored the superficialities of the Auld Lichts in order to evade the problems of exposing their inner lives. The townsfolk are ostensibly seen through the eyes of the Thrums schoolmaster, Barrie's fictional narrator; but the mask of the persona frequently drops as Barrie's irony plays over his simple-minded puppets. When laughter is invited, it is at the Auld Lichts and not with them. Religious belief, love, courtship, marriage, and death are treated on a farcical or mock-serious level. Only when Barrie directs his gaze at scenes of the wild Scots countryside from which man is conspicuously absent does a hint of deeper feeling enter his writing.

Barrie's first chapter, "The Schoolhouse," is a tantalizing glimpse of a style that might have challenged the best work of Richard Jefferies, the British master of landscape description in prose. But the prose-poem is jettisoned almost immediately in favor of a series of fictional sketches that lack both the vigor and narrative interest of comparable writing by Arthur Morrison and Israel Zangwill. The remaining eleven chapters contain a series of disconnected impressions of Thrums rather than a comprehensive panorama. Barrie maintained that the various sketches comprizing the book had been reworked before their appearance in *Auld Licht Idylls*; but this reworking was never taken beyond the stage of improving individual chapters. There was no refashioning of the book as a whole in order to give it even the semblance of structural unity. This careless indifference to the coherence of his narrative material is typical of all of Barrie's fiction until the publication of *Sentimental Tommy* (1896), and reflects the haste of the journalist who slaps together a book from previously published articles, while, at the same time, he pours forth a fresh flow of similar material as long as the fashion for it lasts.

Generally, Barrie's critics have been kinder to *Auld Licht Idylls* than the book deserves. This infectious paralysis of the critical faculties that has afflicted so many of Barrie's commentators began with the impact of this book and was to reach its climax with P. R. Chalmers's remark: "It is a mistake to go to plays, to those of Barrie or to those of anyone else, and seek for meanings. . . ."[2] Far too many of Barrie's so-called critics have been mere apologists; "fans of J. M. B." have hastened to overpraise his best qualities and to gloss over his deficiencies. Thus, Thomas Moult, while conceding that *Auld Licht Idylls* was a "piecemeal product," whose "haphazard chapters" reveal "an inexperienced observer and awkward craftsman," insists that the book shows its author to be "a writer of imagination and adequate technique."[3]

Sir John Hammerton, who admits that the work lacks coherence, also argues that the "great merit of the *Idylls* is the success with which its author assumes and maintains the role of schoolmaster in the glen of Quharity,"[4] which, in fact, is the major device aiming at coherence! The book's most vigorous critic has been George Blake, who, while noticing that Barrie was and still is "so confoundedly readable" and "admirable" in his "purely visual descriptions," remarks that Barrie puts on pathos "with a trowel" and that very little is sacred to this showman, for despite his whimsy, Barrie's treatment of death and suffering reveal "the way of a sadist." Blake sees the author of *Auld Licht Idylls* as a writer working "below his own standards in order to achieve the quick, cheap effects. . . ."[5]

II *The Kailyard*

Since Barrie the artist was so soon to emerge from the constricting cocoon of the journalist, some justification seems necessary for dwelling at length on a collection of ephemera. That justification is to be found in hitherto unmentioned aspects of *Auld Licht Idylls.* The book is seminal to all of the subsequent Thrums stories: *When a Man's Single, A Window in Thrums, The Little Minister*, and the two "Tommy" novels: *Sentimental Tommy* and *Tommy and Grizel.* Characters and themes, situations and plot-fragments briefly sketched in *Auld Licht Idylls* are often developed in the later books, so that Barrie's first studies of Thrums are to be regarded in retrospect as the working notes of an incipient novelist. The careful reader also notices how the most trivial incidents or details in *Auld Licht Idylls* have a habit of reappearing a decade or more later as significant elements of a novel or a play. Thus Hooky Crewe, driver of the Thrums mail-coach, is to be transformed into the notorious Captain Hook, while Joey Sutie, the Thrums pedlar who strangles himself in his pack-strap, becomes a model for the death of Sentimental Tommy.

The immediate popular success of *Auld Licht Idylls* elicited different responses on each side of the Atlantic. By 1898 several enterprising American publishers had dug their way into the rich quarry of Barrie's uncollected journalism and had begun to publish unauthorized collections of essays and stories, modeled on the Auld Licht book.[6] *A Holiday in Bed and Other Sketches* (1892) and *An Auld Licht Manse* (1893) included plundered Barrie material that had first appeared in *The British Weekly* and *The Edinburgh Evening Dispatch; A Tillyloss Scandal* (1893), pirated from the same sources, also went farther afield to collect Barrie articles from *Good Words, The Scots Observer,* and *The National Observer; Two of Them*

(1893) widened the field of plunder by ransacking *The Graphic* and *The Illustrated London News;* but by now the quarry was almost worked out. Hence *A Powerful Drug* (1893) pirated the pirates by publishing material from *A Tillyloss Scandal* and *Two of Them. Jess* (1898) was also a straightforward reprinting of many chapters from Barrie's *A Window in Thrums* (1889). It is notable that the publishers of the pirated collections relied for titles or subtitles on associations between their books "by the author of *Auld Licht Idylls*" and the authorized Thrums works. These associations were emphasized even when the pirated collections had included material that had little or no Scots interest.

On Barrie's side of the Atlantic, *Auld Licht Idylls* was to become a model for the studies of small-town life by Scots novelists "Ian Maclaren," Neil Munro, J. J. Bell, and S. R. Crockett. These were the most notable writers of the Kailyard or "Cabbage-patch" movement, which, without producing a Scots counterpart to Mrs. Wiggs, nevertheless managed to popularize the shabby glories of provincial existence. According to F. J. Harvey Darton, the term "Kailyard" was "based upon a quotation by 'Ian Maclaren' from an old Jacobite song about 'the bonny brier bush in our kailyard'—his *Beside the Bonnie Brier Bush* (1894) standing worthily high in the products of the [Kailyard] school."[7]

Like Barrie, the other Kailyard writers observed the superficialities of life and character in a spirit of gentle irony. They subordinated plot to an extensive use of dialect. And they created a fictional Scotland that bore no more relationship to their own age or to the real past of pre-industrialized Scotland than did *Auld Licht Idylls.*

Since a survey of the whole Kailyard school is irrelevant to this study,[8] it suffices to remark that Barrie stood in relation to the Kailyard writers as a master to his disciples. But his *Better Dead* (1887), published in the year previous to *Auld Licht Idylls* but nevertheless a work of later composition, is not a product of the Kailyard: the book is heavily indebted to Robert Louis Stevenson. When Barrie measured his stature as a Scottish novelist, it was invariably against the achievements, the reputation, the influence of Stevenson. Sir Walter Scott and Thomas Carlyle he had no desire to emulate; their manner and tone were alien to him; but he envied Stevenson as a master of romantic fiction; Barrie admired the technical skill with which he had integrated Scots idiom and character into his novels, not as a curiosity, but in the natural course of creating a body of fiction that had been accepted into the mainstream of British literature. Like Scott, Stevenson had brought a Scottish past to life. And it was unnecessary for him to forget that he was a Scotsman when he wrote for the widest possible reading public. He had made Scotland an exciting place even to those who had not been fortunate enough to be born there.

Better Dead is inspired by the first adventure of "The Suicide Club" from Stevenson's *New Arabian Nights* (1882). Stevenson's tale concerns a club whose members are tired of life but afraid to commit suicide. Each evening, during a gambling session, two members are selected—one to be a killer; the other, his victim. On a subsequent evening the killer in his turn becomes the victim. In this way members are relieved of life without having to face the horror of self-annihilation. Out of morbid curiosity, Prince Florizel, Stevenson's hero, becomes a member of the Suicide Club. To his horror, he is selected one night as a victim. Similarly, Andrew Riach, the Scots hero of Barrie's story, becomes a probationary member of the Society for Doing Without Some People, a secret organization centered in London and concerned with finding out who the superfluous people are, and then with persuading them that they would be "better dead" and should eliminate themselves as soon as possible. The society arranges for the murder of superfluous individuals who are reluctant to commit suicide. During his probation, Andrew tries unsuccessfully to persuade several celebrated political figures that they would be better dead. He then endeavors, with equal failure, to assassinate those who will not be persuaded. Meanwhile, his own end is being plotted; and he narrowly escapes destruction by evading his attacker and taking the express back to Scotland.

The two works have numerous similarities of plot; but here the resemblances end. Stevenson's story is the framework for a series of ingenious tales. Its infrequent flights of humor do nothing to impair the comparatively serious tone of the story. The characters are quite deliberately of little intrinsic interest, for it is the thrilling twist of the narrative that must command attention. Stevenson's singleness of purpose results in the relegation of every element of his story to serve the needs of the plot.

By contrast, *Better Dead* is a highly confused, unprofessional piece of work. Barrie himself hesitated to include it in the standard edition of his fiction, but his doubts were overruled by his American publisher. The style of *Better Dead,* its abruptly handled episodes, its clipped two- and three-line paragraphs again betray the journalist at work, that journalist "persona" Barrie later nicknamed "M'Connachie." Young Barrie, full of bright ideas, was in love with all of them, for he had not yet learned the desirability of wielding the pruning knife. Thus from page to page we are never quite certain whether mystery or satire is intended. Barrie's humor is frequently a juvenile mockery of violence: the tale of suspense and terror is reduced to farce. Unfortunately, even this level of humor is not consistently sustained. Much of the story is a mélange of topical, political, and literary jokes which might in 1888 have seemed entertaining, but have since become obscure. The early chapters contain the heavy imprint of student "gag-writing" and a great parade of plots for unwritten stories. In the account of Andrew's first experiences in London, there are also abundant, though obviously distorted, autobiographical allusions to a difficult period in Barrie's life which he ultimately romanticized in a speech entitled *Courage,* his Rectorial Address to the students of St. Andrews, Edinburgh: "The greatest glory that has ever come to me was to be swallowed up in London, not knowing a soul, with no means of subsistence, and the fun of working till the stars went out."

Barrie's commentators tend either to pass over *Better Dead* as rapidly as possible or to ignore it. However, at least two apologists have discerned notable merits in the work which is rather more than its author ever managed to do. Sir John Hammerton considered its satire "essentially Barriesque," though he somewhat inconsistently condemned its "cold, hard, sophisticated" qualities and its lack of "the softening relief of humour and sentiment. . . ."[9] Thomas Moult, on the other hand, praised the book for its wealth of "quips and comicalities," which seem to have been lost on Hammerton. Moult theorized that De Quincey's celebrated essay on murder as a fine art might have inspired Barrie's story, and he also noted that a contemporary critic (unnamed) had facetiously suggested that *Better Dead* was the outcome of a collaboration between Bernard Shaw and the Oscar Wilde who had written *Lord Arthur Savile's Crime.*[10] Nevertheless, Barrie himself had no illusions about the work. In the 1930's, when asked by P. R. Chalmers whether he would like to see the book in print again, Barrie replied, "No. Better dead!" The novelette is really of little consequence as fiction or satire. It retains our interest on the one hand as an index to its author's shortcomings as a would-be Stevenson, and on the other, like *Auld Licht Idylls,* as a work in which the seeds of future writings had been sown. As we shall see in subsequent chapters, it was the first of many works to be preoccupied, though far less superficially, with trying to do without some people.

III *Collected Trivia*

Before turning to the novels, we should note two works that were considered by Barrie to be worthy of inclusion in the collected editions of his writings, but which belong in the category of ephemeral journalism, long and deservedly ignored. These are *An Edinburgh Eleven* (1889) and *My Lady Nicotine* (1890).

The first of these books is a collection of eleven studies of eminent professors and alumni of the University of Edinburgh, Barrie's alma mater. To the British reader, Barrie's title for the book suggests a cricket team, which is what its author, an ardent cricketer, doubtless intended. However, the title is the only thing about the book that indicates coherence or unity. Barrie had simply assembled the volume by selecting eleven of his articles from *The British Weekly,* giving them an eye-catching title, and slapping them between two covers. With the exception of the pieces on Lord Rosebery, Professor David Masson (the great Milton scholar), and Robert Louis Stevenson, the subjects of the articles are too obscure or local to be of contemporary interest. But they are still readable by indomitable spirits who appreciate Barrie's anecdotes and pyrotechnic displays of wit, regardless of his subject matter. The article on Lord Rosebery is an excellent example of Barrie's mastery of the vignette form; as a piece of political analysis, it is virtually worthless. The value of the essay on Masson may be indicated by quoting one sentence from it: "This is no place to follow Masson's career, nor to discuss his work." The essay does, however, deal with Masson's personality which, curiously enough, was not a little like Barrie's. Most disappointing is the section on Stevenson, for the admirer takes over from the wit, and superficial criticism replaces the display of anecdotes, which in the other selections often make up in liveliness what is lacking in significance.

My Lady Nicotine is a collection of trivial sketches and tales—first published in *The St. James's Gazette*—that parade the virtues of tobacco smoking. As all of Barrie's biographers have noted, the Arcadia Mixture, the fictional brand of tobacco celebrated in *My Lady Nicotine*, was actually Craven Mixture, a real brand patronized by Barrie. Mr. Yapp, the tobacconist who made and sold Craven Mixture, made in three years a fortune of one hundred thousand pounds after getting Barrie to endorse a statement declaring publicly that the Craven and Arcadia Mixtures were one and the same. This incident might suggest the worth of *My Lady Nicotine* as an advertiser's "gimmick," but it says nothing of its significance as a work of literature. One of Barrie's kindest critics, James A. Roy, compared the book in 1937 with the work of Jerome K. Jerome (author of *Three Men in a Boat*, 1889) and George Grossmith Senior (co-author, with his brother Walter Weedon Grossmith, of *The Diary of a Nobody*, 1894); but he admitted that it was dated and stated his belief that it would have been forgotten long ago if anyone but Barrie had written it. Thirty years later, there seems no reason to make even this qualification about the book. It also is, in Barrie's own words, "better dead."

CHAPTER 2

The Novels: Theme and Variations

I *The Prototypic Story*

"THE abortive adventure into the affairs of the Little Minister apart, Barrie really wrote throughout his Kailyard period for, out and from his mother. The complex was more than maternal; it seems to have been positively foetal."[1] So observes George Blake in 1951, after referring to *Margaret Ogilvy* (1896)—Barrie's testament to his mother—as the book, debatable as "a positive act of indecency," which "really spills the beans" about its author. Blake, who limits this "complex" to the Kailyard period, excludes Barrie's drama; yet it is evident in and integral to everything that Barrie wrote. Blake also points to *Margaret Ogilvy* as a revelation of Barrie's attitude to his mother rather than a study of Margaret Ogilvy herself. Yet the book reveals not only its author but also the source of much of his creative material. It recounts certain prototypic experiences that must be closely examined if we are to understand the interrelationship of all Barrie's non-journalistic work and the "positive act of indecency" with which it is preoccupied.

In January, 1867, Barrie's brother David was fatally injured from a fall on the ice. The boy had been visiting his married brother Alexander. It was the first time he had been out of the care of his parents, and ever afterwards they—and Barrie—held themselves accountable for what had occurred. David's death was Margaret Ogilvy's great tragedy. He was her favorite son, only thirteen years of age but already showing qualities that suggested a future career as a teacher or a minister.[2] He had been named for her husband, David Barrie, a stolid weaver whose life was to be troubled not only by the death of the child but also by its shattering effects on Margaret's already enfeebled state of health. Her invalid condition persisted until the end of her life. When she moved about, she did so with the aid of a staff which Barrie prized after her death as his

YEARY LIBRARY
LAREDO JR. COLLEGE

most valuable possession. Barrie was only seven when David had his fatal accident, but its effects, his mother's reactions, and his involvements with it as son and brother were to remain indelible experiences.

Margaret Ogilvy, in presenting Barrie's own version of this family situation, provides the prototypic story discernible through numerous variations in all of his novels and plays:

> She had a son who was far away at school. I remember very little about him, only that he was a merry-faced boy who ran like a squirrel up a tree and shook the cherries into my lap. When he was thirteen and I was half his age the terrible news came, and I have been told the face of my mother was awful in its calmness as she set off to get between Death and her boy. . . . Margaret Ogilvy had been her maiden name. . . . Often when I was a boy, 'Margaret Ogilvy, are you there?' I would call up the stair.
>
> She was always delicate from that hour, and for many months she was very ill. I have heard that the first thing she expressed a wish to see was the christening robe, and she looked long at it and then turned her face to the wall. That was what made me as a boy think of it always as the robe in which he had been christened, but I knew later that we had all been christened in it. . . .
>
> My mother lay in bed with the Christening robe beside her, and I peeped in many times at the door and then went to the stair and sat on it and sobbed. I know not if it was that first day, or many days afterwards, that there came to me my sister [Jane Anne], the daughter my mother loved best, yes, more I am sure than she loved me. . . . This sister . . . told me to go ben [the direction in which the loom-shop was situated] to my mother and say to her that she still had another boy. I went ben excitedly, but the room was dark. . . . I heard a listless voice that had never been listless before say, 'Is that you?' . . . I thought it was the dead boy she was speaking to, and I said in a little lonely voice, 'No, it's no him, it's just me.' Then I heard a cry, and my mother turned in bed, and though it was dark I knew that she was holding out her arms.
>
> After that I sat a great deal in her bed trying to make her forget him, which was my crafty way of playing physician. . . . At first, they say, I was often jealous, stopping her fond memories with the cry, 'Do you mind nothing about me?' but that did not last; its place was taken by an intense desire (again, I think, my sister must have breathed it into life) to become so like him that even my mother should not see the difference. . . . Then I practised in secret. . . . I secretly put on a suit of his clothes, dark grey they were, with little spots, and they fitted me many years afterwards, and thus disguised I slipped, unknown to the others, into my mother's room. Quaking, I doubt not, yet

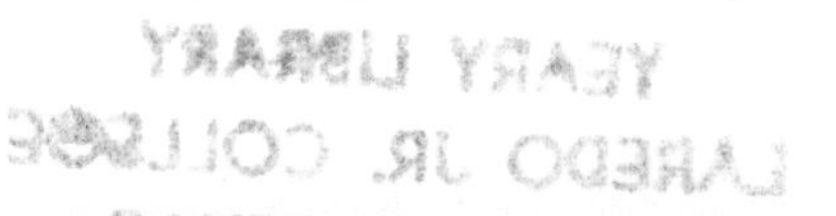
YEARY LIBRARY
LAREDO JR. COLLEGE

so pleased, I stood still until she saw me, and then—how it must have hurt her![3]

A later chapter of *Margaret Ogilvy* is of major importance in understanding Barrie's work, for it is devoted to identifying his mother with the heroines of all his plays and novels, from Lucy White (*The Professor's Love Story*) to Jess McQumpha (*A Window in Thrums*), and, by implication, to such later heroines as Mary Rose. By contrast, David Barrie, the father, is virtually ignored in *Margaret Ogilvy.* Instead of the writer's giving us an impression of his parents' relationship, we are offered what is tantamount to a lover's eulogy of his beloved. Margaret is the object of his conscious rivalry with the dead brother. He is jealous when he sees her in bed caressing the christening robe that symbolizes David the deceased brother, and so he climbs in to take David's place. He does not think or speak of his mother as a married woman, never as Margaret Barrie, but always as Margaret Ogilvy, using her maiden name in fanciful implication of her youth and virginity. And the character he sketches is that of an immature girl often coyly unwilling to admit her true feelings even when they are transparently obvious behind her subterfuges. There is no hint of the staid matron about Margaret Ogilvy; indeed, Barrie attributes his fantasy virgin-mother with the characteristics of his elder sister, the spinster Jane Anne, and his younger sister Maggie (Margaret).

The prototypic story is very clearly an Oedipal situation. Barrie's prose hymn to Margaret Ogilvy sometimes seems like an expression of the repressed incestuous impulses of the child. In his later writings, father and brother (both named David) are sometimes fused into one character; at other times, the father is patronizingly dismissed as a simple soul, or branded as a wretch who has neglected his own children. Mother and sisters may be fused into another character; or different characteristics of the mother are separated into two figures, each identifiable with one of the two sisters. Barrie himself is seen as the assassin or would-be killer of his brother; for the brother's death, if not consciously desired, certainly removes a rival—or seems to do so until Margaret's memories and dreams of the more virile boy David loom up to create a more formidable fantasy-rival. In *The Interpretation of Dreams* Freud notices how "Many persons . . . who now love their brothers and sisters, and who would feel bereaved by their death, harbor in their unconscious hostile wishes, survivals from an earlier period, wishes which are able to realize themselves in dreams. . . . I have never failed to come across this dream of the death of brothers or sisters, denoting an intense hostility. . . ."[4] Earlier in the same book Freud explains that "Many adults who today are devoted to their brothers and sisters . . . lived with them in almost continuous enmity during their childhood. The elder child ill-treated the younger, slandered him, and robbed him of his toys; the younger was consumed with helpless fury against the elder, envied and feared him. . . ."[5]

As this study endeavors to show, the basic material of Barrie's mature work was to be developed out of the imposition of the personal involvements of 1892-94, the years in which *Sentimental Tommy* was gestated, upon the prototypic story.

Barrie's opposition as a child to his fantasy-rival first took the form of diversions or entertainments for his mother: he would try to make her laugh and thereby forget David. In so far as all of Barrie's books and plays were written for and inspired by his mother, his works may be regarded as a lifelong diversion intended to counteract or obliterate the fantasy-rival. (When Barrie's wife began to enter his fantasies as a rival to Margaret, he tried to suppress her image in similar ways.) The second stage of opposition to David took the form of deliberate deception, a recurring motif in the plays and novels. Barrie tried to supplant the fantasy-rival by taking over his identity, by so impersonating the dead brother that his mother would be completely deceived. When the deception was exposed, she would understand (or was expected to) that there was no difference between the two brothers, since James could be David as well as himself. However, the obliteration of the rival or the deception of absorbing David's character into his own were both felt as guilty acts. Guilt feelings also arose from Barrie's double image of his mother: on the one hand as the virginal Margaret Ogilvy whom he desired, and on the other as the "promiscuous" woman consorting with the father-brother (David). Another but later source of guilt was his desertion of Margaret for another woman. As his fantasies endured, Barrie's wife, the actress Mary Ansell, entered them as the seductress who tried to entice the son away from the virgin-mother.

In 1892, Barrie's younger sister, Maggie, named for her mother and later imaginatively fused with her in the character of Elspeth (*Sentimental Tommy*), had been engaged to marry the Reverend James Winter. This clergyman became linked in Barrie's mind with his brother David; and Gavin Dishart, the Little Minister in the novel of that name, may, perhaps, be regarded as an extension of the potential clergyman (David) into the real one (James Winter). The death of David was horrifyingly re-enacted for Barrie in 1892 when Winter was suddenly thrown from his horse and killed. But Barrie's second "rival" for Margaret was soon replaced by a third, for in 1893 Maggie became engaged to Winter's elder brother William, another clergyman.[6] All the available details suggest that Barrie's ensuing illness was psychosomatically induced. He was being oppressed by guilt feelings involving his sister and the second "rival" whom he had killed by wish if not by deed. But perhaps his deepest guilt feelings were connected with his mother, for months passed before he could tell her that he planned to get married. He had repressed his identification of himself with the cause of his mother's illness as well as his inner resentment at being "defeated" by a third rival for the younger "virgin" Margaret. His marriage to Mary Ansell in 1894 was probably an unconscious response to being "deserted" for the new rival.[7] The marriage lasted until 1909 when Mary divorced Barrie to marry the critic Gilbert Cannan.

We assume that Barrie harbored resentment against his mother for "rejecting" him for David, just as he must, later, have harbored resentment against Mary for rejecting him for Gilbert Cannan, whom she subsequently married. However, though Barrie considered both women guilty of the same "crime" against him, his idealization of Margaret prevented him from making her the object of his animosity. Thus, in Barrie's fantasies Mary served the very useful function of receiving the resentment intended for Margaret as well as for herself.

To balance or relieve his frustrations, Barrie provided himself with an imaginary outlet symbolized by his magic woods and fantasy-islands.[8] "I should feel," he once told an audience of critics, "as if I had left off my clothing, if I were to write without an island." On Barrie's imaginary islands anything is possible, and everything is countenanced as long as it mitigates or excludes his guilt in the prototypic situation. Hence the fantasy-island is sometimes the place where the lost brother David lives, and where he is free to love Margaret without being suppressed by his rival, where the lure of the seductress may be transformed into an innocent diversion, where the lost child may actually desire to be separated from his mother, and the mother lose her baby without missing him.

Many of Barrie's critics have noticed the recurrence in his novels and plays of a character typified by Peter Pan: the boy who will not grow up. Peter Pan is regarded frequently as a mouthpiece for Barrie himself, expressing a hopeless nostalgia for his lost childhood or offering the notion that men always remain boys at heart. However, the prototypic story indicates that the idea of Peter Pan as an alter ego of Barrie is quite untenable. The fictional boy who will not grow up is identifiable, like most of Barrie's other "lost" children, with David, the rival-brother who literally did not grow up. The dream of one of Freud's patients provides a remarkable parallel to Peter Pan's flight to the Neverland with Michael, John, and Wendy: "A number of children, all [the patient's] brothers and sisters with her boy and girl cousins, were romping about in a meadow. Suddenly they all grew wings, flew up, and were gone." Freud observes that his patient "had no idea of the significance of this dream; but we can hardly fail to recognize it as a dream of the death of all the brothers and sisters, in its original form, and but little influenced by the censorship."[9]

In Barrie's work, images of the dead brother recur: he is a lost child; a baby who dies or is stolen; he is dropped out of the perambulator, falls into the Round Pond in Kensington Gardens, or is deserted by his mother. Barrie's lost children "live" underground or in coffin-like boxes, in magic woods and on fantasy-islands. When the David figure is represented as an adult, he is often named David in addition to being reduced in some way to an appropriate stature. Thus David Gemmell in *Tommy and Grizel* is "reduced" by being presented as a nondescript, colorless character, while Gavin Dishart, the hero of another novel, is reduced physically to appear as the Little Minister.

The Margaret figure, the most complex of the prototypic characters, appears on the one hand as a promiscuous woman, a Painted Lady, the defiled or debauched object of desire, and on the other as the virginal girl who is invariably a heroine. Two aspects of the virginal Margaret are also discernible as a result of the fusion of the mother image with separate attributes of Barrie's sisters. In consequence, there are two recurring heroine types: the domestic-maternal-serious and the impractical-flirtatious-happy-go-lucky. This contrast in types of heroine is, of course, the contrast between Grizel and Elspeth in the "Tommy" novels.

The Grizel figure is usually linked closely and tragically with a character who is representative of Barrie himself, typified in the fiction by Sentimental Tommy Sandys. Tommy characters are always "magerful" (masterful) in their treatment of the heroine. They impose their will upon women by deception or by exerting their superior authority. And their "magerful" natures are invariably responsible for the sufferings of virgin-mothers and Painted Ladies. Tammas Haggart, the burlesque hero of many of the Thrums sketches in *Auld Licht Idylls* and in *A Window in Thrums,* is the first appearance of the Tommy character in Barrie's fiction. The name fixes the type at once: Tammas (Tommy) and Haggart—evocative of "braggart" and "hag"—and suggesting the characteristic Tommy preoccupations with boasting and with promiscuous women. The Tommy impostures frequently assume the form of plausible self-deceptions —masks created by the character and adopted by him because they are more attractive and more positive than the true personality they replace or conceal. All of the characters conceived in the Tommy image are natural actors who strive to efface their own personalities in the act of believing in what they pretend to be. In this respect they approximate to Barrie in his attempt to assume the identity of his brother as a means of capturing Margaret Ogilvy's attention.

II When A Man's Single

When A Man's Single (1888), its author's first attempt at a novel, weights the balance of sympathies toward Barrie by presenting him in the guise of the idealized character, Rob Angus. *A Window in Thrums* (1889) and *The Little Minister* (1891) tilt the scales toward the mother and brother, respectively. In idealizing Barrie, the first novel parodies the prototypic situation, depicting the major characters—apart from the transformed hero—as deceivers or imposters. Throughout the book its hero, Rob Angus, is more sinned against than sinning, if beyond the first episode he can be said to sin at all. His career in journalism, rising from insignificance at Silchester to eminence in London, is closely modeled on Barrie's own remarkable progress from his apprenticeship on *The Nottingham Journal* to a highly successful career in Fleet Street.

The novel first appeared serially in *The British Weekly* during 1887-88 under the author's pseudonym, Gavin Ogilvy: the name of the fictitious narrator of all the Thrums stories (apart from the two "Tommy" novels) and the father of the Little Minister. Barrie was subsequently to offer serial publication as an excuse for the novel's structural weaknesses, although the book is superior in structure and coherence to *A Window in Thrums* and *The Little Minister*, for which no apologia was offered. Despite a general recognition of its "disjointed nature," the novel has been widely praised as "a book rich in entertainment," and "the work of an unrivalled humorist."[10] Exceptionally, Moult, who condemns the work for its inconsistencies and inexplicable shifts of mood, remarks: "Rarely in the history of tale-telling can a work have baffled and disappointed an audience so completely." The novel, he declares, marks the triumph of Barrie the journalist over Barrie the imaginative artist."[11]

Nevertheless, except where the plot is reliant on coincidence and where Barrie endeavors to be serious and declines into mawkishness or melodrama, his first novel holds the attention through page after page of gentle irony, wit, and mock-heroic parody. All the serious elements are foredoomed by Barrie's persistent mockery of the conventions of romantic love as his contemporaries found them in the novels of Ouida, Marie Corelli, and other queens of the circulating library. Incongruously, Barrie himself, in his first novel and elsewhere, often lapses into the very conventions that he parodies—one of the major reasons for his now almost total neglect as a novelist. However, if *When A Man's Single* is good only in parts, the parts that are good, particularly the author's asides and commentaries on the action, exhibit Barrie at his sprightliest, puckishly deflating the male ego and exalting the superior intelligence of the female in a tone of mock pomposity.

The very first chapter introduces the prototypic material. David is represented as Davy, a little girl with a boy's name. Like all the other characters apart from Rob, he is given a "mask" symbolic of the deception imputed to the prototype. Little Davy should have been called Margaret, but was mistakenly baptized as a boy by the Little Minister, Gavin Dishart. Her Uncle Rob, the sawmiller, sets his heart on going to college; but, when the girl is left an orphan, he gives up his ambition and becomes the child's guardian. Davy dies accidentally while trying to deliver a letter offering Rob his first chance of a position on a newspaper. He is able to accept the job when Davy's conveniently timed death sets him free from the responsibilities of being a foster father. In fantasy Barrie here tries to jettison his brother while expressing his awareness that David's death is the *raison d'être* of his creativity as a writer. Rob finds the dead child clutching the letter, and guiltily, if irrationally, relates the child's death to his own desire to be "free." Rob's guilt feelings reflect those of Barrie in the prototypic situation.

This first episode of the novel is out of harmony with most of what follows. Tragedy gives place to a mainly lighthearted account of Rob's career as a writer and the vicissitudes of his love affair with Mary Abinger. Little Davy and Rob's guilt feelings over her death are, for the most part, forgotten or suppressed. But, significantly, another representation of David appears in the form of Dick Abinger who provides an important link between Rob's love affair and his career in journalism. Unaware that Dick is the brother of the woman he loves, Rob first encounters him as the successful journalist from whom he learns the tricks of the trade. (Another apt pupil of Dick Abinger was H. G. Wells who, in *The Experiment in Autobiography,* acknowledges the influence of *When A Man's Single* on his early career as a journalist.) Dick "masks" his real identity under the name Noble Simms, a device to prevent the legal profession, of which he is an unsuccessful member, from discovering how he makes his living.

Rob is immediately impressed by Dick's ability to make newspaper copy out of any trivial object or incident. This remarkable gift is exemplified when Dick prepares an article from the disclosure that Rob has a walking stick which produces a mysterious disease in the palm of the hand. Later we learn that this article catches the fancy of other journalists who perpetuate the story of Rob's stick in countless articles—just as it is perpetuated by Barrie in other works. If we accept the psychological interrelationship of Barrie's writings, it is apparent that this stick, which is also of special significance in *A Window in Thrums,* represents Margaret Ogilvy's staff, the symbol of her invalid state after the death of David. Barrie identifies himself with the cause of his mother's condition, for it is only in Rob's (Barrie's) hand that the stick produces a disease. When the stick is discussed in Dick's article, it is perpetually ridiculed. Dick Abinger, a fantasy grown-up David, simultaneously destroys the disease and displays Rob to public mockery.

In a later episode, Rob imagines that Dick is his successful rival in love when he chances upon Dick kissing his sister Mary. Then, in what is virtually an inversion of the prototypic situation, Rob almost kills himself inadvertently. Later, he discovers the truth about Dick, only to learn that he has a real rival in the haughty baronet, Sir Clement Dowton. The final chapters recount the rivalry of these two men for the hand of Mary Abinger, Rob's triumphs over Sir Clement, the class barrier, and the misfortunes that beset his rise to eminence in journalism. Rob's love for Mary is mocked by the comedic subplot in which a barber named Josephs impersonates Sir Clement and plays for his own amusement the kind of unrequited lover that Rob imagines himself to be. Rob later unmasks the impersonator, but he never unmasks the enigmatic nature of the woman he loves. The unconvincing development of the hero's relationship with Mary and the incredible coincidence by which he succeeds in business precisely when it becomes necessary for him to be affluent enough to support a wife from the upper classes convey the impression that the happy ending is the kind of pipe dream mocked earlier in the novel. All the twists of plot leading to the fairy-tale finale demonstrate how noble, hardworking Rob Angus achieves happiness not by his own efforts but through a series of unlikely coincidences that Barrie took no pains to render plausible.

Rob Angus never strikes us as the potential literary genius he sees in himself; it therefore comes as no surprise to the reader when, as a crowning irony, the hero is offered the promotion he desires precisely because he is not a genius. The notion that getting what we want is a disillusioning or disappointing experience is a recurring motif in the novel just as it is in so many of Barrie's plays. It is the literary equivalent of Barrie's discovery in the prototypic situation that the death of David, though a realization of what he had desired, did not bring him his mother's love: for Margaret Ogilvy could never forget the child she had lost. In the novel, Rob's desire to be "free" is realized at the heartbreaking cost of little Davy's life; Josephs' obsession for sampling the life of a gentleman is satisfied at the price of discovering that such an existence is unendurable for more than two or three weeks a year; Dick Abinger's desire to marry Mary's friend, Nell Meredith, is realized at the expense of discovering that he would rather remain single; and Mary's dream of marrying a true gentleman is achieved at the cost of discovering that titles and distinctions do not make the gentleman.

Mary's impenetrable character is the reason for the implausibility of her relationship with Rob. Barrie tells us that her cynicism is a cloak for her true nature but omits to reveal what her true nature is. Mary is an early portrait of the woman Barrie was soon to marry. Her cynicism is only one of the masks she assumes. When Rob first meets her, she has temporarily adopted the character of the disdainful heroine of her novel, *The Scorn of Scorns,* whose plot is apparently plagiarized from Henry James's *Washington Square.* When Rob rereads her novel after blasting it in his first review, he imagines that he has discovered Mary's true nature and the reason he loved her at first sight. Significantly, in relation to the prototype story, *The Scorn of Scorns* is the tale of a woman deserted by her lover; but Barrie ridicules it for its melodramatic and "courtly love" conventions, thereby mocking the fantasies of Rob, his own alter ego, who believes that the woman he loves is what he wants her to be.

On the houseboat, one of the three "islands" of the novel, isolated from the conventions of society, the social barriers are lowered; and Rob masters his humility sufficiently to declare his love for Mary. Later, in lonely Glen Quharity, another "island," he claims her as his wife. Tagg's Island, the third region of fantasy, is an anticipation of the Island that Likes to be Visited in *Mary Rose* (1920). When Mary Abinger gazes from the houseboat across the water, she shivers inexplicably at the sight of Tagg's Island bathed in moonlight and looking like fairyland. Another time, looking across the same stretch of water, she stares in an enraptured state without seeing the man she loves. Tagg's Island also casts its spell on Dick Abinger: when he takes a stroll on it, his mind becomes a complete blank and remains so until he returns to the houseboat.

Aside from its anticipation of *Mary Rose, When A Man's Single* also provides an earlier and more optimistic view of the leading theme of *The Admirable Crichton* (1902). *When A Man's Single* argues that the true gentleman is not the exclusive product of the upper classes and that a man of talent and nobility of character can rise above class barriers as soon as society recognizes him for what he really is. After 1894, the years of his ill-fated marriage and the death of his mother darkened Barrie's fantasies. Where *When A Man's Single* accepts the fantasies of the island as realities tolerable by society, *The Admirable Crichton* puts fantasy in its place and corrects the earlier notion by insisting that a true gentleman knows his place in society and respects the limitations imposed on him by class barriers. On an island anything is possible; and, when a man's single, as Barrie was when he wrote his first novel, he is on an island from which marriage may sometimes rescue him and bring him to reality.

III A Window in Thrums

The prototypic story is patently the basis of Barrie's next attempt at an extended work of serious fiction. "Serious fiction" is about the closest we can get to a description of the kind of work Barrie offers his readers in *A Window in Thrums* (1889), or at least of the story of Jess that forms the core of the book. It could hardly with justice be described as a novel. It is rather a collection of journalistic sketches struggling to become a novel and failing miserably in the attempt. The book is formless. And it is not, as Hammerton maintained, "a triumph of the episodic manner" with each chapter (excluding the seventeenth, which is misplaced) being "an articulated part of a whole and yet . . . complete in itself."[12] From the standpoint of construction, there is little to commend *A Window in Thrums.* And we must look for other qualities if we are to understand why this incoherent book was received with such acclaim when it was first published.

In place of Hammerton's notion of the novelist shaping his material with meticulous care, we have an impression of Barrie caught between his delight at having turned out a sensitive work of fiction (the Jess story) and his despair at realizing that it was too short even to make up a volume the length of *Better Dead.* It was Barrie the journalist who attempted to solve the dilemma for Barrie the artist by inserting the serious fiction in a padding of previously uncollected sketches of Thrums. Commenting on Barrie's book in a letter to Henry James, Stevenson found "Genius in him, but there's a journalist at his elbow—there's the risk."[13] George Blake, who discerned not genius but mere "technical dexterity" in *A Window in Thrums,* remarks that the book "is sorry stuff in terms of life . . . a farrago, prefabricated; a debauch of sentimentality."[14] And certainly the story of Jess rests uneasily in its setting as an unworkable effort to combine the quaintness of the Kailyard with a poignancy that borders on tragedy.

Chapters VI, XVI, and XVIII through XXII are the essence of the book. The remaining fifteen chapters even when they concern Jess McQumpha's family—and many of them do not—are extraneous to the story of Jess and her faithless son. It is this tale, scattered through seven chapters, that evoked Stevenson's praise. "Jess is beyond my frontier line," he wrote to Barrie. "I could not touch her skirt; I have no such glamour of twilight on my pen. I am a capable artist; but it begins to look to me as if you were a man of genius."[15] Several American publishers, who shared Stevenson's high estimate of Barrie's latest work but were unwilling to pay the genius his price, showed their discernment by pirating the Jess chapters and discarding the padding. Since Barrie was to write several novels before overcoming his aversion to the pruning knife, the padding remained in all the authorized editions, testifying as much to his unconscious desire to conceal the special significance of the serious fiction as to his conscious intention of giving permanence to his journalism. The special significance of the Jess chapters is apparent in their fidelity to the basic elements of the prototypic situation. In *Margaret Ogilvy* Barrie records with almost scientific detachment his mother's silent anguish in reading Jess's tragedy. She could recognize in it the virtually undisguised story of her own misfortunes.

Jess is a fictional equivalent of Margaret Ogilvy. Her name conjures up associations with the biblical King David whose *father* was named Jesse; but then Barrie's Jess assumes the importance of *both* parents since the weaver Henders McQumpha, her husband, is as insignificant as Barrie's father in *Margaret Ogilvy.* Another biblical association is to be found in Jess's fondness for the text of Genesis 15:13, "Thou God seest me," which has significance not only as the favorite text of her dead son, but also as part of the story of the lost mother and child, Hagar and Ishmael.

Jess, like Margaret Ogilvy, is an invalid; she also has a stick and a favorite son, little Joey, who sleeps with her and dreams of becoming a minister. Part of Jess dies when Joey is run over and killed by a passing cart. Jamie, the son born to her after Joey's death, is not accepted as a replacement for his brother—except by Henders, the father, who often calls Jamie by his dead brother's name. Jamie becomes a barber and eventually leaves Thrums to make his fortune in London. But every year, during his vacation, he returns to Jess and the companionship of his unmarried sister, Leeby.[16] On one of these vacations, when Jess finds a woman's glove among Jamie's belongings, she rightly suspects it to be a love token from a woman in London, but she never imagines that Jamie will desert her. Her faith in him proves ill-founded.

After Jamie returns to London, tragedy strikes at the family in Thrums. Henders and Leeby die within a short time of each other. Jess writes to her son, but her letters are intercepted by the London woman. Years pass and Jess sits at her lonely window awaiting the return of the prodigal son she is destined never to see again. Long after she has died brokenhearted, Jamie arrives in Thrums. He goes to his former home in the old house at the top of the brae and finds it occupied by strangers. From them he learns the bitter truth. He advises the strange woman who lives in his former home not to set her heart on her child because he might grow up to murder her. Then, before leaving Thrums, he goes to the dominie, Gavin Ogilvy of Glen Quharity, and obtains from him Jess's stick which had been sold when all her possessions were auctioned. With this stick in hand, Jamie takes a last look at the window where his mother had sat waiting for him until she died; then he passes forever out of the sight and knowledge of Thrums.

Curiously, it is in connection with this book rather than with *Auld Licht Idylls* that Barrie has been frequently commended or criticized for his use of Scots dialect. "Not yet," writes Moult, ". . . was the author aware that if the dialect speech of a 'regional' story is to be artistically introduced, it must not be literally reported, but idiomatically suggested."[17] Hammerton, a great admirer of *A Window in Thrums,* rejects Moult's criticism as evidently that of an ill-informed Sassenach. In fact, Hammerton insists, Barrie has succeeded in this and other Thrums stories, in presenting to English townsfolk the lives and language of a people as foreign in many respects as Finns or Norwegians.[18] At least he, another Scot, had no doubts about Barrie's fidelity to Scottish life and language.

Stevenson, writing to Barrie from Valima, remarked, "I read

(for the first time—I know not how) the *Window in Thrums;* I don't say that it is better than *The Minister;* it's less of a tale—and there is a beauty, a material beauty, of the tale ipse, which clever critics nowadays long and love to forget; it has more real flaws; but somehow it is—well, I read it last anyway, and it's by Barrie. And he's the man for my money. The glove is a great page; it is startingly original, and as true as death and judgment."[19] Stevenson's concluding words are unerringly prophetic. Five years before bringing himself to propose to Mary Ansell, Barrie expresses in Jess's story his foreboding of the effect his marriage would have on Margaret Ogilvy.

IV The Little Minister

Aside from *Peter Pan,* Barrie's next novel, *The Little Minister* (1891) is his most celebrated work of fiction. The heroes of both are fantasy-images of the boy David. But it was the fantasy of character and situation that caught the public imagination. The immense success of *The Little Minister* prompted Barrie to prepare a dramatization of the story, and it proved as popular as the novel. In contrast, the success of the play *Peter Pan* inspired Barrie to produce the equally successful fictionalization, *Peter and Wendy.*

The Little Minister—which George Blake has not inaccurately described as a "hopeless and utterly impossible—tangle . . . in the coldest fact ridiculous . . . to say nothing of its technical blemishes"—is the least typical of the Thrums narratives despite its strict adherence to the regional setting. The earlier "idyllic" presentation of the Auld Licht community did not preclude an effort to give Thrums and its people at least the semblance of reality; but *The Little Minister* makes few concessions to credibility. The love affair of the minister and the gypsy is played against a vague background of a Chartist-inspired uprising of Thrums weavers. The novel's half-dozen or so subplots are welded to the main narrative in fragmentary and implausible ways. Throughout the book there is much tiresome padding, especially in the narrator's asides and in the middle chapters focusing on the events in Nanny Webster's cottage. And, where it is not verbose, the novel is often absurdly melodramatic. Barrie avoids the proliferation of coincidence that marred *When A Man's Single,* but falls instead into the error of exaggerating his characters in order to make their implausible relationships seem plausible.

Even Barrie's most loyal apologists have found it difficult to commend *The Little Minister.* Both Moult and Hammerton admit that Barrie seems to have lost control of his novel's structure. Moult further notices that the original intent of the book goes inexplicably astray, so that we have an implausible romance with "heavily plastered sentiment" instead of the "portrayal of the life, manners, and religious sentiment of the now famous weaving community. . . ."[20] And even Hammerton, who worshiped Barrie almost to idolatry, is at a loss to defend the novel against charges of implausibility, incoherence, and crude melodrama, though he insists that it possesses an "inherent beauty" and states, despite much evidence to the contrary, that it is "the most truly Thrumsian" of Barrie's works.[21] Only Chalmers has been generous in some measure to *The Little Minister,* and his generosity is the product of hindsight; for he discerns in its hero and heroine, Gavin and Babbie, the prototypes of Adam and Julie, the memorable lovers in Barrie's ghost story, *Farewell, Miss Julie Logan* (1932).[22]

As in the earlier books, the fictional narrator of *The Little Minister* is Gavin Ogilvy, the dominie of Glen Quharity. For the first time, however, the dominie is directly involved in the main narrative. The name Ogilvy links him with Barrie's mother, and he is married to a Margaret long enough to become the father of Gavin Dishart, the David-hero of the novel. These details point to the interplay of the prototypic story through two generations: first, the "Enoch Arden" subplot and antecedent story involving Gavin Ogilvy, Margaret, and Adam Dishart; secondly, the story of Gavin Dishart, the Little Minister. In the first-generation story, Margaret is the helpless victim of Gavin and Adam, her two lovers. Gavin Ogilvy's love is deeper but less assertive; he is too bookish, too reserved to counter the masterful rivalry of Adam Dishart. So braggart Adam marries the girl despite her love for Gavin.

Subsequently, Adam disappears and is believed drowned at sea. His presumed death is actually a deception enabling him to live an uninterrupted life of pleasure without any obligations to Margaret. Now Gavin marries Margaret in good faith, believing her to be a widow. (The Little Minister's mother thus literally becomes Margaret Ogilvy.) The child born to them is named Gavin after his father, just as Barrie's brother David was named for Margaret Ogilvy's husband. Six years later, Adam suddenly reappears. His long absence has "killed" the spirit of the old Margaret as Jamie's absence had literally killed Jess. Adam enters the house with his lanky black dog and once more asserts his mastery over Margaret and Gavin. In his weakness, Gavin retreats from his home; the child is persuaded to reject him; and Adam's mastery is confirmed by his changing of the child's surname to Dishart. (Since Adam here becomes Gavin's new father, it is relevant to notice the appropriateness of Dishart's first name. Margaret's "first man" is that of the biblical father whose son Cain killed his brother, Abel.) Barrie's desire to usurp David's place is fulfilled in the assimilation by Adam of all the rights of Gavin Ogilvy. Rejected by his own child, Ogilvy now effaces himself by disappearing in the same manner that his rival had vanished years before. When, shortly afterward, Adam actually does lose his life at sea, Ogilvy decides never to return to his wife although secretly he hovers in the background like her guardian angel.

The second generation story, forming the main plot, concerns Ogilvy's son, the Little Minister. David Barrie had shown qualities that indicated a probable career as teacher or minister, and these potentialities are represented in the novel by making Ogilvy the dominie-father, and Gavin Dishart the minister-son. A more complex version of the prototypic story is now presented by showing Gavin in relation to two women (a splitting of the character of Margaret Ogilvy) and to Lord Rintoul, a "reincarnation" of the Barrie-figure earlier represented by Adam. The two women are Margaret Dishart, the Little Minister's mother, and a mysterious gypsy, Babbie, the girl with whom he falls in love.

Ogilvy, the narrator, speaks of two "phantom" women who distract men from their purpose. One is the evil woman who tests man and may debase his love by reducing it to a passion that can destroy him. The other is the ideal, man's superior, who may bring him a pure love that is not incompatible with the love of God. (Woman, Gavin explains later, is not an "undeveloped man" but an improvement on him.) The ideal clearly has affinities with the Holy Virgin; she is also identifiable with Barrie's own "virgin-mother." Earlier in this chapter we noticed that there are two aspects of the virginal Margaret Ogilvy, and in the course of *The Little Minister* it becomes evident that Babbie is the "happy-go-lucky" aspect while Margaret Dishart is the "domestic-serious" figure.

In the first chapter Ogilvy tells us that the Little Minister and his mother were "as one far more than most married people." In his childhood, Gavin Dishart resembles his mother; later, her character reflects his. He sits beside her when she goes to bed and is delighted when she tells him that, although he is not a tall man, he is just the height she likes. Babbie, the more frivolous figure, makes less reassuring comments on his diminutive stature. Like Jess, Margaret watches her son intently from the window. And, like Jamie, Gavin tries to conceal his interest in another woman; in each case, the mother considers the girl a sexual rival. While she is still unaware of Gavin's love for Babbie, Margaret tells her son that every woman wants her firstborn to be a boy. But, if a son is born she immediately begins to think of him as a man being ensnared and taken away from her by a young girl. In this fashion, Margaret declares, neglected little girls eventually get their revenge on mothers. Gavin, however, trying to ignore his passion for Babbie, assures his mother that she has effectually prevented him from ever caring for another woman whom he would have to compare, always unfavorably, with Margaret.

Later in the novel, the motif of the deserted mother is shifted into the subplot. The Little Minister encounters Babbie at the secluded cottage of an old villager, Nanny Webster, whose name indicates that she is a substitute mother. Nanny, like Jess, seems to be heading for the poorhouse; for her only means of support, her brother Sanders the mole catcher, is dead. Sanders is described, like Adam, as a braggart. Gavin Dishart, who knew him, hated the man. The brief account of Sanders makes it clear that his death is the last of his desertions of the obligations he owes to Nanny. This subplot—a variation on the story of Adam, Margaret, and Gavin—resurrects not merely the Jess tragedy but also the tale of Nanny Coutts, one of the chapters of *A Window in Thrums* that belongs outside the main narrative of the McQumpha family.

In "The Tragedy of a Wife," chapter twelve of *A Window in Thrums*, Nanny Coutts appears as the deserted victim of her cruel husband, Sanders. Nanny's "tragedy" is partially the outcome of her own deception in concealing the hypocrisy and viciousness of her braggart husband from those who believed they knew him. Nanny Coutts is left to her fate, but Nanny Webster is more fortunate. Gavin is the savior of both mother characters in *The Little Minister*. By becoming a minister, he had rescued Margaret from the poverty in which she had been left by Adam Dishart; by satisfying the whims of Babbie, he gets her to supply the money necessary to save Nanny from the poorhouse. In each case, however, the method of salvation is too incredible to be taken seriously.

Similarly, it is impossible from the outset to believe in the character of Babbie. She is the most obvious example of the inflation to the level of fantasy of characters in any story in which the brother David appears as hero. Gavin's love for Babbie and his success in snatching her from his rival are also unbelievable. Gavin and Babbie are married three times—twice in impossible ways (by a "Scottish marriage" in which Gavin is duped into passing Babbie off as his wife, by a "Gypsy marriage" over the tongs at the camp fire) and once in a conventional manner. But this last, conventional marriage is the only one of the three that is never described, for Gavin's marriage to Babbie represents the union of Margaret Ogilvy and her favorite son, a triumph of the rival that Barrie seemingly finds too painful to face in a realistic setting.

The fantastic elements of the novel are compounded by the theme of the deception. Long before Gavin's suspicions are aroused, the reader is also deluded into believing that Babbie is not the gypsy she seems to be. Throughout much of the novel Gavin appears to be on the verge of discovering what the reader has known since the end of the fourth chapter: Babbie is the fiancée of Lord Rintoul. But Babbie's deception takes the complicated form of pretending to be an impostor, for she really *is* a gypsy. As a child, she had dropped out of her cradle under the caravan, unnoticed by her gypsy parents whom she was never able to find or identify. The lost child was adopted and raised by Lord Rintoul. He offered her neither love nor pity; but, as she grew up and showed signs of becoming beautiful, he determined to make her his wife. Before her meeting with Gavin Dishart, Babbie had resigned herself to marrying the austere, loveless aristocrat.

The prelude to Gavin's first meeting with Babbie in the wintry loneliness of Windyghoul is his recollection of the legend of Caddam (the name suggests a conflation of "Cad" and "Adam") about a maiden who is pursued by an evil man into the depths of a wood where both are lost. The man's bones are found beneath a beech tree; but the voice of the girl still echoes through the woods weeping or singing, depending on whether she is unhappy or joyful. The death of the evil man, like the triumph of Gavin over Lord Rintoul, signifies a fantasy defeat of Barrie by his rival-brother. Fantasy is also indicated in the "island" location. Caddam is isolated; the wood is a remote place set apart from Thrums as an island is removed from the mainland. Caddam Wood, like Lob's wood in *Dear Brutus,* actualizes what might have been. David might have been the successful rival, and Barrie in his fictional pursuit of the mother might have been the one to die like the evil man who pursued the virgin.

Every episode that crucially involves Gavin occurs in an isolated or island location. Windyghoul, where he first meets Babbie, is an extension of Caddam Wood. Babbie comes joyfully through the trees to meet Gavin, unlike the girl in the legend of Caddam who had fled through the trees to avoid her evil pursuer. As we learn subsequently that Babbie is a "lost" girl, her emergence from the wood to meet Gavin is, in effect, an epilogue to the legend of Caddam. Babbie is dancing through the wood in her happiness at escaping from the "evil man," Lord Rintoul, whom she evades whenever she sneaks away from his home (the Spittal) dressed as a gypsy. Gavin and Babbie later meet in the isolation of Nanny's cottage, and here the Little Minister's love for the gypsy overcomes his suspicion that she is a "sinful woman." During the storm that follows the gypsy wedding, Babbie is kidnapped while Gavin is again isolated—this time in Ogilvy's cottage which is surrounded by floodwaters. Here Ogilvy discloses that he is Gavin's father, recounts the story of his involvements with Margaret and Adam Dishart, and identifies himself with Gavin's interests. Gavin in turn tells his father that he is not going to repeat the tragedy of Margaret and Ogilvy by showing indecision and weakness. But the "island" location signifies the fantasy of David–Gavin's resolution. Ogilvy's life stands for the actuality, the eclipse of the David-figure; Gavin represents only what might have been. In the climax that follows the great storm, Gavin is isolated with Lord Rintoul on an island in a ravine left by the floodwaters.

Rintoul is helpless as the floodwaters erode the little island; but Gavin, in an unselfish attempt to rescue his rival, exhibits a show of bravery that overcomes the Auld Lichts' determination to denounce him for associating with a gypsy girl. The crumbling of the island leaves the rivals equally powerless and exposed to the horrified gaze of the public. Gavin now makes a declaration that he is married to Babbie, and he expects it to be his last utterance. But, as the floodwaters rise over the island, the frustrated Rintoul and his diminutive rival are rescued by a villager, Rob Dow, who kills himself in the act of jumping into the ravine to bring them a rope.

The rivalry of Gavin and Lord Rintoul for the hand of Babbie has a parallel in the rivalry of Rob Angus and Sir Clement Dowton for Mary Abinger in *When A Man's Single.* Significantly, Gavin and Rintoul are rescued by another "Rob." However, the heroes of the two novels represent different prototypic figures: Barrie, in the earlier novel; David, in *The Little Minister.* The villainous aristocrats of both works are alter egos of Barrie. Indeed, Lord Rintoul is demonstrably a "reincarnation" of another Barrie-figure, Adam Dishart, to the extent of being accompanied by the latter's lanky, black dog.

From the final pages of the novel it transpires that Ogilvy has been recounting the story of the Little Minister to his granddaughter, the child of Gavin (Ogilvy) Dishart and Babbie. The girl, eighteen-year-old Margaret, is addressed by Ogilvy as "my little maid." She reciprocates for the story of her parents by telling the tale of a minister and his wife who want a daughter. God is so sorry for them that he puts a little girl inside a cabbage in their garden. The story, which anticipates the dream-child scene in Act Two of *Dear Brutus,* is the first of Barrie's children's fantasies. In *The Little Minister,* however, it is lost to the readers for whom it is most appropriate. Thirteen years were to pass before Barrie captured his audience with *Peter Pan.*

V *The "Tommy" Novels*

Barrie's most ambitious venture into fiction took the form of two closely linked novels in which he set out to expose the fundamental weaknesses of the artistic temperament. Usually known as the "Tommy" novels, these books achieved a notable success in disarming critical reaction. Hammerton, who was unsettled by Barrie's unpredictable flights into mawkishness and cynicism, prefers not to discuss these aberrations; and he actually asserts that "No good purpose would be served . . . by entering into an exposition of those points in which *Sentimental Tommy* fails as a novel. . . ."[23] Darton goes even further in rejecting criticism by insisting that "Such novels—and there have been few at all like *Sentimental Tommy* and *Tommy and Grizel* —are to be felt, not dissected."[24] Even Moult, who sometimes remembers that he is supposed to be writing a critical study of

Barrie, rhapsodizes about the *Tommy* books as the work of "an English Gogol."[25] Certainly *Sentimental Tommy* is an entertaining tale, and it is, arguably, Barrie's best work of fiction; but there is nothing sublime about it, nothing that puts it beyond criticism. It reveals Barrie's tongue-in-cheek whimsy and puckishness at their most engaging; but it does not reveal a profound thinker exploring and illuminating the artistic temperament. The only temperament enlightened is Barrie's, and it is therefore absurd to over praise the novel as a kind of universal *kunstlerroman,* like Joyce's *Portrait of the Artist* or Mann's "Tonio Kröger." Tommy Sandys is an alter ego of Barrie but of no other literary artist. And the fundamental weakness of the two novels in which he appears is that, except for Tommy himself, the only character Barrie really understands, the characters are, for the most part superficial or implausible, or both.

Barrie spreads the saga of Tommy Sandys through two novels, but in respect to the prototypic story it is convenient to treat *Sentimental Tommy* (1896) and *Tommy* and *Grizel* (1900) as one continuous narrative. As in *The Little Minister,* the prototypic story is played through two generations. The tragedy of Tommy's mother, Jean Myles, pieced together over many chapters, is a prelude and contrasting subplot to the main narrative. Jean's involvements with the weak lover Aaron Latta and with "magerful" Tam Sandys, who becomes her husband, repeats the situation of Margaret Dishart in all essentials aside from the "Enoch Arden" situation in the earlier book. Margaret's weak-willed second husband fathers the David-figure (Gavin Dishart); Jean Myles's "magerful" Tam fathers Tommy, who is an alter ego of Barrie. This triangle of braggart-victim-weakling in the first generation gives way in the second generation to several other triangular situations involving all the main characters.

Similarities of the two consecutive generations are also reflected in the repetitions of situation and character that abound in both novels. The constant reworking of the prototypic material results in a cyclical treatment of locations. If we start with the story of the hero's mother, Jean Myles, the action begins in Thrums and moves to London. With her son Tommy, Barrie's hero, the action then moves back to Thrums, returns to London, and later concludes at Thrums. Tommy and Grizel, the heroine, are "repeated characters" insofar as they embody the most notable qualities of their parents: Tommy is "magerful" like his father and a deceiver like his mother; Grizel, like her mother, is born to suffer after first being misled into believing that she is truly loved. Above all, Tommy is obsessed with the desire to repeat his childhood dream of getting back to Thrums; and when, as a man, he goes back there, he tries to relive his childhood adventures.

The account of Tommy's childhood and adolescence shows Barrie the novelist at his best. Except for the brief story of Davy in *When A Man's Single,* the full-length portrait of Tommy, his first study of the mind of a child, is at once credible and entertaining. Tommy first toddles into view in London, where his mother has gone into hiding after shamefully deserting the weak-willed Aaron Latta to marry the braggart "magerful" Tam. The name of Tommy's father recalls that of another braggart, the comic character Tammas Haggart, who for the first time makes no appearance in a Thrums story. When *Sentimental Tommy* begins, "magerful" Tam is dead, leaving Jean Myles destitute, as the braggart Sanders Coutts had left his wife, Nanny. He has also left her pregnant. When Tommy learns that his mother is expecting a child, he is determined to dispose of the rival for his mother's affections.

Ignorant of the "facts of life," he assumes that the first baby he encounters is the one his mother is expecting. It is actually an infant who has strayed from a neighboring house. Tommy "disposes" of this baby by taking it for a walk and losing it. Years later, in Thrums, Tommy witnesses a Punch and Judy show during which Punch tosses his offspring out of the window. He is caught and punished, and then the showman gives the moral of the story: "Let this be a lesson to you never to destroy your offspring." When Elspeth is born in spite of Tommy's efforts to lose the baby, he tries to persuade his mother to creep away from the house and leave the child behind. Later, Tommy learns that Reddy, the baby he had taken for a walk, has died of a childhood ailment. Nevertheless, as Elspeth becomes old enough to interfere in Tommy's boyish games, he constantly keeps her in check by threatening to exchange her for Reddy.

Tommy's deception of his sister is among the earliest of the many deceptions pervading both novels. Jean Myles writes to Thrums describing her "affluent" life in London when she is actually dying in poverty. Tommy surpasses his mother by actually believing in his own fabrications. In his childhood he believes in the fantasy of a Thrums he has never seen. An "enchanted street," an island of Thrums weavers who live in

London, helps to sustain his fantasy. In response to their stories about the Auld Lichts, he tells lies about himself. When he arrives in Thrums and becomes aware of the difference between his fantasies and reality, he drives away his disappointment by creating new self-deceptions. In all of his childhood exploits Tommy "lives" the parts he creates for himself. He gate-crashes a party given for juvenile criminals and steals the show by masquerading as a "boy with two mothers." He creates deceptions and deceptions swarm about him. The London neighbor who dresses as a gentleman turns out to be a waiter. Jean takes Tommy backstage at the theater where she works as a cleaner, and there he observes pantomime girls dressing as boys. He thinks of his baby sister as the "deceiver in the back of the bed," and he knows that his mother is lying to him when she affects delight in a worthless gift on which he has spent his money.

Yet it is Jean who shatters Tommy's first illusions. Before she dies, she takes him into the bed where the "deceiver" had been born and tells him the truth about her involvements with "magerful" Tam and Aaron Latta. Aaron responds to the dying woman's plea by coming to London to adopt her children. Jean does not speak to her former lover but stands at the window, staring at him before they part forever. It is now evident to everyone in Thrums that Jean's letters from London were lies. And it soon becomes apparent to Tommy and Elspeth that his dreams about Thrums bear no relation to reality. But Tommy adjusts to the situation by creating new self-deceptions; he is, however, unable to adjust to Aaron, a little silent man who works a loom in his own house—like Barrie's father. Aaron, who can always penetrate Tommy's "masks," despises him for being a "showman" like his father.

In Thrums, Tommy's fortunes become linked with Grizel, the persecuted child of a "Painted Lady." Grizel, like Aaron, can see through Tommy—at least until she falls in love with him; but Tommy's misfortune is to be incapable of returning her love. Tommy is Grizel's only friend; she is never on intimate terms with Elspeth, her antiself. Grizel is a born housewife, but Elspeth is never good at domestic work—only at loving and being loved.

The children play together, always led by Tommy, who decides the nature of their make-believe. And they all attend the Hanky School, an establishment whose blue and white room reappears as a setting in the play *Quality Street* (1902). In lieu of a brother, Tommy has a friend, Corp (the corpse), who is always overshadowed by the former's vitality and superior imagination. Their most notable exploit as children is re-enacting the Jacobite Rebellion in which Tommy inevitably plays the role of the Young Pretender. (It is not irrelevant to notice that Charles Edward Stuart claimed the throne as a descendant of the *younger brother* of Charles II). Tommy as the Pretender hurls his defiance at Queen Victoria, mother of empires. Later, in *Tommy and Grizel,* when they try to play the same game as adults, Tommy's illusion is shattered by the cry of Corp's baby.

Tommy fails the public examination that would have secured him the means of gaining a college education. He can only achieve success on his own terms. What these terms are becomes evident when Tommy also fails the Blackadder essay prize because he wastes too much time searching for the *mot juste,* the consequence of being too involved imaginatively in what he is supposed to be writing about. About this time Cathro, his teacher, dubs him "Sentimental Tommy" when he observes him weeping while writing a letter of condolence for a stranger. Tommy's departure from Thrums to seek his fortune coincides with his own recognition that his true métier consists in creating plausible fantasies.

The opening of *Tommy and Grizel* finds Barrie's hero embarking on his meteoric career as a writer. He has taken Elspeth away from Aaron, in repetition of his father's enticement of Jean Myles, and fled to London where he at last exploits his talents socially and creatively as a writer. His first book, *Letters to a Young Man about to be Married,* is an immediate success, and Tommy earns a reputation as an expert on women by capitalizing on his fantasies about them and their own fantasies about themselves.

All that follows—Tommy's triumphant return to Thrums as a literary lion, the death of Dr. McQueen (Grizel's guardian), Tommy's abortive romance with Grizel, Elspeth's marriage to Dr. Gemmell (McQueen's successor), and Tommy's liaison in Switzerland with the seductress Lady Pippinworth—was developed out of the imposition of the personal involvements of 1892-94, the years in which *Sentimental Tommy* was written, upon the prototypic story.[26]

The middle chapters of *Tommy and Grizel* focus on Elspeth (the younger Margaret Barrie) and the two doctors, McQueen and Gemmell, who are projections of the two clergymen in Margaret Barrie's life. Like the "replacement" of the dead clergyman James Winter by his clergyman-brother, old Dr. McQueen, who dies in Grizel's arms, is replaced by another doctor. McQueen's further identification with David is clear from his paradoxical references to the child Grizel as his "mother." He loves her unselfishly but openly dislikes Tommy; the latter, in turn, masks his aversion to the doctor. After the older man's death, Gemmell's unselfishness takes the place of McQueen's. The former's willingness for self-sacrifice—shown in his offer to marry Grizel (whom he does not love) when he thinks she has been deserted by Tommy—corresponds to Barrie's conception of William Winter's marriage to his dead brother's fiancée. But, in spite of Tommy's resentment, Gemmell actually marries Elspeth (whom he does love)—a development that patently corresponds with the actual marriage of William Winter and Maggie. Tommy's belief that he is sufficient for Elspeth motivates his resentment toward all men who find her attractive. He resolves that neither of them is to marry; but, when Elspeth deserts him for David Gemmell, his fantasy-romance with Grizel, Elspeth's antiself, is shattered; and he flees from Grizel into the arms of the seductress Lady Pippinworth.

Denis Mackail, Barrie's biographer, maintains that the aristocratic seductresses who recur in Barrie's works are "little stabs of vengeance" directed against the fashionable parasites of London society. However, we need not go beyond the Barrie family to see who these characters really are. An image of the wife-seductress has been imposed on the fantasy of the prototypic situation: there is specific evidence pointing to an identification of the wife-seductress with Mary Ansell. The first example in Barrie's work of the aristocratic seductress is Lady Pippinworth who works her charms on Tommy in Switzerland—where Barrie took his bride for their honeymoon. Grizel stumbles upon the seduction scene, and the shock of discovering Tommy's infidelity unhinges her mind .When Tommy returns to her in Thrums, she has reverted mentally to her childhood. This episode of the novel is clearly related to the last year of Margaret Ogilvy's life. Barrie's book about his mother makes no mention of Mary Ansell. But Margaret Ogilvy was present when Barrie and his bride were married in his parents' home in Kirriemuir (Thrums), and in the final chapter of *Margaret Ogilvy* we are told how Barrie's mother mentally reverted to childhood during her last illness. She died within a year of her son's marriage.

In the novel, Tommy tries to expiate his guilt by marrying Grizel and nursing her back to sanity. He is now faced with the consequences of extending his fantasy life into reality. But the tower of deceit he has built is insurmountable. In the last chapters of the book it topples onto him. A manuscript and an overcoat, two of the many "masks" behind which he has concealed his true nature, lead him again to Lady Pippinworth and thence to his death. The manuscript of his second book, one full of lies denounced by Grizel, had mysteriously disappeared during the intrigue in Switzerland. But one day he receives a letter from Lady Pippinworth inviting him to claim the manuscript which she had stolen as an assurance of his continued interest in her. When Tommy leaves Grizel to claim the missing book, which he calls "his baby," he is wearing Dr. McQueen's old overcoat, symbolic of the usurpation of the rival's identity, which he had obtained from Grizel by the "mask" of affecting a love for McQueen that was contrary to his true feelings. He confronts Lady Pippinworth only to learn from her that she has deliberately destroyed the manuscript. On leaving the seductress who has "killed" his fantasy-baby, he finds himself trapped inside her locked garden, enclosed in an island of flowers. He endeavors to escape by climbing over the garden gate, but his overcoat catches in the iron spikes; and he is suffocated inside it. Thus Barrie—as Tommy—destroys himself inside his "brother's" clothes, and the manner of his hero's death recalls the child of the prototypic story dressing up as his dead brother in order to assume David's identity. The iron spike and the overcoat that kill Tommy anticipate and help to explain the iron hook and the crocodile that destroy the villainous captain in *Peter Pan.*

Tommy's literary legacy to the world takes the form of his third book, which he had completed shortly before his untimely end: *The Wandering Child,* a story of a lost child who has fled joyfully from his parents into the depths of a wood where he can be "free, free, free." The message is unequivocal. Barrie could "destroy" himself in the character of Tommy, but the fantasy-David was indestructible. The Wandering Child is the precursor of Peter Pan.

Barrie is so frequently dismissed as a sentimentalist, according to the conventional usage of the word, that is bound to surprise readers of the "Tommy" novels that he uses the word "sentimental" in a special sense. Tommy's sentimentality is his belief in the masks that he creates at the expense of his own personality. Sentimentality, which makes him as a writer, destroys him as a man. He starts out as a hero and becomes an object lesson, a late Victorian equivalent of Walter Mitty or Billy Liar. Like these more recent characters, he believes the parts he plays more than he believes in himself. Ironically, Barrie's representation of himself in the character of Tommy Sandys is a mask additional to those assumed by Tommy and torn away by his creator. Barrie's own involvement with the novels made it impossible for him to see this objectively. But, in laughing bitterly at and with Tommy, the adult-boy, he was laughing at himself, the adult writer unable to escape from the childhood experience that provided his creative material. He was also trapped, like Tommy, by the glamor of popular success. The irony of his position, represented in Tommy's relations with Grizel, is that the masks which brought him success as a writer acted as barriers to love. The fictions he created in his psychological rivalry with David became progressively more elaborate, but we know from *Margaret Ogilvy* that Barrie's mother saw through them just as Grizel eventually saw through Tommy.

CHAPTER 3

Peter Pan

I *Development of a Legend*

BARRIE'S preoccupation with childhood experience indicates an inevitable progression toward the writing of a children's story. To the majority of readers *Peter Pan* is the essential Barrie. Everyone has encountered it in one form or another. Yet beyond the nursery it is frequently as unfamiliar as *Gulliver's Travels.* To reacquaint ourselves with Barrie's "legendary creation," it is first necessary to forget the pantomime and Walt Disney perversions of the original stories. We must then follow Peter through several of Barrie's works; for, although Peter was never to grow up, he nevertheless developed as a character from book to book and through more than one genre.

Peter Pan's story passed through three distinct stages: (1) a children's story in six chapters carved out of an "adult" novel, (2) a children's play similar in only a few respects to the children's story, and (3) a children's story in seventeen chapters based closely upon the play and its separately published sequel. Barrie first brought Peter Pan to life in a long digression, occupying chapters XIII-XVIII of an "adult" novel entitled *The Little White Bird, or Adventures in Kensington Gardens* (1902). The title of the book was evidently taken from the Grimm brothers' familiar folk tale "Hansel and Gretel," in which the lost children are guided first to the gingerbread house and then out of the forest by a little white bird. Two years later, using substantially different story material, Barrie completed a three-act play entitled *Peter Pan, Or The Boy Who Would Not Grow Up.* A final published version of this play, revised and extended to five acts, was not to appear for many years. But in the interim, he turned back in 1906, to *The Little White Bird* and excerpted the six "Peter Pan" chapters, which he published in a slightly adapted form as the children's story, *Peter Pan in Kensington Gardens,* illustrated by Arthur Rackham.

In 1911 another children's story, *Peter and Wendy,* appeared.

This was a narrative based on the unpublished play, using practically all the dialogue, and adding a final chapter about what happened "When Wendy Grew Up." The book was later reissued as *Peter Pan and Wendy,* or simply as *Peter Pan.*[1] Barrie's five-act play, *Peter Pan, Or The Boy Who Would Not Grow Up,* was not given its definitive form until 1928, nearly a quarter of a century after the original production.[2] By this time the text had undergone numerous changes[3] and had been provided with a long dedication in which the author gave a tongue-in-cheek account of the genesis of his play. *When Wendy Grew Up: An Afterthought,* published posthumously in 1957, completed the dramatic version of the Peter Pan story. Barrie wrote this sequel to his play in 1908. It was performed only once, in honor of the American producer, Charles Frohman, and was excluded from published editions of the play. Nevertheless, it patently belongs with the story, as Barrie indicated when he turned it into narrative form for the final chapter of *Peter and Wendy.*

II The Little White Bird

In *Peter and Wendy* Barrie compares Mrs. Darling's romantic mind to a Chinese box, a comparison equally appropriate to the structure of *The Little White Bird,* in which several plots are enclosed, one within the other, among them the children's story which was to be separately published as *Peter Pan in Kensington Gardens.* The various plots are loosely framed by the story of a narrator, never mentioned by name, who is a thinly disguised persona for Barrie himself. This character is substantially a resurrection of the type of unsuccessful lover previously represented by Ogilvy, the dominie, in *The Little Minister* and Aaron Latta, the weaver, in *Sentimental Tommy*: a middle-aged bachelor who, having been frustrated in his own love affair, cherishes a guardian angel's interest in two young lovers. The framing story obscurely sketches this bachelor's affair of long ago; and at one point, (Chapter 5), it vaguely associates him with a beautiful but sulky girl named Margaret.

Enclosed within the framing story is the main narrative that opens with the love affair of a young maidservant Mary A—— (named for Mary Ansell, Barrie's wife) and an impecunious artist. The narrator, standing at the window of his London club, observes the daily vicissitudes of their courtship; and, using the simple device of a "lost" letter, he intercedes to mend the inevitable lovers' quarrel. Later, when Mary marries her impoverished artist, the narrator redeems the beloved doll's house she had been forced to pawn and returns it to her anonymously, chiding her in a mock-serious note for forgetting that she would have some future use for it. When David, her firstborn, arrives, the narrator becomes virtually a second father to the child. Mary has, by this time, ascertained her benefactor's identity, but he maintains throughout most of the book an elaborate pretense of indifference to her sentimental interest in him. She vainly and mistakenly assumes that his concern for her is the whim of an unrequited lover, but the narrator has insisted from the outset that he prefers spirited old ladies to young girls. By the end of the book Mary has gained sufficient understanding of his taste in women to try to interest him in some female acquaintances of his own age.

However, the main narrative is not so much a love story as a conflict of shadow and substance, a rivalry between the Creator-Artist (the narrator) and the Creator-Mother (Mary), in which a writer's literary fantasies are unfavorably contrasted with reality, represented by a living child. This rivalry, a fundamental aspect of the duel of the sexes, has been explained in another context by Weston La Barre: "A woman can give proof of her femaleness in a very simple and irrefutable way, by having a baby—but a male must always *prove* something, his manhood within the group. What reason, indeed, would press women to create great poetry, music and art—when they can do better than that and make real human beings!"[4]

Early in the book the narrator invents a fantasy-child, Timothy, as a rival to the real baby, David. He then conveniently "kills off" Timothy so that he can, without embarrassment, give baby clothes, presumed to have belonged to the dead Timothy, to the real child. In effect, these clothes are intended to conceal the real baby in a fantasy-identity created by the narrator. The narrator, who introduces the story of Peter Pan to entertain David, brings the fairy story to an abrupt conclusion as soon as he anticipates David's emergence from childhood (symbolized by the baby clothes that he outgrows) and his consequent unwillingness to listen to the narrator's fantasies. Finally, discovering that Mary had abandoned her intention of writing a book about Timothy, whom she had believed to be real, he decides to write a fantasy of his own and to present it to her after she has given birth to her second child. His book is entitled "The Little White Bird," for, as he explains, all children were once birds, and children who have never had mothers—dream children—are little white birds (a notion that recalls both Grimm and Peter Pan's flying exploits in *Peter and Wendy.*) When David's mother reads the book—an artistic creation to rival her own maternal creation—she concludes that it is, after all, about Timothy, but that Timothy was only a dream-child and therefore a pitifully insignificant comparison to David or the new baby.

Framed in its turn by the main narrative is the story of little David's adventures with the narrator and his dog, a melancholy St. Bernard named Porthos. From the outset we learn that the narrator's interest in the child is heightened because David calls him "father." The real father is quickly dismissed as an inconsiderable "lout," while the narrator assumes "paternity" as a natural right, since his letter device for reconciling Mary A—— and her lover was eventually responsible for the making of David. The real child of the story is thus seen, from Barrie's whimsical standpoint, to be a sort of literary creation, an attitude equivalent to a relegation of the prototypic David to the status of literary creation dependent on his literary creator.

The identification of the two Davids (prototypic and fictional) is never left in any doubt. Not the least interesting of the numerous details reinforcing the association fiction and prototypic story is Barrie's description of David's tree-climbing abilities, which compare with those of David Barrie, and which both terrify and thrill his mother. The narrator, aware of her fears, mentions that he once maliciously sent Mary A—— a photograph of her son being hanged from a tree.

Thus Barrie in his fantasy can destroy David as easily and painlessly as he kills Timothy. The fictional child is entirely at his mercy; and, to precipitate a flashback, Barrie's narrator "destroys" him temporally by utilizing a time machine device in the form of a hansom cab that conveniently drives David back six years to a time before the child was born—in spite of his fears of getting "littler" and then evaporating into nothingness. Throughout the book, Barrie emphasizes David's possession by, dependence on, and "creation" by the narrator who furnishes his clothes, invents his fantasies, takes him to a pantomime in which he witnesses a clown making and unmaking fantasies, "kidnaps" him, and later borrows him from his mother so that he may undress and sleep with the child. The narrator in effect seeks to usurp the function of the mother as well as the father, and the episode that culminates in David's climbing into bed to sleep with his mother's benefactor is plainly a wishful adaptation of the prototypic situation in which Margaret Ogilvy slept with the christening robe that symbolized her favorite son.

Contained within the David story are two fantasy-tales: one, the Peter Pan narrative in its earliest published form; the other, the story of the dog Porthos who was eventually to become Nana of the *Peter Pan* play and *Peter and Wendy.* While the first appears as the substance of the narrator's entertainment of David, the Porthos tale is the narrator's own fantasy experience. It concerns the brief transformation of a dog who is almost human into William Paterson, a simple, honest, doglike man. Porthos as William Paterson is a tragic failure: he attempts to identify himself with the narrator and to adapt himself to the world's harsh realities, but he soon reverts to the old canine form in which he can remain oblivious to the shortcomings of man and continue to perform his duties as guardian of David. When Porthos reappears in *Peter Pan* and *Peter and Wendy,* he has undergone a change of sex and a change of name; but his function as guardian is retained. The name of Nana for a dog who is pushed out of the house into a lonely kennel recalls the deserted women, Nanny Coutts and Nanny Webster of the Thrums novels, who were left alone in their little cottages.

But, in the later developments of the Peter Pan story, Barrie definitely points to an identification of Porthos-Nana with the prototypic father. Mr. Darling uses the dog as a substitute for himself by feeding it his own medicine. Ultimately, he expresses his understanding of his relationship with the dog by climbing into its kennel to take its place. Mr. Darling's faults are evidently those Barrie ascribed to his own father: he is "dog-like" and an unsatisfactory guardian for allowing his offspring to fly away. As dog or as man, the character is an ineffectual one. The world flows on indifferently past William Paterson as it had done past Barrie's father. The dog-man loses all faith in human nature and then recoils from the world, accepting a life of mindless servility comparable to the Thrums weaver's. Nana is unable to save the Darling children from flying away with Peter Pan any more than the senior David Barrie was able to save his son from a fatal fall on the ice. The dog's attempts to alarm the household and drive away the intruder are suppressed by Mr. Darling when he leaves Nana chained in the yard. In departing with Mrs. Darling for a pleasant evening with the neighbors, he has unwittingly shackled his own guardian instincts, as did the senior David Barrie in allowing his son and namesake out of his care to stay with Barrie's elder brother, Alexander.

The wishful alternative that might have been if the father had assumed his responsibility is represented in *The Little White Bird* (chapter XIII) by the story of Malcolm the Bold. Malcolm, like young David Barrie, was his mother's favorite. His closest companion was Sooty, a chimney-sweep who killed bears—the dangers that menace children. One day while he was playing in Kensington Gardens, Malcolm fell into St. Govor's Well; whereupon Sooty leaped in to the rescue, and young Malcolm was saved from an untimely death. When Sooty climbed out of the well, he was washed clean and stood revealed as none other than Malcolm's long-lost father. Thus, without accepting his role or being recognized for what he really was, the father had always been present. Before the revelation Malcolm had taken his father's place in the mother's affections. But, after Sooty had assumed his responsibilities and washed away his voluntary disguise, Malcolm refused to tolerate his mother's cuddles. This episode, however, is pure fantasy; and as such belongs where it is assigned in the book—in the world of Peter Pan.

III *Genesis of the* Peter Pan *Story*

As a synthesis of fairy, adventure, and pirate story, *Peter Pan* is a perennial children's favorite. In writing it, Barrie imposed a collage of childhood enthusiasms and a wide range of elements from popular children's literature upon the prototypic material. Children who enjoy the story are not, of course, consciously aware of its psychological substructure, but its enduring popularity among young people must be attributed in part to the story's correspondence to their own ineffable Oedipal fantasies. Like speaks to like, and *Peter Pan,* blending autobiographical, fantasy-psychological, and literary material makes its wide appeal on many levels.

In the 1890's, while Barrie was living near Kensington Gardens in London, he became acquainted with the young children of Sylvia Davies, daughter of George du Maurier. Barrie would take daily walks in the park accompanied by Porthos who was a real dog before he became a character in a story; and sometimes the children joined him to listen to his stories about a little boy who refused to grow up. In 1901, when the Davies children were vacationing near Barrie's holiday cottage at Black Lake in Surrey, he again kept them entertained with stories; but this time the tales were about pirates and shipwrecks in locations based on Black Lake. As a memento of that summer of storytelling, Barrie later compiled an unpublished volume of photographs of Black Lake, had it bound with a printed cover in the style of an R. M. Ballantyne story, and gave it the title "The Boy Castaways of Black Lake Island." The Davies children had thus been treated in two stages to the basic of the Peter Pan story, for in Kensington Gardens Barrie had evolved his hero; at Black Lake he had turned his attention to the pirate-adventure story that would become integral to the narrative involving that hero.[5]

However, the fusion of hero and pirate-adventure story was not to occur until after the publication of *The Little White Bird.* In using as publishable material the stories he had told the Davies children, Barrie first concentrated on his hero as he had emerged in the Kensington Gardens setting. Chapters XIII-XVIII of *The Little White Bird* present a Peter Pan who is different in many respects from the hero of *Peter and Wendy* and the play on which it is based. The reader who requires a vivid demonstration of this difference should compare Arthur Rackham's illustrations of Peter in *Peter Pan in Kensington Gardens* (Barrie's separately published adaptation of chapters XIII-XVIII of *The Little White Bird*) with the familiar hero in *Peter and Wendy.*

Rackham's charming pictures show the earlier Peter to be a newborn baby clad in an infant's nightdress—a character totally unlike the heroic boy, usually dressed in a modified Robin Hood costume, who is, feasibly, old enough to defy Captain Hook. The baby Peter is depicted as an inhabitant of a fairy world populated with Brueghel-like diminutive individuals, gnarled elflike creatures and furry animals. Obviously, the earlier story is directed at readers who are far younger than those who may be expected to enjoy *Peter and Wendy.* When Barrie came to write the later work, he rejected most of the material concerning the baby Peter as too infantile for older children. The eternal boyhood of the hero, his encounter with the heroine, and the building of the heroine's house are among the few elements that are unaltered from *The Little White Bird.*

IV Peter Pan in Kensington Gardens

Associations between Barrie's hero and the goatlike Pan of Greek mythology are definite in *The Little White Bird* but more obscure in the later books. The baby Peter, in *Peter Pan in*

Kensington Gardens, rides a goat and plays an instrument that corresponds to the syrinx, Pan's musical pipe of seven reeds. When the narrator of *The Little White Bird* takes off David's socks, the child puts his toes to its mouth as if to play them like the reeds of a pipe. The mythological Pan lived in an Arcadian grove where he fell in love with certain nymphs who did not requite his affection, but Barrie places his baby Pan in an island on the Serpentine in Kensington Gardens and sometimes in a wooded area in the same park where the eternal child comes upon the little girl Maimie, who returns his affection but eventually leaves the garden to go back to Mommy.

Variations on Barrie's version of Pan in the grove with a "nymphet" had appeared previously in the first meeting of the Little Minister and Babbie and in Tommy Sandys' tale of "The Wandering Child." And, as Barrie had in his earlier book provided adequate reasons for our identification of the Little Minister with David Barrie, so in *The Little White Bird* he points clearly to the identification of David with Peter Pan. Maimie whom Peter-David marries according to fairy ritual is the "Mommy" of the prototypic story, but her name also suggests Jaimie (*i.e.,* James Barrie), which is in keeping with the book's preoccupation with the wishful identification of artist and mother in the story of the narrator and Mary A——.

Younger than her braggart brother Tony (*cf.* Tommy), Maimie is subjected to his bullying (which recalls the sufferings of Jean Myles and Margaret Dishart in the Thrums novels); but she admires him and tries to imitate his magnificent swagger. At night, however, Tony reveals another side to his character: the braggart is a coward in the dark. Maimie terrifies him with fantasies of a monster who is coming to bore into him with its horns. This "monster" is presumably Peter's goat.

Maimie decides one day to remain in Kensington Gardens after lockout time when the fairies hold their court and Peter Pan comes out to play. Tony also agrees to stay behind, but, when the hour arrives, he deserts Maimie. When the fairies find her alone sleeping in the snow, they hit upon the idea of building a house around her. When Maimie wakes up to find herself inside a fairy house built exactly to her size, she knocks her head against the roof in a manner that recalls an early episode of *Alice in Wonderland.* But, where Alice outgrows her house, Maimie's shrinks slowly away; she stands aside to watch it disappear and bursts into tears as it vanishes into nothingness. At this precise moment a naked little Peter Pan appears to comfort her. Barrie's description of his appearance before Maimie is a fantasy account of an immaculate childbirth: the house (womb) shrivels as the naked newborn infant arrives.

This episode recurs with some elaboration of sexual imagery in *Peter and Wendy.* There the house is built not by fairies but by lost boys who acquire a mother in Wendy (Maimie), when one of their number shoots her down (impregnates her) with an arrow. Peter Pan pulls the arrow from Wendy's breast and is relieved to discover that she is still alive. While the girl remains unconscious, the house is built round her and a chimney is provided by placing Mr. Darling's (*i.e.,* father's) top hat on the roof. Peter Pan, who shows more understanding of the significance of the house than most of Barrie's commentators, wants to order babies to come out of the house before Wendy wakens, but the other lost boys prevent him from doing so:

> We've made the roses peeping out,
> The babes are at the door,
> We cannot make ourselves, you know,
> 'Cos we've been made before.

Peter knocks on the door; and, as Wendy emerges, the children appeal to her to become their mother. At night, the lost boys sleep underground, in a womb-tomb of earth, like the dead David Barrie. Wendy retires into little house, and Peter Pan stands guard outside with a drawn sword.

The image of the womb as house or nest is recurrent in *The Little White Bird* and in *Peter Pan in Kensington Gardens.* Near the beginning of *The Little White Bird,* before David is born, the narrator sends Mary her doll's house. Mother Mary is directly associated with the fairy house-builders, for we are told that she too speaks in the affected "fairy way," pronouncing all her *r*'s as *w*'s. When Mary's baby is born, the narrator bemoans his loneliness, regretting that alone one cannot build a nest. Later, the narrator's "baby," Peter Pan, escapes from his island in the Serpentine to the little wood where he meets Maimie by sailing across the lake in a thrush's nest. While talking to Maimie, Peter, stroking the fur on her pelisse, tells her that he loves her because she is like a beautiful nest. Peter's own nest, in which he sleeps in a foetal position, evidently symbolizes the "womb" of artistic creation—the poet's "nest"; for the narrator informs us that it was made by the thrushes out of a five-pound note discarded by the poet Shelley. Patently, Barrie's emphasis is repeatedly on birth: the birth of babies, of a book, of a house.

With Mary's triumph at the conclusion of *The Little White Bird,* the exaltation of the mother-creator over the artist, Barrie shifts his focus of interest away from problems of birth or rival creativity to revert, in *Peter Pan* and in *Peter and Wendy,* to the old theme of usurpation of identity. The new emphasis—indebted to the conclusion of *The Little White Bird* that artistic creation is the sterile equivalent of maternal creation—represents Barrie as a pirate bent on stealing a mother, a monstrous thief whose missing hand, replaced by an iron hook, was devoured by a crocodile. Peter Pan here confronts an adversary who, in his passion to destroy his rival, will reach into the Neverland, down even into the womb of earth where the dead David sleeps in the guise of Peter Pan.

V *The Play,* Peter Pan

Barrie's most enduring dramatic success, *Peter Pan,* was first presented in London by Charles Frohman and produced by Dion Boucicault at the Duke of York's Theatre, in December, 1904, with Nina Boucicault as Peter and Gerald du Maurier as Captain Hook. The only hostile critic amid a chorus of acclaim was Max Beerbohm. The American premiere—with Maude Adams as Peter—was also presented by Frohman. It opened in Washington D.C. and was transferred to New York's Empire Theatre, in November, 1905. The play proved so successful that, as Hammerton has remarked, "America even more than the land of its birth was to take *Peter Pan* to its heart. . . ."

There have been innumerable productions and revivals of *Peter Pan* in many countries (see further R. L. Green, *Fifty Years of Peter Pan,* 1954). R. L. Green estimates that fifteen million people had seen the play by 1950, and this figure may now be doubled or trebled if we include all those who have seen motion picture versions of Barrie's most famous work. There have been two films of *Peter Pan*: a silent movie, produced by Famous Players-Lasky in 1925, and starring Betty Bronson as Peter, and a Walt Disney cartoon version, released in 1953. Several musicals have also been based on *Peter Pan,* the most recent being a lavish Broadway vehicle for the talents of Mary Martin. Among the many notable actors who have appeared as Captain Hook are Charles Laughton, Alastair Sim, Sir Ralph Richardson, and Sir Donald Wolfit. Peter Pan has been played by Fay Compton, Gladys Cooper, Margaret Lockwood, and many others.

The play, *Peter Pan,* written prior to *Peter and Wendy,* though not published until many years after, provided Barrie with the basis of the prose narrative that augments the Peter Pan story in *The Little White Bird.* All that will be said about *Peter and Wendy* later in this chapter applies to the play. The dramatic dialogue and, in one form or another, most of the stage directions were incorporated into the story, so that the play exists embedded within *Peter and Wendy* as well as in its separate published form. How the original three-act play became transformed through numerous reworkings and productions into the five-act play incorporated into the definitive edition of Barrie's dramatic works is a complex subject beyond the scope of this book. There is no published collation of the extant manuscripts, but in his book, *Fifty Years of Peter Pan,* R. L. Green summarizes the development of the play through its various manuscript drafts. Our concern is with the relationship of the play in its final, five-act form to *Peter and Wendy.*

With the exception of chapter IV, "The Flight," every episode in the story is fully represented in the play. All the characters are also retained, though it is notable that in actual productions the same actor usually doubles the roles of Mr. Darling and Captain Hook. And, for obvious technical reasons, productions of *Peter Pan* limit the flight to a brief spectacular performance by actors suspended from wires. The prose narrative is not subject to such technical restrictions, and so Barrie was able to recount dialogue and incidents occurring in mid-flight en route to the Neverland. The episodic and chronological parallels between play and story are remarkably close. Chapters I, II, and III of *Peter and Wendy* correspond to Act 1 of the play; Chapters V and VI relate to Act 2; Chapter VIII relates to Act 3; Chapter X (with its material slightly transposed) and Chapters XI through XIII are the narrative equivalent of Act 4; Chapters XIV and XV represent Act 5, Scene 1, and Chapter XVI represents Act 5, Scene 2. The final chapter is a narrative version of the dramatic sequel, *When Wendy Grew Up,* which Barrie excluded from the definitive text of the five-act play.

Barrie's skill at transforming fiction into drama was as considerable as his talent at adapting drama from fiction. He had already turned *The Little Minister* into a play with the same facility apparent in his transformation of *Peter Pan* into a story. Curiously enough, Peter's adventure on the vanishing island in the Mermaid's Lagoon is derived from the climax to the novel of *The Little Minister.* Barrie omits Gavin Dishart's dramatic confrontation of Lord Rintoul from the dramatic version of *The Little Minister*, but he returns to it again in the guise of the first encounter of Hook and Peter Pan. The adaptation of *The Little Minister* exhibits Barrie's ingenuity in pruning the prodigality of material that swelled the pages of the novel. The play of *Peter Pan* is as lavish in incident and detail as the first form of *The Little Minister*, and Barrie in writing it exercised all his skill as a dramatist in shaping a profusion of episodes into a manageable number of scenes.

The measure of his achievement becomes impressive when we compare *Peter Pan* with *Peter and Wendy* and discover that the story is scarcely richer in detail than the play. The whole of the Neverland is gradually revealed over the last four acts, each of which is located on a different part of the island or on Hook's ship, the *Jolly Roger*. The setting of Act 4 provides for a simultaneous view of the Home under the Ground and the wood above it in which redskins battle with the pirates. Act 5, Scene 2, is a little structural masterpiece, developing what becomes a crowded chapter of narrative through three brief inner scenes arranged with a fluency that anticipates screen-writing at its best. Excluding the sequel, Barrie requires only eight scene changes for the dramatic version of a story he later tells in sixteen chapters.

In three respects *Peter Pan* is more enlightening to a student of Barrie's work than *Peter and Wendy*. It is only in the dramatic version that we find the long dedication "To the Five" Davies children, with its whimsical account of the genesis of the Peter Pan legend. The dedication also alludes briefly to *Mary Rose*, and in the play of *Peter Pan* and nowhere else do we learn from Mr. Darling that his wife's first name is Mary A—— the name of Barrie's wife and the heroine's in *The Little White Bird*. Finally, in the first scene of Act 5, where there are a number of minor differences from the story,[6] Captain Hook communes with his ego in a long soliloquy that was not to be worked into *Peter and Wendy*. At the heart of this soliloquy the significance of the prototypic situation to the adult Barrie comes plainly to the fore. Hook complains that no little children love him: "they play at Peter Pan . . . the strongest always chooses to be Peter . . . they force the baby to be Hook."

Countless revivals of *Peter Pan* have ensured that Barrie's most enduring theatrical success is also the world's most popular children's play. None of its notable rivals—Maurice Maeterlinck's *The Blue Bird*, A. A. Milne's *Toad of Toad Hall* (a dramatization of Kenneth Grahame's *The Wind in the Willows*), and the adaptations of L. Frank Baum's stories of the *Wizard of Oz*—has proved to be a formidable challenge. The numerous critics who have scoffed at its lapses into sentimentality have not prevented it from becoming a theatrical institution. The play's perennial success confounded even Shaw who tried without success to drive it from the boards with *Androcles and the Lion.* Shaw told his biographer, Hesketh Pearson,

> When *Peter Pan* was in its first great vogue Max Beerbohm caricatured Barrie reading it to a circle of elderly people and children. The elderlies were beaming with enjoyment: the children were all asleep. I agreed, and wrote *Androcles* to show what a play for children should be like. It should never be childish; nothing offends children more than to play down to them. . . . Like all other [great children's] plays and tales it should go over the heads of the audience occasionally because this makes them feel that they are superior people with highbrow tastes.[7]

Unfortunately for Shaw, most children are not Shavians. They prefer *Peter Pan* to Shaw's *Androcles,* and will presumably go on doing so as long as there are Christmases and theaters for pantomimes.

VI *Peter and Wendy*

Compared to *The Little White Bird, Peter and Wendy* has a basically simple structure. There are no Chinese boxes here, no fairy-tale digressions within an adult novel. The chapters located within the Darling household and framing the Neverland episodes—the narrative equivalent of *Peter Pan in Kensington Gardens*—are integral to the story they enclose. Instead of a series of loosely linked episodes, we now have a coherent children's novel whose three structural divisions—Peter's arrival at the Darling household, the adventures in Neverland, and the return of the Darling children—embody the prototypic story stripped of the artist-mother theme previously imposed upon it.

Few elements of *Peter Pan in Kensington Gardens* are salvaged for *Peter and Wendy*. In the later book, Peter is more evidently based on the prototypic David than on the Kingsley "water-baby" called Peter Pan in *The Little White Bird.* The new Peter is courageous and clever, but also conceited; and his "cockiness," which reminds us of Tommy Sandys, infuriates Captain Hook more than the injury Peter inflicts on him. Scarcely a hint remains of earlier associations with the mythological Pan. Peter still has his pipes, but there is no mention of the goat. The earlier Peter had flown away from his mother when he was seven days old, and he was still a naked newborn babe when Maimie encountered him in Kensington Gardens. The new Peter had fled from home when he was a day old, but he appears fully clothed and about Wendy's age when he arrives at the Darling household.

The locale of Peter's greatest adventures is now an elaborate fantasy-island, a child's dream world reached by taking the second turning to the right and keeping straight on until morning. (The direction seems to anticipate the route to the fantastic world of James Branch Cabell.) Rejected with the original locale are the fairies who have been replaced by the "predatory" island population of crocodile, beasts, redskins, and pirates. Wendy is substituted for the lost girl Maimie Mannering; and, like Maimie, she supplies Peter with thimble-kisses and is provided in turn (though under somewhat different circumstances from Maimie) with a wonderful makeshift house-in-the-woods. Of Malcolm the Bold and his long-lost father Sooty not a trace remains. *Peter and Wendy* is a children's story; but, unlike its predecessor, it is directed at an audience that is beginning to outgrow the nursery—and at the incipient maternal instincts of little girls and at the adventurous and belligerent spirits of little boys.

A detailed plot summary of Barrie's most famous story should be unnecessary, but readers who left the nursery behind more years ago than they care to remember may need to be reminded that the plot of *Peter and Wendy* turns mainly on the rivalry of Peter and Captain Hook for the possession of the substitute mother, Wendy. The scene of this conflict is the Neverland where lost boys sleep in a subterranean home. Manifestly, the island represents more than unactualized possibilities, the Lob's Wood of *Dear Brutus*: it is also Barrie's Hades, a land of the dead. The lost boys who "live" there have left the maternal womb for that of the earth.

Attracted by stories told to the Darling children by their mother, Peter, on one of his flights from Neverland, hovers about the window of the nursery. In effect, fiction keeps him from returning immediately to his tomb-home—just as Barrie kept David alive in his books. Peter had first left the Neverland in order to return to his own mother whom he had deserted years before. But his return home was long overdue; another baby had taken his place, and the window was barred against him. (The cold glass of the window recalls the ice on which David Barrie fell to his death.) While visiting the Darling household, Peter conceives the idea of taking both the stories and Wendy back with him to Neverland where they can be anything he desires them to be.

While Peter is eavesdropping at the Darling household, he suddenly has his shadow cut off when Nana the dog slams down the window. Nana, whom we have already identified with Porthos and William Paterson as a father-figure, is appropriately the boy's "killer": the one who severs shadow from substance. The dog, being a brute, does actively what the prototypic father was supposed to have done passively through neglect. Thus we are shown the "truth" that had been evaded in the fantasy-story of Malcolm the Bold whose duty-conscious father rescued him from St. Govor's Well. The dull nature of David Barrie senior and his imputed guilt are subsequently depicted in Mr. Darling's humiliating retreat to the dog's kennel. In *The Little White Bird* Kensington Gardens magic had transformed dog into man, but in *Peter and Wendy* the "guilt" of the father who remains permanently outside the Neverland turns man into brute.

The severed shadow of Peter, recalling the memory of Peter-David, is retained by mother Darling. Before stuffing the shadow into a drawer (the equivalent of keeping children in boxes in the plays *Little Mary* [1903] and *A Kiss for Cinderella* [1916]), Mrs. Darling hangs it out of the window. She soon withdraws it because she fears that its exposure to the public gaze would lower the tone of her household or, in other words, that it would create a public spectacle of the Darling home as Barrie and Margaret Ogilvy had done through their preoccupation with David's memory. Later, Wendy, a virgin mother like Grizel, sews Peter's shadow back on his feet, thereby effecting a fusion of memory and reality, of shadow and substance, that makes Peter complete and enables him to return to the Neverland. Wendy's act of attaching the shadow to Peter expresses Barrie's own desire for his mother to give up the memory of the dead son and become free for the attentions of the younger brother.

Apart from Hook, Peter's relations are mainly with female characters. In one way or another, all the male figures other than Peter and Hook are minimized. Michael and John, inconsequential characters named for the two older Davies children, are relegated to subordinate positions in Neverland; Mr. Darling is reduced to the level of a dumb animal; and in the sequel,

"When Wendy Grew Up," the heroine's husband is never characterized.

The female figures who surround Peter are based on the inevitable prototypes: the girl-mother (Wendy), the inveterate spinster (the fairy-light Tinker Bell), and the desirable "blood sister" (Tiger Lily). Barrie specifies that Tinker and Tiger are both Bell(e)s, Tinker by name and Tiger as "the belle of the Piccaninnies." The former is the bell(e) of light, the latter the belle of darkness. Like Barrie's sister Maggie, Tiger Lily is pursued by young "braves" who desire to marry her; but she is "coquettish, cold and amorous by turns" and staves off her admirers with a hatchet. Like Barrie's sister Jane, Tinker Bell is the "useful" spinster (a fairy who mends pots and pans) who dies young and is buried beside Peter in her subterranean boudoir situated beside Peter's bed.

At the climax of the book Peter kicks his rival into the crocodile's maw and then proceeds to assume Hook's identity by donning the pirate's clothes and by imitating his stance and his hook. Peter fights Hook in order to "become" Hook; he adopts the personality of his dead rival as Barrie had assumed the identity of David in the prototypic story. The "substitutions" that pervade the book signify that the two male figures of the prototypic situation are now interchangeable.

Peter, the boy who "becomes" Hook, is also the lad who will never grow up and the rival who returns repeatedly from the Neverland to claim the girl-mother as his own, like Pluto ascending from Hades to retrieve Proserpine. Numerous related images reinforce the themes of identity assimilation and "eternal return" or rebirth. In the assimilation of identity, dog becomes nurse; man, dog; girl, mother; hand, hook; "tomb," home and womb; thimbles, acorns; buttons, kisses; hollow trees, tunnels or "suits of clothes"; and a top hat and a mushroom, chimneys. In exemplifying the theme of rebirth, the lost boys lose their mothers and find mother-substitutes (Wendy, and later Mrs. Darling); and, as we have previously noticed, they are symbolically reborn at the conclusion of the house-building episode: Peter loses Wendy and finds a new "Wendy" (the heroine's daughter Jane, who subsequently provides him with yet another new "Wendy" in the person of her daughter Margaret); Mr. Darling, who was previously William Paterson who was Porthos, "becomes" Nana, thus transforming repeatedly from dog to man, and back again. Finally, the inhabitants of Neverland are described as living in endless pursuit of one another: the lost boys who are pursued by pirates (the stealers of mothers); redskins (the conscience) scalp or unmask the pirates; beasts (uncontrolled passions) seek to devour the redskins; and a crocodile consumes James (Hook's first name). Birth, uninhibited passions, conscience, and illicit desire for the mother pursue the lost boys. The pattern of pursuit on the island manifestly conforms to the psychological development of a child.

In *Peter and Wendy* Barrie had endeavored to entice his mother from the memory of David. *Tommy and Grizel* had suggested the consequences of such an attempt. Tommy Sandys suffocated in the coat that symbolized the identity he had tried to assume. But Peter-David assumes the identity of another and survives. Since the identity he assumes is that of the pirate-thief Hook (Barrie), it appears that Barrie had come to regard his attempted assimilation of David's identity as a gradual destruction of his own. Once Barrie had thought to contain David; but now David threatened to overwhelm or to absorb Barrie.

VII *Envoi to Fiction*

Farewell, Miss Julie Logan: A Wintry Tale (1932), published twenty years after *Peter and Wendy,* which had long seemed to be Barrie's swan-song as a writer of prose fiction, does not belong to the legend of Peter Pan; however, it is convenient to discuss it before turning to Barrie's dramatic work. There is nothing very original or impressive about this tale for anyone who has read Barrie's earlier work. Curiously, though written over forty years later than *Auld Licht Idylls, Farewell, Miss Julie Logan* reads like a belated publication of a long chapter omitted from Barrie's first book about Thrums; for Adam Yestreen, the story's hero and narrator is, to all intents and purposes, the snow-bound dominie of *Auld Licht Idylls,* though Barrie has decided to turn him into a snow-bound minister.

The glen in which Adam lives patently belongs in Thrums country, while some of the minor characters who inhabit the area have their replicas among the Auld Lichts. The love story of Adam and Miss Julie Logan is strongly reminiscent of a romance in Thrums between another minister, the Reverend Gavin Dishart and his equally strange mistress, the gypsy Babbie (*The Little Minister*). Dr. John, Adam's friend, is merely Dr. McQueen of the "Tommy" novels parading under a new name. This patchwork of repetitive characters and motifs could be continued at length. The tale is, however, a ghost story; and in this respect might be thought an unusual departure for Barrie, though we hope we have already made it clear that all of Barrie's works are best understood as "ghost stories." Moreover, prior to *Farewell, Miss Julie Logan,* Barrie had, in his play *Mary Rose,* handled the more conventional notion of ghost story with conspicuously greater plausibility and success.

Farewell, Miss Julie Logan is, however, worth readings for its beautiful description of the ghostly Jacobite banquet and for the eerie twist of plot with which it concludes. An earlier twist—Barrie's joke about the Protestant Minister's (Adam) suddenly discovering that he is in love with a Papist (Julie)—misfires because it provides a climax to episodes that are too protracted. The outcome of this unfortunate affair is no surprise: merely another variation on the old, familiar fantasy. Shocked at discovering his sweetheart's terrible secret, Adam dumps her into the burn. Then, though he is forever haunted by her, he nevertheless lives on to form a "blessed union" with a lady called Mima (a transparently obvious misspelling of what Barrie, as a boy, usually called Margaret Ogilvy) whom he decides never to tell about Julie.

Farewell, Miss Julie Logan has been grossly overpraised by Barrie's admirers. James A. Roy, for example, compares it, inexplicably, to James Hogg's *The Confessions of a Justified Sinner* and to R. L. Stevenson's *Thrawn Janet.* "It is," writes Roy, "a beautiful and tragic vision, a dream of loyalty to a lost cause, of fidelity to an ideal." Readers who are unable to discern these remarkable qualities are rather more likely to conclude that Barrie's last work of fiction is merely a short ghost story that has been stretched into a hundred-page novelette. Old journalists never die.

CHAPTER 4

One-Act Plays

I *Themes of the Playlets*

IT is not surprising that a novelist who had begun his literary careers by mastering the vignette should have been attracted by the potentialities of the one-act form when he turned to drama. Barrie's first play, the four-act *Richard Savage,* written in collaboration with H. B. Marriott-Watson, was virtually stillborn: its only performance occurred in 1891 at a special matinée at the Criterion Theatre in London. But in the same year, Barrie caught the public taste with two one-acts: *Becky Sharp,* an adaptation of part of Thackeray's *Vanity Fair,* and *Ibsen's Ghost,* a skit on the current vogue of Ibsenism. During the following year, Barrie embarked on a succession of longer plays, beginning with *Walker, London,* and continuing until 1904, the year of *Peter Pan,* when he turned once again to the one-act form. The new playlet was *Pantaloon,* a variation on the Harlequinade, originally produced in 1905 in a double-bill with Barrie's *Alice Sit-By-the-Fire. Pantaloon* and eleven other short plays written between 1905 and 1921 are the only essays in the one-act form that Barrie decided to include in the definitive edition of his plays; and these are, therefore, the only playlets that are discussed at some length.

Barrie's one-acts are neither ephemeral *pièces d'occasion* nor shavings of intractable material discarded from the longer plays. With few exceptions they are sensitive treatments in miniature of fantasy themes developed at length in his major dramatic works: most notably the theme of what-might-have-been and the theme of woman's inscrutability. Most of the playlets turn on episodes of sudden recognition, significant realization, deception, discovery, or self-discovery. And these recurrent motifs are sometimes associated with contrasts of youth and age, and sometimes with contrasts between desirable ideals and practical or material necessities.

II *Pantomime and Mystery*

Conceived as a salute to the deathless tradition of *commedia dell'arte, Pantaloon* (1905), written eleven years before the full-length play, *A Kiss for Cinderella,* is the shorter of Barrie's two essays in pantomime. Chapter XXII of *The Little White Bird,* containing the episode of *Joey* the circus clown who makes sausages out of dogs and dogs out of sausages, had already suggested what Barrie might do if he decided to turn his dramatic talents in this direction. The actor-clown is evidently the supplanter of the serious Joey of *A Window in Thrums,* Jess' son who had been "dead this twenty years." So, as we should expect, for Barrie it is not Pantaloon, Harlequin, or Columbine but the undying clown (Barrie himself) who perpetuates the pantomime tradition.

The two scenes of the playlet are located in the private home of Pantaloon and Columbine. No one, as we are told, has ever been certain about the relationship of Pantaloon to Columbine. Barrie decides to make them father and daughter. It would be "cruel" to make them husband and wife, for Columbine would then be deprived of a love affair. Her secret lover is Harlequin, "a lovely boy with no brains," in contrast to the chief member of the Harlequinade, Joey, the unlovely clown, who is all brain. This Joey would not debase himself by being seen with sausages; he has appearances to maintain: he lives at a good address, wears a Savile Row suit, and smokes cigars with bands round them. But the old man, Pantaloon, has become a vulgar sausage eater; and he indulges to his heart's content, never suspecting that his daughter hates sausages. Poverty has compelled the two of them to live in a poor district, to make their home in a ground-floor flat with sitting room and kitchen combined, a place somewhat reminiscent of the "ben" and "but" of the house in Kirriemuir where Barrie himself was reared.

The curtain goes up to reveal Columbine alone, toasting bread by the fire. When Harlequin enters, they play hide-and-seek, a wordless game because, except through the magic of their dancing, they have never been known to talk. The game ends as Harlequin slips an engagement ring on Columbine's finger. A moment later they are interrupted by the arrival of Pantaloon, who is shocked to see that Columbine is engaged; for he had come to tell his daughter that Joey wants to marry her and that the wedding is arranged. They dare not defy Clown Joey; he is their only means of livelihood in the theater since only he can hold an audience and make it laugh. The other members of the Harlequinade are his flunkies, debasing themselves to satisfy him, and being caned by him when they fail to give satisfaction.

When Joey appears, ready to claim his bride, he struts about in braggart fashion and ogles Columbine through his monocle. She is instantly repelled by his nauseous manner. The clown kisses her with "the sausage look" in his eye, and is about to drag her away to the wedding when "love turns timid Boy into a man." Harlequin waves his magic wand and freezes Joey, Pantaloon, and Columbine into immobility. Then, gathering up Columbine in his arms, he carries her off to the sound of wedding bells.

The next scene occurs several years later. The dilapidated state of the room expresses the destitution of Pantaloon, now the sole occupant of the apartment. The clown enters and starts to gloat over the old man's misery. Ostensibly, he is looking for Pantaloon in order to offer him employment; but the halfhearted offer is a job as sandwich boardman advertizing a new Pantaloon. In fact, the clown has come to increase the old man's grief with a tale of the misfortunes of Columbine and Harlequin. After their elopement, the couple had never had a day of success. They had wandered starving from town to town, and soon the burden of a child had added to the wretchedness of their lives. Satisfied at the effect produced on the old man, the clown leaves, chewing on a sausage as if it were a cigar. Hardly has he disappeared from sight when the door opens and Columbine and Harlequin enter. Ragged, pale remnants of their former selves, they can no longer dance. The child accompanying them catches sight of Pantaloon and instantly darts beneath the table. The old man is on the point of turning the couple out for bringing misfortune upon all of them, when the child emerges, rubs Pantaloon's legs with a poker, and strikes at him with a sausage. Momentarily, Pantaloon recoils; then a surge of joy overwhelms his grief. The child is a new clown! The spirit of the Harlequinade is born anew! All are dancing merrily as the curtain starts to descend, and Barrie urges the prompter to bring it down quickly "before we see them all swept into the dust-heap."

A fantasy situation has been created in this playlet by Barrie's reordering of the original sequence of the plot. As prototypic material the last sequence belongs at the beginning of the work, to give it the following significance. David (Harlequin) and Margaret (Columbine) were the "makers" of Barrie (Joey), his inspiration as a man of the theater. But, because David won Margaret, Barrie took his revenge by deserting them for the sake of his public; in effect, he killed them by remaining indifferent to their fate. Appropriately, the dead mother and brother are represented by dumb characters and the ineffectual father by Pantaloon. Harlequin's freezing of the troupe is a vivid image for the effect of David's death on the Barrie family, and the abduction of Columbine is, significantly, an act of taking her through a window—one that is comparable to Peter Pan's departure with Wendy for the Neverland.

The action of *Shall We Join the Ladies?* (1921) develops through one scene, located in Sam Smith's country house in the evening, toward the end of a delightful dinner party. Sam Smith, a diminutive bachelor, radiates good humor and hospitality, beaming at his twelve guests "like an elderly cupid." This is how his guests think of him, but they are shortly to be rudely awakened to a different impression. Lady Jane Raye suddenly notices that there are thirteen seated at the table, and Sam Smith thereupon recalls the old superstition that, if thirteen people sit down at table, death will befall one of them before the night ends. It is a disturbing thought in the midst of such conviviality, but Miss Isit has the bright idea of persuading the butler, Dolphin, to sit at table, thereby adding one to their number and breaking the spell.

Dolphin, having obliged the guests with his presence at the dinner table, proceeds to fill their glasses with wine. After Sir Joseph Wrathie has called for a toast to Sam Smith, the host rises to speak. Captivating his guests with his "Pickwickian smile," he asks them whether they had ever wondered why he had invited them to his country house. He brushes aside Miss Isit's assertion that the guests were invited because he liked them, and then Smith begins to mystify the assembled company by querying whether he is as simple a person as they suspect him to be. Can one person ever really know another? Even the simplest person has his own secret. When Miss Isit urges Sam to reveal his secret, Mrs. Castro, a widow from Buenos Aires, intercedes with the suggestion that their host, as an inveterate bachelor, must have lost his first and only love. Sam obligingly admits that he had once loved a woman, but he has forgotten her name. The person he had loved the most and could never forget was his brother, Dick, who had died two years ago.

Having inflamed the curiosity of his guests as part of his

diabolical purpose, he now reveals some of the details of his brother's death. Dick, who was as attractive as Sam was commonplace, had died in Monte Carlo. The official verdict was death by natural causes; but, since Dick had died in suspicious circumstances, Sam had gone to Monaco to investigate the affair. After prolonged inquiries, he had concluded that Dick had been poisoned. It then became his mission in life to hunt down his brother's murderer. The evidence that he had assembled showed that the criminal, who might have been a man or a woman, was someone who spoke English and who had been at the gaming tables in the Casino on the night of the crime. The suspects, all of whom were outwardly respectable people, had, after unsuspected investigations of their private lives, been invited as guests to his country house; they are, he reveals, now sitting before him, listening to his story.

When the consternation subsides, Sam explains that he proposes to try a little experiment to trap the guilty person. It will take place during the after-dinner recess when the men join the ladies. Meanwhile, with one innuendo after another, Sam devastatingly discloses an intimate knowledge of the scandalous secrets of each one of his guests. In their embarrassment and horror, they hurl violent recriminations at one another while feebly attempting to conceal the truth that Sam relentlessly exposes. As the moments pass, his unwaveringly genial comments, now received as bitter cynicism, clearly imply that everyone present has had some shameful association with Dick. (To this point the playlet is a striking anticipation of J. B. Priestley's *An Inspector Calls.*) Every allusion that Sam makes traps one or other of the guests into an incriminating response. To heighten the terror, he gets Dolphin to pass round the handcuffs that are to be used on the murderer. When the guests attempt to leave the house, they find a policeman blocking the exit.

Smith now orders the ladies to wait in Dolphin's room. In their absence the men ponder over the suspicious reactions of their fiancees and wives. While they are speculating about whether a woman could have killed Dick Smith, they suddenly realize that the ladies must be having similar discussions about the men. Smith casually discloses that Dolphin had been working hand-in-glove with Scotland Yard in collecting evidence against the men. Their suspicions about one another are now aroused, and conversation among themselves produces the impression that they have at least as much to fear and hide as the ladies.

Sam, now ready for his experiment, invites them to join the ladies. As they rise from the table, a piercing sound of a woman's shriek comes from the direction of Dolphin's room. When the dining-room door is flung open, Dolphin reappears; his face is livid, and horror has made him totally inarticulate. The men dash past him, out of the room. For a moment Dolphin gazes at his master in a mood of mingled supplication and terror; then he withdraws, leaving Sam, his back to the audience, to sit down to a glass of brandy as the curtain falls.

This one-act play was one of Barrie's most notable successes. It received its premiere at the opening of the theater of the Royal Academy of Dramatic Art in May, 1921, when it was performed by one of the most impressive casts ever assembled for the presentation of a dramatic work. Two years later, at the St. Martin's Theatre, London, it ran for 407 performances. Described by its author as the first act of an unfinished play, *Shall We Join the Ladies?* tantalized the public and provoked ingenious "solutions" to the mystery. A. E. Wilson, who supplied the foreword to the definitive edition of Barrie's plays, queried "whether it was just a brilliant *jeu d'esprit* or whether Barrie ever intended to complete it. . . .[1] Barrie's critics have been sharply divided on whether or not to take this playlet seriously. For some, it is a clever trifle. Darton, for instance, considers it "a perfect little Grand Guignol mystery play" which "leaves the reader or hearer tense, horrified, and—not bewildered, but faced by a fascinatingly insoluble riddle."[2] James A. Roy observes that "the play can hardly be called a serious treatment. It is partly social satire, partly a detective story, and partly jesting. Perhaps," he adds, rather more provocatively than he seems to be aware, "the moral of this playlet is that each of us has a conscience which haunts us, and that there are secrets in the lives of the most unlikely."[3] Moult, on the other hand, is one of a number of commentators who consider the playlet to be a "brilliant" but puzzlingly significant piece, an unfinished work related somewhat obscurely to the full-length Barrie play, *Dear Brutus*, whose Lob is an earlier incarnation of Sam Smith. Moult assumes, as Roy suggests, that Sam is a symbol of conscience.[4] But whose conscience?

The question of what the play is really about has been generally ignored, yet an adequate answer explains why the play is unfinished and why Barrie had no intention of completing it. In brief, Sam (Barrie) is investigating the death of his brother Dick (David). Those who applaud Sam—his guests and the theater audience—are identified as the killers and are tormented by their erstwhile entertainer. Barrie has wishfully transferred his own fratricidal guilt feelings to the public conscience, satisfying himself that it was the public who acclaimed him who had "killed" David.

III *Domestic Dramas*

In *Pantaloon* the young and beautiful Columbine was forced to choose between her love for the penniless Harlequin and marriage to the prosperous but braggart Clown Joey. In *The Twelve-Pound Look, The Will,* and *Half an Hour,* Barrie asserts unequivocally that love and material success are incompatible, that material success is a destructive force, a "black spot" that kills everything that makes life worth living. The first and last of these playlets associate the braggart—a "reincarnation" of "magerful" Tam and Captain Hook—with material success. The heroines of both plays face Columbine's choice. The correct decision, as Barrie saw it, was conventionality itself: one should marry for love if one desires happiness; but, if one marries for security or success, one should honor one's commitments within the marriage bond. The woman who marries for money is usually aware of her "obligations," but Barrie insisted that in such a marriage certain less obvious obligations also devolve upon the husband: he must respect his wife's spirit of independence. She must never be allowed to feel that she is merely a piece of his personal property. In *The Twelve-Pound Look* Barrie's view of women and marriage is evidently indebted to Ibsen's *A Doll's House*.

The Twelve-Pound Look (1910) is concerned with two women who married for material security and with what that experience taught them. Harry Sims, a conspicuously successful middle-aged financier, is shortly to be knighted. When the play opens, he is rehearsing his role in the forthcoming ceremony. His wife Emily is a mere adornment to his success, a piece of property he had acquired in the course of a meteoric business career. He has hitherto assumed that he fully understands her and that he alone is the center of his wife's selfless, devoted interest; but he is on the threshold of disillusionment. A typist turns up to answer the letters of congratulation. A complacent, businesslike woman, she is unimpressed by the news of the knighthood or by the opulence of the Sims household. Her presence comes as a shock to Harry Sims, and Barrie temporarily deludes his audience into the belief that the typist is Harry's mistress. But this false assumption is soon corrected, for, unknown to Harry's second wife, the typist is none other than Kate, the first Mrs. Sims, whom Harry had divorced after she had deserted him—evidently to join her lover.

When Harry observes that his former wife is a poor working girl, his exultation is as great as Joey's over the misfortunes of Columbine. He concludes that her lover, having tired of her, had left her to fall on hard times. As Harry is happily remarried, he has no regrets; but, given this chance encounter with Kate, he must satisfy his curiosity as to the identity of his first wife's lover. For whom could she have been so foolish as to give up a prosperous and successful husband? (Similar questions were raised the year this play was written, when Mary Ansell departed Barrie.) The answer comes as a crushing blow to Harry's pride: there was no lover. Kate had simply grown tired of being treated as a piece of property. She had craved independence and eventually achieved it, in secret, by learning how to make a living as a typist. The signal to desert her husband had not been the voice of a lover but the moment she earned twelve pounds—the purchase price of a typewriter—by her own unaided efforts. The law, as administered in the divorce courts, had been as deluded as Harry in believing that it could interpret the motives of Kate or of any other woman.

When Emily enters, Harry tells her that the typist is unsatisfactory and will have to be dismissed. He recovers his pride in a bravura display of authority and possessiveness toward his second wife. And, when the typist has gone, he contrasts the happiness and good fortune of the future Lady Sims with the wretchedness of the working girl. But Harry's wife has had a very different impression of the typist: she had seemed so full of vitality while working at her machine. A light has begun to dawn upon Emily; and, just before the curtain falls, she asks her husband whether a typewriter is very expensive. Harry is visibly startled, for his second wife also has the twelve-pound look.

Barrie's critics have frequently singled out this playlet as the best of his one-acts, and it is indeed a model of economical and effective writing in this form, skillfully constructed and vivid in its characterization. Darton admired it as a "delightful comedy, verging on farce, but not devoid of pathos. It has a glorious *double entendre* for its ending."[5] Braybrooke was one of the few critics who detected autobiographical elements in the piece:

"Barrie shows . . . how the successful man does so often fail to be the successful husband, not through malice, but through thoughtlessness. For Sir Harry is not malicious, he merely puts his own success before everything else. . . ."[6] Moult is among the minority who rank *The Twelve-Pound Look* "among Barrie's lesser works. . . . It is a mere anecdote about a wife who inquires the price of a typewriter because she sees a way, through its aid, out of her unutterably tedious marital existence, but many people have taken it seriously."[7]

Half an Hour (1913) depicts the other side of the medal: a wife's decision to abandon her secure marriage, and the desperate situation through which she recovers what she had hoped to lose. The unfeeling husband is again the middle-aged financier, a wealthy businessman who had "acquired" a young wife as if she were another piece of merchandise. When the curtain rises on a tense and bitter scene between husband and wife, the beautiful Lady Lilian has already reached the end of her tether. The couple has no illusions about marriage; but Lady Lilian cherishes a secret of which her husband, Richard Garson, has no suspicions. She has a means of escape—not through financial independence—to a realm of happiness through eloping with a man she really loves. There is no question of a life of independence for Lady Lilian; her upbringing has made her unfit for a career as a working girl. She must have the security of a husband or protector; and Garson, realizing his wife's helplessness, has no compunctions about playing the authoritarian and mocking her misery. In half an hour he is to entertain some guests, and Lady Lilian is expected to prepare herself to receive them. But she has other plans. Unseen by her husband, she encloses her wedding ring in an envelope along with a final message; then, divesting herself of her jewelry, she throws it, together with the letter, into her huband's desk and leaves.

In a mews near the Garson residence lives Hugh Paton, Lady Lilian's lover. The Garson house and Hugh's apartment in the mews each occupy half of the stage and may be illuminated in turn as they become the setting for the action. Lady Lilian arrives at the apartment with the happy news that she has left her husband and is ready to go to Egypt with Hugh. The young lovers are jubilant, but their joy is short-lived. Hugh goes out to call a taxi. Moments later he is dead—run over by a bus. Confronted by Dr. Brodie, who breaks the tragic news, Lady Lilian stifles her grief and has the presence of mind to conceal her identity.

Now that Hugh is dead, she cannot face the consequence of being revealed as his mistress. There is no explicit indication that adultery was committed, but even mere suspicion of adultery would mean divorce, insecurity, disaster. . . . She has to retrieve the letter and her wedding ring before Garson learns the truth. The rest of the play is concerned with Lady Lilian's frantic race to save herself. She returns home sickened by Hugh's death, distraught with fear at the consequences of Garson's discovery of the letter. But the dinner guests have arrived, and she has to mask her emotions. Meanwhile, Garson has found the jewels in his desk without noticing the letter. Deciding to have a joke at Lady Lilian's expense, he pockets the jewels and locks the desk drawer.

Among the last guests to arrive is Dr. Brodie. When Lady Lilian sweeps elegantly into the room, having dressed for dinner in record time, he recognizes her at once; but he says nothing to betray his suspicion of her adulterous intrigue. She is introduced to the doctor and listens to his story about the strange woman who ran away from a dead man's flat, unable to face either suicide in order to join her lover or a working life of independence, apart from the husband upon whom she lives parasitically. But Lady Lilian is too anxious about the letter to concern herself with Dr. Brodie's innuendoes. She is uncertain how much Garson has discovered when he casually asks her what she has done with her jewels. Following his furtive glance at the drawer, she takes his keys and opens it. The jewels are, of course, missing; and, in the midst of her consternation, Garson suggests calling the police. As his wife now seems to be on the verge of fainting—though for reasons other than Garson suspects—he brings the joke to an end by producing the jewels from his pocket and placing them around her neck. Lilian's crisis is over. As the guests go in to dinner, Lilian tosses a letter into the fire and slips on her finger the wedding ring she had taken out of the envelope.

In Hugh's apartment Brodie had told Lady Lilian that those who risk everything must be prepared to take the consequences of losing. But Lilian was unwilling to accept this fact. Her own security was all-important. *Half an Hour* and *The Twelve-Pound Look* emphasize that for some women security, for others independence, can mean more than love or self-sacrifice; that women's motives, although invariably misunderstood by men, are usually sound and practical, directed by self-interest and seldom by romantic illusions. Both playlets are fantasy distortions of Mary Ansell's divorce from Barrie and her subsequent marriage to Gilbert Cannan. In the first, Barrie had denied the existence of his wife's lover; in the second, he accepts the lover's existence but destroys him in the character of Hugh Paton.

Half an Hour, a little model of the well-made play, subordinates the development and interplay of character to the contrivances of the plot and the exigencies of split-second timing. Structurally the playlet is unusual for its period. It has three scenes; but, by eliminating formal scene divisions, Barrie has suggested a unity of place without actually providing it. There are no scene changes. Lilian merely walks across the stage from Garson's house to Hugh's apartment, and then back again when she returns home to retrieve the letter.

Written in the same year as *Half an Hour, The Will* also spreads its action over three brief scenes. But, where the former playlet packs a swift succession of episodes into a mere thirty minutes (in what may have been unconscious conformity to the unity of time), the latter spans some half a century in the lives of its characters. The married couple of *The Will* are Philip and Emily Ross. Barrie locates each scene in the offices of Devizes Senior and Junior, the lawyers who draw up Philip's will. The general appearance of the office remains unaltered throughout the play, but the period is indicated from scene to scene by a framed engraving on the wall: one which changes from Queen Victoria through Edward VII to George V. The passing of time is also indicated by the aging of the characters.

In the first scene the Ross's are comparatively poor newlyweds whose generosity to others is a natural extension of their unselfish love for each other. The gaucheries of the young couple, their romantic ideals, their indifference to material values, their ridiculous fears that making a will brings death nearer, charm the sentimentalist in Devizes Senior as he helps them make a will that bequeathes their meager savings to needy relatives and deserving charities. After their departure, the enchantment fades; humorless old Surtees, the faithful office clerk who had been hovering gloomily in the background, discloses to his employer that his days of faithful service are numbered. The "black spot" that was always in him, as it is in all of us waiting for a chance to spread, is on the verge of destroying him. When he was younger, an operation might have saved him; but he had allowed the black spot to grow unchecked when he should have been ever on the watch for it. Barrie was to reiterate this notion of the "black spot" some fifteen years later, on June 20, 1928, in an address to the Rhodes Scholars at Oxford: "The beginning of all you are to be already lies inside you—a little speck that is to grow while you sleep and while you are awake and that in fulness of time is to be the making of you or destroy you."

In the second scene, Surtees has been dead for many years; and a brisk young clerk, Sennett, has taken his place. Devizes Junior, a middle-aged man, has begun to replace his father as the controlling partner in the law firm. Mr. and Mrs. Ross arrive to discuss a new will. Philip Ross is now a successful city magnate and Emily Ross a self-confident woman determined to obtain the maximum security for herself in the event of Philip's death. Money has come to mean more to them than their love for each other; they have lost their romantic idealism as they have grown affluent. The generosity of the former newlyweds has given place to cavilling over niggardly bequests to the same needy relatives and to "charitable" endowments to gain publicity.

When the third scene opens, Devizes Senior, now a feeble old man who lives mentally in the past, has wandered out of his place of retirement into the office. He perplexes the new clerk, Creed, by calling for Surtees. But soon Devizes Junior arrives and coaxes the old man into a comfortable seat beside the fire. When Creed now announces the entrance of *Sir* Philip Ross, the knighthood underlines the contrast of public success and domestic failure and suggests the parallels of Sir Henry Sims (married to another Emily) and Sir James Barrie. Philip's business career has been a long success story; but he is an ill-tempered, abysmally discontented man. Emily had died before she could become Lady Ross. But his love for her had died even earlier. Fame and fortune have not brought him happiness. Something had gone wrong with Philip's life. He expresses his disillusion in a last will that bequeathes his wealth and his hearty curses to his business rivals.

Devizes Senior wakes up while his son and Ross are discussing the will. He fails to recognize Philip; but, when the name Ross stirs his memory of the young couple who had come to his office half a century before, he regrets that their lives ended unhappily. Philip asks why this should have happened, and the old man explains: the black spot had spread within them. If they had been on the watch, they could have checked it; but the spot, the "accursed thing," the disease of materialism, gets nearly everyone in the end. Philip leaves the office with the desire to save some young people from the evil that had blighted his own existence; and he knows that it cannot be done with money.

"There is," writes Braybrooke, "undoubtedly an underlying cynicism in this play. . . . [It] lies in the fact that Barrie shows . . . that a state of having a moderate income is better than a huge fortune, whereas nine out of ten people would consider the contradictory to this, much more true."[8] Roy ignored the cynicism; for him the play is "a parable, the moral being as in *The Twelve-Pound Look,* that money is far from certain to bring happiness."[9] Moult, who dismisses most of Barrie's one-act plays as "trifles" or "pot-boilers," dwells at some length upon *The Will,* noticing how the dramatist "deals with its subject with a fine skill . . . it moves with consummate ease. . . . Light sentiment darkens here to pathos and irony, and the economy of change in scene and personae is superb."[10]

It would be out of place to discuss here the possible influences of this playlet on *Milestones* by Edward Knoblock and Arnold Bennett and on *The Long Christmas Dinner* by Thornton Wilder. Of greater relevance are the anticipations in *The Will* of Barrie's own plays. *Dear Brutus* is already discernible beyond Philip Ross' suggestion of what-might-have-been in the closing scene of the playlet. And *Mary Rose* looms in the shadow of Old Devizes as he assumes that time stands still, that change cannot occur; indeed, part of the later play's plot is already implicit in Barrie's contrasting of the threshold of marriage with that of death.

With *Old Friends* (1910) Barrie returns to an attack on the negligent father. The entire action of this one-act occurs one evening in the living room of the Brands' country house. It is a special occasion, for the Brands' only child, Carry, "an engaging girl of twenty," has become engaged earlier in the day. A visitor, the Reverend J. Carroll, has been enjoying the celebration; but it is time for him to leave; and Mrs. Brand and Carry are about to go to bed. Mrs. Brand is particularly anxious that the girl should not get overexcited as she has only recently shown signs of recovering from a prolonged illness aggravated by incessant headaches. Mother and daughter sleep in the same room; but Mr. Brand, who sleeps alone downstairs, is unwilling to be left to himself. He urges his guest to remain a little longer; whereupon Carry mischievously tells the minister that her father is afraid of the dark. Mrs. Brand, strangely disturbed by her daughter's remark, explains that the girl had seen her father sleeping with the light on one evening when she had wandered downstairs in search of a book. Carroll obligingly remains while mother and daughter retire for the night.

The men's conversation now turns upon the subject of Brand's alcoholism, a chapter in her father's life of which Carry knows nothing. Brand had tried to cure himself of a lifelong addiction to alcohol; his wife had done her utmost to assist him, but the vice had controlled him until, long after Mrs. Brand had given up her efforts to cure him, he had suddenly and inexplicably mastered it, alone. But he had not conquered his fear of the dark to which Carry had referred. He discloses to Carroll that he is terrified of shadows that creep about the house, ones that appear to have some mysterious connection with him. When his guest departs, Brand settles into an armchair beside the fire and quickly falls asleep. As the firelight flickers about the room, Carry in her nightdress enters, holding a lighted taper. The girl, hovering among the shadows that terrify Brand, is to bring the old vice back into his life again. She removes her father's keys from his pocket and unlocks the liquor cabinet. At this moment Brand awakens. Realizing what his daughter is doing, he cries out and startles her. The nature of his daughter's "illness" now dawns upon him; and, unconvinced by her attempts to explain her presence at the liquor cabinet, he is immediately anxious lest his wife should learn about the girl's secret vice. But Carry reveals that her mother has known about it for a long time. That was the reason for their sharing a bedroom.

When Mrs. Brand appears, she explains why she had withheld from Carry the fact that alcoholism was a legacy the girl had inherited from her irresponsible father. She had presumed that a struggle against the vice would be more effective if Carry believed the blame was hers. When Brand tries to give his daughter hope of recovery comparable to his own, his wife dismisses the notion that he was ever cured. Brand had never given up alcohol; it had given him up. The vice had tired of him; but, being too old a friend to desert the family altogether, it had returned to claim Carry. Mrs. Brand agrees that Carry's fiancé (another Dick) must be told about the girl's vice if she has not been cured within the engagement period. The Brands resolve henceforward to keep a close vigil on their daughter in the hope of overcoming the "old friend's" temptations.

Another delayed spark of Ibsenism, *Old Friends* takes from

Ghosts the theme of the father's sins being visited upon the child; but Barrie transfers the focus of evil from hereditary syphilis to hereditary alcoholism. The name "Brand" is patently derived from an earlier Ibsen play, while the characters of the Reverend J. Carroll and Mrs. Brand are reminscent of Pastor Manders and Mrs. Alving. However, Ibsen's influence is too inconsequential to prevent *Old Friends* from being anything more than Barrie's weakest one-act play. All motivation is moved to the realm of the inexplicable. The curse of alcoholism is treated implausibly, melodramatically, and sometimes ludicrously as a mysterious "it" that loosens or tightens its grip on the individual regardless of human will or impulse, and irrespective of the nature of the victim. In consequence, the play reads like a temperance tract that has somehow missed the point because alcoholism is actually Barrie's "substitute" vice for sexual promiscuity.

The characters—mother, father, daughter, "absent" financé, and minister—play out a fantasy about Barrie's sister Maggie who had married the Reverend James Winter after the sudden death of her fiancé, Winter's brother, William. Barrie's revulsion at this marriage is first expressed in *Tommy and Grizel.* In *Old Friends* Carry (Maggie) is not married to the minister, although their association is indicated in the similarily of names: Carry/Carroll. Carry is engaged to Dick (one of Barrie's names for a dead brother, as in *Shall We Join the Ladies?*) who never appears throughout the play; and Mrs. Brand suggests that Dick may be repelled when he learns of Carry's vice (Barrie himself believed that William Winter would have been revolted by Maggie's marriage to his brother.) The fantasy is completed for Barrie by the severing of all sexual contacts between the characters: the parents sleep apart, Dick (William) is kept out of the play and given a dead man's name, and the minister is turned into an old man.

In *Rosalind* (1912), Barrie's most poignant one-act play, the playwright interweaves two themes that relate closely to the prototypic story. The first, inspired by the character of his mother, is the idea that a young woman always remains inside the older one; the second is that love is only possible when illusion prevails. Charles, the young man of the play, does not recognize the woman he is in love with when he sees her as she really is. (Barrie himself was in love with the illusion of an eternally young Margaret Ogilvy.) Mutability, the destroyer of illusions, is, like material success, a destroyer of love. This last theme is a variation on the motif that appears in the last act of *Mary Rose* in which a mother lost in the illusion of an irrevocable past fails to recognize the son she loves.

Mrs. Page, the heroine of *Rosalind,* is a middle-aged lady vacationing in the seaside cottage of Mrs. Quickly. (The names of the female characters are, of course, drawn from Shakespeare.) The two women envy each other in a friendly way: Mrs. Page wants to be a grandmother, like her hostess; Mrs. Quickly wants to be contented with middle age, like her guest. It seems not unlikely that Mrs. Page's desire will one day be fulfilled, for beside the sofa where she is resting stands a photograph of her beautiful daughter, Beatrice. While Mrs. Page is pretending to doze, a young man named Charles Roche (the surname is identical with that of a man Sir Harry Sims had suspected of being his first wife's lover) arrives at the cottage seeking shelter from the rain.

Mrs. Quickly allows him to remain in the living room on condition that he does not disturb Mrs. Page. But Charles recognizes the photograph as that of the young actress with whom he is infatuated; and, learning from Mrs. Quickly that the sleeping woman is the girl's mother, he wakes her up and insists on discussing Beatrice. Mrs. Page unexpectedly tries to dampen the young man's ardor for her daughter; but Charles remains constant until Mrs. Page reveals that there is no daughter: Beatrice is her masquerade. As Beatrice, she is a slave of the public that will never allow an actress to be herself and a slave of the theater that decrees that there are no parts for actresses between the ages of twenty-nine and sixty. The middle-aged Mrs. Page is her real self which she can only discover by running away from her public image, the Beatrice who must remain eternally young. Becoming Mrs. Page has enabled her to discover all that she has missed by not being a nobody. Success in the theater has been bought at the expense of having a real daughter instead of the illusion that she creates out of herself.

As Charles is recoiling from the sudden revelation, a telegram arrives summoning the famous actress to London where she is to appear as Rosalind in *As You Like It.* Leaving the stunned Charles to recover from his first serious heartbreak, Mrs. Page disappears from view only to sweep into the room a few moments later as the enchanting Beatrice. As desirable and as unattainable as Dante's ideal, Beatrice-Rosalind instantly captivates Charles, overwhelms his grief, and flouts all that Mrs.

Page had said. For Beatrice everything is real except middle age; having a family is of no consequence; the public, all that matters, is her slave, her plaything to whom she tosses nuts when she pleases. As the sound of a distant train is heard, Charles follows his Rosalind—to London, or perhaps to the Forest of Arden; but she has ears only for Touchstone, the Fool, whose voice she hears in the whistle of the train that will take her back to her beloved theater.

Seven Women (1917)—a revised version of an earlier playlet called *The Adored One* in England and *The Legend of Leonora* in the United States—was withdrawn by Barrie two weeks after its American premiere, on September 4, 1913, when it achieved the distinction of being the only play by Barrie to be hissed after the final curtain. The play was reworked, and was given its premiere, as *Seven Women,* at the New Theatre, London, in 1917. The inspiration for this work is an idea also developed in the full-length play, *What Every Woman Knows* (1908): the complexity of a woman's nature is beyond man's simple powers of comprehension. But, where *What Every Woman Knows* is a subtle treatment of the idea in terms of the interplay of character, the one-act play exploits it superficially as a means of holding together a series of comedic reversals.

Mr. Tovey, a man with a bizarre sense of humor, is wont to entertain himself by observing the consequences of informing credulous guests that a murderess has been invited to his house parties. Mrs. Tovey, who considers her husband's idea of amusement to be in bad taste, warns him against trying to be funny at the expense of his old friend and guest of honor, Captain Rattray. But Tovey's sense of fun is irrepressible; and the Captain, whom he has not seen for twenty years, is an easy target. Tovey tells his friend that seven women guests are expected at the party that evening: a lady who has no sense of humor and another who has too much sense of humor; a woman with strong political commitments who is easily recognizable because she drops things all over the place; an "old-fashioned, obedient clinging kind of woman"; a woman who is all mother and nothing else; a coquette; and a murderess.

As the first lady arrives, Tovey slips out of the room, leaving the Captain, a bachelor who is terrified of women, to face her alone and discover which of the seven women has arrived first. Leonora, the "unspeakable darling" who appears, looks like the clinging woman; but Rattray has no sooner identified her as such than she begins to talk about her political interests and drops her handkerchief to the floor. Evidently, then, she is the politician. But as Rattray comes to this conclusion, Leonora starts to rhapsodize at length about the two Tovey children and her own six offspring. Presumably she is the one who is a mother and nothing else, or so it seems to Rattray until she begins to drop things again, behaves like a coquette, and fails to respond to his best joke. Rattray is now certain that there are only two of the seven women she could not possibly be: the lady with too much sense of humor and the murderess. At this point Leonora realizes that she has somehow become an unwitting party to one of Tovey's jokes. Deciding to keep the fun going, she confesses to being the murderess. Her account of the murder she claims to have committed indicates to the audience, if not to Rattray, that she could also be the lady with too much sense of humor. The Captain is horrified to learn that she had pushed a man out of a railroad carriage when he had refused to close the window and shut out the cold air that was blowing on her sick child.

As the Toveys enter, Leonora turns on the Captain and denounces him for accusing her of being a murderess. Rattray, in his confusion, appeals to his host; Tovey, realizing that his little jest has gone far enough, explains that Leonora is not a murderess but a devoted mother; the murder she had described is merely the sort of crime she *might* commit if she had any criminal instincts. But so far the Captain has seen through only half of Tovey's jesting. He still expects six other ladies to arrive. His host therefore to enlighten him by pointing out that there are no other ladies—Leonora is all seven—and more than that. In particular, as Rattray is delighted to learn, she is a marriageable widow.

IV *Echoes of the War*

The New Word and *A Well-Remembered Voice* are the most closely related of Barrie's four war playlets. The names of the main characters change from play to play; but, aside from this fact, these two one-act plays are essentially the first and third acts of an unfinished tragedy. An enterprising reader may make up the deficiency by regarding the closing scenes of R. C. Sheriff's *Journey's End* as a kind of second act; then the play as a whole would provide a unique dramatic chronicle of the changing mood of England during the years 1914-18. Beginning with a youthful buoyancy, an eager straining for the conflict, the action would pass through disillusionment and death in battle to the dark memories and cold comfort of the elders who survived at home.

It is significant, however, that Barrie himself never wrote the sort of "middle act" that Sheriff's play supplies. There is not the slightest hint that, as a dramatist, the war gave him anything more than a public situation in which to express his private psychological problems. Certainly the poetry and the pity of war never replace the familiar old sentiment and whimsy. In none of Barrie's "war" playlets is there a sense of the brutality of battle. Barrie has no trench scenes, no allusions anywhere to the mud and blood of the western front. Where there is pity, Barrie seems to have found it not for the victims of war but for bereaved English fathers whose characteristic restraint prevents them from expressing their emotions. Both *The New Word* and *A Well-Remembered Voice* are, therefore, largely irrelevant as "echoes of the war," and the latter playlet in particular is so wide of the mark as to be sacrilegious. The hero of this piece goes into battle looking forward to a great "lark"—like Peter Pan's expecting that to die will be an awfully big adventure—and anticipating, quite accurately, an extension of the public-school spirit and the manner of the cricket field. Death, when it comes, translates him into a public-school heaven and an eternal place at the right hand of his schoolboy cricket hero.

The New Word (1915) takes place in the home of the Torrance family, but Barrie observes that the scene could be in any room where father and son confront each other. It is 1915; and, although we are not immediately aware of it, Roger, the son, is upstairs donning his second lieutenant's uniform for the first time. The curtain rises on the living room where Mr. Torrance is reading the evening paper while his wife and seventeen-year-old daughter, Emma, are eagerly listening to Roger's footsteps in the bedroom above. Mr. Torrance, the only member of the family who is outwardly calm, takes private pleasure in making ironic comments on his wife's maternal solicitude for the son who is at that moment stepping out of his boyhood. Mrs. Torrance urges her husband to be "nice" to the "boy": Roger has always been shy of his father.

When Mr. Torrance queries whether his wife has ever realized that he is somewhat shy of Roger, she passes over that remark as a sample of his usual sarcasm. She does not expect a father to have a relationship comparable to a mother's intimacy with her son (the same attitude is expressed by the mother in *A Well-Remembered Voice*), but she wants her husband to show more warmth toward Roger than he has exhibited in the past. Above all, she expects no more sarcasm. In return, she will contrive to leave father and son alone together to reach an understanding before Roger joins his regiment. At this moment, Emma flings open the door to reveal Second Lieutenant Torrance in his resplendent uniform, armed with a ceremonial sword. Despite Mr. Torrance's occasional lapses, his wife is as good as her word. But she does not depart before reminding her son of his brother Harry—only two years older than Roger—who had died at the age of seven. Roger can no longer recall him, but he is proud to hear his mother say that, if Harry had lived, she would gladly have seen him serve his country in its hour of peril.

Now Roger and his father are left alone. At first there are embarrassing attempts at superficial conversation punctuated by long and even more embarrassing silences. By awkward steps, however, Roger gradually realizes that his father understands him more profoundly than anyone else—certainly more intimately than his mother. This fact does not surprise Mr. Torrance; for, as he explains to Roger, "I know because you are me." All that is now lacking in their new relationship is Roger's willingness to express his affection for his father. Mr. Torrance observes that Roger's mother would be overjoyed to hear him say "dear father." But the most delighted person would, of course, be Mr. Torrance himself. Roger, however, is unwilling to oblige by saying anything so "effeminate." Mrs. Torrance returns as the growing strain of the new relationship is beginning to inflame the tempers of father and son. On querying the situation, she is told by her husband that he has been helping Roger to take his first trench. They had taken it together, but no doubt it would be captured by the enemy in the night. Mrs. Torrance, though unable to identify herself in the role of adversary, comprehends dimly that there is now a private understanding between her husband and her son from which she has been excluded. She is unaware that Roger has, at last, established a true relationship with each of his parents. "Good-night, dear father," he says, using the new word for the first time as he passes out of the room. Mr. Torrance, left alone, rubs his hands victoriously as the curtain falls.

The séance that opens *A Well-Remembered Voice* (1918) has been arranged to give Mrs. Don the opportunity of trying to communicate with her dead soldier-son (another Dick). Mr. Don, a professed agnostic, has been excluded from the mystic rituals. Reminding us of our first glimpse of Mr. Torrance, he sits to one side of the stage, in the great ingle-nook of his artist's studio, endeavoring hopelessly to read his evening paper by firelight. His wife, younger than himself and a domineering personality, has browbeaten him into a conviction of his own deficiencies as a husband and his insensitivity to the death of their son. As the séance proceeds, the people at the table remain oblivious of Mr. Don's presence.

Letter by letter, a message is rapped out. Mrs. Don deciphers the puzzling words as "Love Bade Me Welcome" (a line from George Herbert's poem, "The Temple"); but she receives no further communication from the dead—evidently because of unsympathetic presence of her husband. When the séance abruptly concludes, Mrs. Don turns upon her husband, who forlornly concedes that he had never mattered very much to his son. Dick had always been his mother's "chum": together they had "shut the door softly on old Don, always anxious not to hurt his feelings, and then ran into each other's arms." Mrs. Don, offended by her husband's refusal to believe in the possibility of communication with the dead, cites his skepticism as a clear indication that sons always mean much less to their fathers than to their mothers.

Left alone in the silence and the deepening shadows, Mrs. Don is suddenly aroused by a well-remembered voice calling out of the darkness "Father." It is Dick's ghost, released temporarily from the land of the dead by the password, "Love Bade Me Welcome." Ghosts are permitted to manifest themselves to only one chosen person, and Dick's choice has been his father. While alive, Dick had always underrated his father; but in death he has come to understand that not his mother but his father had missed him most of all. At his father's request Dick describes the veil that is drawn between the living and the dead; he recounts his own experience of death in battle which had come suddenly, without agony, and which had drawn him into a peaceful world of eternally lost young men, the Neverland of older boys.

Looking about the room, Dick comes upon some scraps of paper on which are written the letters of incomplete words received during the séance. When he reads aloud the letters H A R, they convey no meaning to him; nor do they correspond to any message received during the séance. Barrie never explains these letters in this play, but we may recall that Harry was the name of the dead child mentioned in *The New Word.* Harry is also the heroine's "lost child" in *Mary Rose,* the play Barrie wrote immediately after *A Well-Remembered Voice.*

When Mrs. Don reappears, Dick refuses to manifest himself

to her, despite his father's entreaties. The mother thus remains unaware of her son's presence. The dead, we learn, cannot rest in peace when their mothers waste a lifetime mourning for them. Dick's glimpse of his girlfriend Laura and his brief encounter with his father are sufficient to convince him that these two will not use the memory of a loved one as an excuse to deny themselves happy, useful lives. The well-remembered voice is a plea for the living to live.

The last two plays of the "war" quartet are less obviously linked than *The New Word* and *A Well-Remembered Voice.* Mrs. Dowey, the heroine of *The Old Lady Shows Her Medals* (1917), is an old Scotswoman (actually a Thrums exile) living in London where she earns a pittance working as a charwoman. Barrie's whimsical foreword refers to her as a "criminal," but the old lady's criminality consists of nothing more than deceiving her fellow charwomen and a clergyman into believing that she, a lonely spinster, has a soldier son. The first of the three scenes reveals Mrs. Dowey entertaining her charwomen friends, three old ladies who provide an occasional choric commentary on the action of the play. This gathering of proud mothers boasts of soldier sons who are away fighting in strange lands. Proudest of all is Mrs. Dowey, who brandishes letters she claims to have received regularly from her son Kenneth, a private in the Black Watch regiment. But unexpected news brought by the local clergyman, Mr. Willings, puts a sudden end to boasting. At the Church Army relief center, Willings had run into a kilted soldier who identified himself as Kenneth Dowey of the Black Watch. As the young man was evidently unaware of his mother's presence in London, Mr. Willings had offered to conduct him to Mrs. Dowey's home. When Kenneth strides into the room, the clergyman and the charwomen friends unsuspectingly leave a quaking Mrs. Dowey alone to face her "son."

At first, the soldier denounces her for being a lying trickster. The letters she claimed to have received from him are old envelopes rescued from waste-paper baskets in the offices where she works as charwoman. His name and regiment she admits having picked out of a newspaper report in which he had been cited for bravery in action. Kenneth, who is unmoved by her explanation of the "invented son" as an old woman's way of getting involved in the war, jeers at her miserable deception and rejects her offer of hospitality. He is about to walk out on her forever and go in search of Lady Dolly Kanister, the benefactress who had sent him gift packages while he was in the front line, when Mrs. Dowey reveals that all the gifts had come from her. Brought to the point of capitulation, Kenneth is now willing to accept the old lady's hospitality without accepting her as a mother. Before he can consider becoming her son, she has to prove herself satisfactory. Mrs. Dowey joyfully accepts a probationary period when she learns that Kenneth is unmarried and an orphan. She has everything ready to make his short furlough as comfortable as possible. Kenneth for his part offers to take the old lady to the theater, and the first scene concludes with a glimpse of her delight as she prepares to adorn herself for the evening ahead.

A few days later the charwomen friends have assembled in Mrs. Dowey's flat with parting gifts for Kenneth who is about to return to the front line. When Mrs. Dowey appears, she is elegantly dressed and radiantly happy. Kenneth has been giving her the time of her life—a few glorious days that had culminated the previous evening in a never-to-be-forgotten champagne supper. Left alone with her young soldier, the old lady knows that she has passed the probationary period. But it is time for their farewells. Mrs. Dowey always knew that men must go out to win their medals; but Kenneth now realizes that women have medals too. Henceforward, he will acknowledge what she is justly entitled to: he will regard the old lady as his mother and report her name officially as his next of kin. As they part, he tells her that she is now what home and England mean to him.

In a brief envoi we observe the old lady alone, a month or two after Kenneth's death in action. She is not dressed in mourning, for it is a working day and she must soon arm herself with mop and pail. But, before leaving for the daily routine, she glances fondly at her medals—mementos of Kenneth—a champagne cork and a package of real letters, souvenirs of those wonderful days they had spent together. She does not weep; she proudly puts her precious things away and, triumphantly grasping mop and pail, trudges off to begin the day's work.

Barbara's Wedding (1927), the last of Barrie's so-called Echoes of the War, was written prior to the armistice of 1918 but did not receive its premiere performance until nearly ten years later. In 1927 Barrie's patronizing treatment of the breakdown of class barriers must have seemed quaintly Edwardian. The play's late production may also have exposed what had been concealed in producing the other "war" echoes during a period of patriotic hysteria: that Barrie was not really concerned with the war and had said nothing of significance about it. The burden of the play is similar to that of *A Well-Remembered Voice*: that the past is too much with the older generation; it must learn to live on in spite of bereavements and to accept the social changes of a new age. In 1918, and certainly in 1927, Barrie needed the message more than his audience.

Of the two scenes in *Barbara's Wedding,* the first is a flashback, though this technique is not evident to the audience until about halfway through the play. The flashback objectifies the old Colonel's memories with all their promise of what-might-have-been. (The second act of *Dear Brutus,* written at approximately the same time, is an obvious parallel.) Throughout the play the old man remains seated at the open windows of his country cottage as visions of the past come to him, then fade, to be succeeded in the second scene with contrasting glimpses of the present.

The Colonel had been disturbed in the early morning by a sound he took to be thunder; but young Dering, the gardener, had heard nothing. His granddaughter Barbara appears, and soon afterward Billy, the boy she intends to marry, accompanied by a German friend named Karl. They have been playing together beside the stream. The Colonel tells them of his vision of Barbara's wedding: Barbara, Granny, and a nurse had appeared in his dream, but not Billy; and there had been something inexplicably sad about what he had seen. The old man somehow imagines that it is Barbara's wedding on that very day, that Ellen, his wife, had told him she was going to church for the ceremony. When Barbara tries to convince him that he is mistaken, the sound of wedding bells is suddenly heard. Billy and Barbara attempt to move close to each other, but cannot. As the bells grow louder, the young people, mere figments of the old man's memory, fade from view.

The bells continue to ring until Ellen comes into the room. We learn from her that it is indeed Barbara's wedding day, but she has not married Billy. Her first love had died in action, probably in the same battle in which Karl, who had become his German enemy, had fallen. The disturbance that had aroused the Colonel in the early morning had not been thunder but the sound of distant guns. Barbara, the joyful tomboy of the Colonel's reverie, appears at the door, a quiet, efficient-looking nurse, arm in arm with her husband, the former gardener, now Captain Dering. Ellen attempts to console the old man by explaining that the world is being remade and that Dering has proved himself "worthy" of Barbara. But the Colonel fails to grasp the situation. Before the couple depart, his mind begins to wander again; and he warns Barbara against going down to the stream where a boy he once knew—"nobody in particular"—used to play. When Barbara and Dering have gone, Ellen assures the old man that boys will one day play beside the stream again. But, like old Devizes in *The Will,* the Colonel's mind has slipped completely back into the past. As the curtain falls, he is laughing to himself at the thought of Billy, Karl, and Barbara playing together, as they were for him when the play began.

Underlying the ostensible subject of his "war" quartet is Barrie's usual preoccupation with the prototypes. His focus is upon the relationship of Barrie Senior, Margaret Ogilvy, and David. *The New Word* and *A Well-Remembered Voice* emphasize the identity or intimacy of David Barrie Senior and Junior and the superficiality of the relationship between the mother and her lost son. This treatment is intended to separate Margaret from David Junior, and the two plays show the desired separation in life (*The New Word*) and death (*A Well-Remembered Voice*). The desired separation is closely linked with the suggestion of the mother's concealed indifference to the death of her son, a wishful fantasy that Barrie develops first through showing the insensitivity of Mrs. Torrance (who thinks her husband is insensitive), a mother who would not hesitate to give two sons to the army, and then through the loathsome character of Mrs. Don, a mother who mourns not out of love but duty.

In *The Old Lady Shows Her Medals,* the lost son is shown to be a means for gratifying a mother's vanity by providing her with a source of pride and a fund of memories to compete with those of other women. Kenneth Dowey's death is no cause for grief to the "mother" who invented her "son." Whether living or dead, he "serves" to enable her to have an involvement with the world at large. She invents him not out of love but out of need—her own. Mrs. Dowey is Barrie's hypothetical mother. Through her example he shows us the maternal instinct as he sees it, or, more accurately, as he wishes to explain it away when it is directed toward a lost son, such as David. In brief, he is saying that if a woman does not have a son she will want to invent one. She will "create" him for what he represents rather than for what he is. The memory is more important to her than the man, and she can sustain the loss of a real son or of a fantasy-child (such as a long dead son may seem to be) with comparative ease—although custom and duty demand that she present the show of mourning or the sense of loss expressed in the need for a séance. In *Barbara's Wedding,* Ellen, the mother-figure, has adjusted herself to Billy's death: she can accept the new world along with her memories. But the Colonel, the play's father-figure, has no future since he had identified himself with what the dead boy was, not with what he had represented. Billy's death is thus, mentally, the end of the Colonel's life.

Insofar as sentimental writing may be said to deny or falsify the existence of unpleasant truth, the "War" quartet explifies Barrie's ever-deepening sentimentality. In these four playlets the truth of the prototypic situation is increasingly distorted: Margaret no longer loves David; she "uses" him, as represented in Mrs. Dowey's use of her invented son. It is but a short step from here to the fantasy of *Mary Rose,* in which the mother tries to kill the son she remembers but cannot recognize.

V *Trifles and Potboilers*

This chapter, as we have already indicated, has been concerned primarily with those one-act plays Barrie himself considered worthy of inclusion in the "Definitive Edition" of his plays. His choice signified the rejection of numerous playlets as trifles and potboilers, most of which have long been out of print and are now of interest to the bibliographer rather than to the critic. Among these we notice *Josephine,* a skit on Joseph Chamberlain and Tariff Reform, and *Punch,* a "toy tragedy," both originally presented in 1905 with *Pantaloon* in a triple bill. *Slice of Life* (1905) parodied the eternal triangle situation in a mock problem play—perhaps as a reaction to *The Wedding Guest,* Barrie's only serious essay in Ibsenism. *The Dramatists Get What They Want* (1913) made a trifling comment on stage censorship, a problem which had never seriously affected Barrie's work.

Among several "War" plays written to raise money for charities were *Der Tag* (1914) and *La Politesse* (1918). The former, a propagandist flight into chauvinism, was directed against the Kaiser; it seems dated and overstrained compared with Shaw's "Playlets of the War." *La Politesse,* suggested by an episode in Henri Barbusse's *Le Feu,* concerned two escaped prisoners of war who seek sanctuary in a home occupied by honeymooners. *Rosy Rapture, the Pride of the Beauty Chorus* (1915), first presented in a double bill with *The New Word,* was a slender dramatic device to exploit the talents of Parisian dancer Gaby Deslys; and *The Truth About the Russian Dancers* (1921) did the same for the famous ballerina, Karsavina. *The Fatal Typist* (1916) and *Reconstructing the Crime* (1917) were trivial skits written for charity performances. *The Real Thing at Last* (1916) puckishly burlesqued a "modern, motion-picture version of *Macbeth.*"

Most deserving of revival is the skit *Shakespeare's Legacy* (1916), written on the occasion of the three-hundredth anniversary of the dramatist's death. In this one-act play Barrie amusingly contributed to the Bacon-Shakespeare controversy by suggesting that *Hamlet* was written by Lady Bacon. Shakespeare himself was really a Scotsman; and for this reason, we are told, he parsimoniously left his wife only the second-best bed. As late as 1925, during a speech to the Stationers' Company, Barrie provided a memorable footnote to this entertaining piece: "I do not know, Sir," he remarked, "whether Bacon wrote the words of Shakespeare, but if he did not, it seems to me that he missed the opportunity of his life."

CHAPTER 5

Major Plays: First Phase

I *Directions of Fantasy: From Farce to Melodrama*

NOT unexpectedly for a young Victorian seeking success as a dramatist, Barrie turned to the writing of full-length plays by trying his hand at farce and comic opera. *Walker, London* (1892) showed Barrie's obvious talents as a farceur; but, when he followed this play, in 1893, by collaborating with Arthur (later Sir Arthur) Conan Doyle on a libretto for a comic opera, it was equally apparent that Barrie was not the potential heir to the mantle of W. S. Gilbert. The result of the collaboration, *Jane Annie, or the Good Conduct Prize,* was named after Barrie's spinster sister, Jane Anne Adamson Barrie. D'Oyly Carte commissioned the piece in an attempt to extend his repertoire of successful Savoy operas, but it was a failure from the outset and the collaboration with Conan Doyle was never repeated. Nevertheless, the experience of writing *Jane Annie* left its mark on several of Barrie's comedies: *The Admirable Crichton,* for example, has more than a hint of the comic-opera libretto. There is a Gilbertian touch to the characterization, and much of the dialogue has the flavor of incipient recitative. In view of the recent popularity of such musical adaptations as *My Fair Lady* and *Half a Sixpence,* it is not surprising that an enterprising composer has now come forward to turn Crichton into the hero of a musical extravaganza.

Barrie's long series of box-office successes began with *Walker, London,* which received its premiere performance in February, 1892, at Toole's Theatre, King William Street in the Strand, London, and achieved a run of 511 performances. The rol̆e of Jasper Phipps, was acted by J. L. Toole, who also produced the play and owned full rights to it, which he bought from Barrie for only two hundred pounds. The American premiere occurred —probably without Barrie's knowledge or Toole's consent—at the Park Theatre, New York, in February, 1894, when Jasper Phipps was played by J. T. Powers. This production ran for only two weeks, and there is reason to believe that Barrie's name was not mentioned as the author of the piece.

"Walker!"—the first word in the play's title—was a nineteenth-century colloquialism signifying, "I'm clearing off before you discover that I'm lying." The play takes its title from the words that conclude the last act. They are spoken by Jasper Phipps, an itinerant Baron Munchausen who exercises his imaginative talents on the inhabitants of a Thames houseboat. Jasper, a bridegroom who has decided "to enjoy the honeymoon before the wedding," escapes from his fiancée, Sarah Rigg, and takes the honeymoon money along with him. Jasper had always earned his living as a barber, shaving the beards of gentlemen; now he wants to sample a gentleman's existence before he returns to Sarah and ties himself for life. Masquerading as Colonel Neil, the intrepid African explorer, he passes himself off as the rescuer of Bell Golightly, a young bluestocking whose mother owns the houseboat. He is soon ensconced in a hammock, telling tall stories of his African adventures to a group of credulous admirers. This part of the play—the houseboat setting and the character of the barber-turned-gentleman—recalls episodes in Barrie's novel, *When a Man's Single.*

Bell Golightly is being courted by Kit Upjohn, a "lowbrow" cricketer. During a scene evidently modeled on a celebrated discussion between Millamant and Mirabell in Congreve's *Way of the World,* Bell and Kit discover their apparent incompatibility and then separate in the heat of a lovers' quarrel. When Jasper frivolously follows up his masquerade by proposing to Bell, she, to his horror, accepts him, although her decision is prompted as much by her pique at Kit as by a sense of obligation to her "rescuer." She soon realizes her mistake when her lover contritely returns to the houseboat.

When Kit makes a passionate appeal to the "Colonel's" sense of honor, Jasper with a fine display of mock-heroic self-sacrifice, releases Bell from the engagement. By now he concludes that his masquerade has gone far enough. Sarah has already located his whereabouts, so he is relieved to be able to retreat hastily before getting involved in any more unwanted amorous entanglements. As he reaches the shore, Bell's mother calls out to him for his telegraphic address; and Jasper obligingly shouts back, "Walker, London." His deception is over; but, like Melville with his Confidence Man, the author will have more to tell us about such masquerades.

Jasper Phipps is a farcial character motivated by non-farcial motives. In running away from his obligations and in assuming the guise of Colonel Neil, he acts out the latent desires that most people repress. Like Tammas Haggart and Tommy Sandys, he is another alter ego of Barrie. In *A Window in Thrums,* Joey, another barber, deserts his mother, Jess, for a woman in London; and Jasper Phipps' flight from Sarah is a farcial re-enactment of the same episode. Sarah conveys the impression of being a mother in search of her lost child rather than a young man's fiancée. The plot and the main characters are developed out of the prototypic narrative. The houseboat setting is merely another form of island on which anything is possible: in this instance, a harmless flirtation with another woman and then reconciliation with the mother-mistress. The farce is thus a fantasy in which the deserter rejects the rival woman and returns home before it is too late. On the houseboat-island Jasper repeatedly asks the other woman (Bell) to be his sister; he is never serious about marrying her. Bell, a fictional equivalent of the girl who was to become Barrie's wife, is speedily repudiated when she looms before him as a possible spouse.

Barrie's critics have generally passed over this play as an early triviality. Typical is the attitude of Roy who remarks that its plot is absurd and its humor dated.[1] By contrast, Darton insists that it retains historical significance because of its link "in feeling" with the later plays of T. W. Robertson, the pioneer of a new, natural style of Victorian comedy. Darton adds: "it is certainly capable of revival. It may become a 'costume' farce in time."[2] On the other hand, Moult emphasizes the play's importance not in connection with any antecedents in comedy, but for "what it leads to" in the work of Barrie. It is, for Moult, the precursor of *The Admirable Crichton;* he sees both plays as works concerned with a central character who achieves "a sudden pathetic accession to power."[3] *Walker, London,* is indeed of elemental importance in relation to Barrie's later drama. Here and there, what was to become a familiar compound of "innocent" impudence, whimsicality, and sentiment breaks the surface of the larger, unsubtle farce. Jasper's exploits turn upon the themes of deception and self-deception and the desire for change that recur so frequently in the plays to follow. Bell's quarrel with Kit is rooted not merely in the perverse logicality of woman which Barrie had mocked in *Better Dead,* but also in the girl's refusal to satisfy the young man's desire to make her a baby-wife—like the heroine of *Mary Rose,* and Margaret Fairbairn in *The Wedding Guest.*

However, when Barrie's farce is not related to a larger context, its limitations became obvious: it is a box of frivolous theatrical tricks as ephemeral as yesterday's newspaper. Barrie was fascinated with dramatic devices, and his early plays in particular abound in masquerades, jokes, and reversals of conventional situations—often at the expense of more significant dramatic elements. But gradually the jokes were outworn, and the successful devices became the conventions of other dramatists. Hence so much of what was once Barrie's most popular work now seems dated or embedded in a morass of effete technique.

The Professor's Love Story (1893), Barrie's next play, was originally commissioned by Henry Irving, but when Irving expressed his dissatisfaction with it, Barrie turned the work over to his new theatrical agent, Arthur Addison Bright, who leased it to an American manager, E. S. Willard, for British and American production. Willard acquired the American rights for a mere fifty pounds and proceeded to make a fortune out of the play. Hammerton maintains that in New York the play was even more successful than in London. The world premiere of *The Professor's Love Story* took place at the Star Theatre, New York, in December, 1893, with Willard himself playing the hero, Professor Goodwillie. In August of the following year, Willard presented the play for the first time in England, at the Comedy Theatre, London. Later, he transferred it to the Garrick Theatre in the same city. The combined run for the British production was 144 performances.

Although *The Professor's Love Story* repeated the commercial success of his farce, it lacked as a comedy the assurance of *Walker, London*: *The Professor's Love Story* fails to resolve the dramatist's ambivalent attitude to his hero. From the outset Barrie could not make up his mind whether Professor Goodwillie was to be ridiculous or lovable, so he tried to make him both. The result is an absent-minded professor totally unaware of the nature of his own emotions, and he is more incredible than ludicrous. As Moult remarks, Professor Goodwillie is the Rev. Gavin Dishart (*The Little Minister*) "grown older and more stupid."[4] Roy, who was irritated by the character, described him as "an absurd caricature of the supposed professorial type . . . the play itself is the sort of play that an intelligent person who can follow Mr. Shaw goes to see under protest."[5] The other characters, especially Lucy White, the heroine, are far more interesting; but their development is restricted by the trivialities of a mechanical situation and by Barrie's eagerness to play for superficial laugher. Lucy White is a more vivid creation than Bell Golightly, but she is out of place as a real woman in love with an amiable but wooden nincompoop.

Again the story is of deception and of the realization of love. But this time the deceiver is the heroine, and it is the hero who comes to understand "the secret yearnings of the heart." When the play opens, the Professor is suffering from a mysterious malady, a severe disinclination for work that prevents him from completing the final chapter of his great scientific treatise. The doctor's diagnosis has already been anticipated by Lucy White, the Professor's pretty young secretary; she is shrewd enough to recognize that the Professor is unwittingly in love with her. But it is not long before Dr. Cosens also guesses the nature of the Professor's affections. When the doctor tries unsuccessfully to convince his patient of the truth of this startling diagnosis, Lucy intervenes to prevent him from revealing the identity of the woman in the case. Eventually, the Professor decides to follow his sister's counsel and return home to Scotland. If the doctor's diagnosis is correct, he will elude the mysterious woman by escaping from London. Accordingly, the Professor departs for home—in the company of his secretary.

But Lucy White is not the only woman interested in Professor Goodwillie. The Professor's sister, Agnes, embittered at the memory of a dead lover whom she believed had been unfaithful to her, is determined to save her brother from the folly of marriage. The Professor's friend, the young dowager Lady Gilding (a character Barrie had borrowed from Wilde), is equally determined to marry him. But Lucy, who had checkmated Dr. Cosens with such consummate ease, is more than a match for both women. As Lady Gilding has no suspicion that the secretary could be her rival for the Professor's affections, she confides to Lucy her plan for fainting in the Professor's arms, thereby arousing his passions. Lucy thereupon outwits Lady Gilding by carrying out the plan herself with immediate success: the Professor becomes aware of his love for Lucy and proposes marriage.

But Lucy now realizes that her duplicity toward the man who loves her is incompatible with the love she genuinely feels for him. Overcome with a sense of shame, she rejects his proposal and prepares to leave Scotland. At this point a missing letter is discovered in an old mailbox. It is addressed to the Professor's sister and turns out to be a final love letter from the lover she had so long suspected of infidelity. With her faith in love suddenly restored, Agnes sets out to reconcile Lucy and the Professor. Her efforts bring the lovers together, and the play ends with a brief glimpse of their blissful happiness.

The Professor's Love Story has a subplot, taken from one of Barrie's Auld Licht stories, about a Scots villager who terrifies his rival out of marrying the girl they both want by depicting the fearsome responsibilities of marriage. The trickster then proceeds to marry the girl himself as a pretended gesture of heroic self-sacrifice for his rival's sake. Amusing as it is, this subplot is never adequately integrated into the play. It belongs, like *Walker, London,* to the world of farce; and it fails to provide a relevant counterpoint to the delicate comedy that is woven about Professor Goodwillie.

In the main plot, the hero's role is again Barrie's. Yet Professor Goodwillie is no Jasper Phipps but a dreamer in an ivory tower of his own construction. Pressure of work has made him insensitive to emotional involvements. He is in love without being aware of it, and he is equally ignorant of being loved. The women of the play pull the strings that make him move, and under their control he can be deceived or seduced without losing his innocence. For Barrie, the role is apologetic. In fantasy he sees his desertion of Margaret Ogilvy as an act of innocence. Work had called him to London and made him a great man. Physically, he had left his mother behind him; but in fact she remained, an inspiration to him, wherever he went, though sometimes he was no more aware of the nature of his inspiration than Professor Goodwillie was of the presence of the woman he loved. He had no suspicion of a rival woman's motives, hence the girl who was to marry him could proceed with her scheme—just as Lady Gilding went ahead with her plan to trap the Professor.

Lucy's identification with Margaret Ogilvy becomes clear when the play shifts to Scotland. Lady Gilding's plan is a symbolic re-enactment of the invalid's role, the helpless mother in the wheelchair being replaced by a fainting woman in a man's arms. But the role is usurped by Lucy. In Scotland, "home ground," the rival woman is frustrated. Two problems still remain, however: Lucy's guilt feelings and Agnes' bitterness toward marriage. The resolution of the second problem is used to overcome the first. Here the dramatic situation approximates closely to actuality, if we accept the fact that Barrie has transferred his own guilt feelings to his mother. Agnes is a fictional equivalent of Barrie's sister Maggie: both women had lost lovers; both have their faith in love restored—Agnes through the discovery of her lover's fidelity, Maggie through marriage to her dead fiancé's brother. Significantly, Barrie soothes his character's bitterness by a literary device: a letter. Agnes, no longer antipathetic to marriage, now becomes the agency whereby the Professor and Lucy are reconciled.

In reality, Maggie had become engaged for the second time—to William Winter—in 1893, the year prior to the first production of the play. While Barrie was at work on *The Professor's Love Story,* he decided to marry Mary Ansell. He returned to Scotland for the wedding in 1894. The play points to Maggie's engagement as a justification for Barrie's marriage. But when Margaret Ogilvy died a few months later, the fantasy suddenly evaporated; Barrie began to see his marriage as the cause of his mother's death. It was to be seven years before he could bring himself to write another comedy.

Despite its commercial success, *The Professor's Love Story* must have seemed to its author a disturbingly unsatisfactory play. Barrie's grip had apparently faltered. The new play moved in an uncertain manner from broad farce to sophisticated Wildean comedy and then settled into an uneasy mingling of lightheartendness and sentimentality. Moult described the work as an "attempt to blend fantasy and satire, but the satire was trivial and the play remained little more than three acts of sentiment."[6] But, when we now read *The Professor's Love Story* in the light of Barrie's entire dramatic output, its apparent incongruities are discernible as the characteristics of Barrie's mature comedic style. Unfortunately, Barrie himself did not have the benefit of such hindsight. At this time he was still so uncertain of the new directions into which the theater was leading him that he retreated to his fiction in search of fresh dramatic material. His next play was to be an adaptation of *The Little Minister* (1897).

Hammerton has stated that the first productions of *The Little Minister* were the foundations of Barrie's fortune. In fact, Barrie made eighty thousand pounds out of the British and American productions. The theatrical presentation of this work also started his profitable association with the American producer Charles Frohman, who was to stage premieres of *The Admirable Crichton, Peter Pan, Alice Sit-by-the-Fire,* and *What Every Woman Knows.* Frohman tried out *The Little Minister* in Washington, in September, 1897; then, in the same month, he shifted the production to the Empire Theatre, New York, where the play had its "official" world premiere, with Maude Adams triumphing in the role of Babbie. Two months later, Cyril Maude and Frederick Harrison presented the London premiere of the play at the Haymarket Theatre (320 performances). Cyril Maude himself played Gavin Dishart, and his wife, Winifred Emery, appeared as Babbie. In reference to this production, Denis Mackail writes: "Maude and Harrison had the biggest success of their nine years' partnership." Subsequently, there were to be three motion picture versions of *The Little Minister*: a version released in 1912 by the American Vitagraph Company, and starring Clara Kimball Young as Babbie, a Paramount production of 1922, directed by Penrrhyn Stanlaws, with Betty Compson as Babbie and George Hackathorne as Gavin, and an RKO "talkie" of 1934, directed by Richard Wallace, with Katherine Hepburn as Babbie.

After his adaption of *The Little Minister,* Barrie, still avoiding a return to comedy, set to work on a serious problem play, written in response to the Ibsen vogue of the 1890's. *The Wedding Guest* (1900) proved to be Barrie's first unequivocal failure, the Ibsenite problem play reduced to melodrama. Evidently it was never professionally produced in the United States. In England it was presented by Arthur Bourchier at the Garrick Theatre, London, in September, 1900. The production closed after 100 performances.

The hero-villain of *The Wedding Guest* is a man whose secret past catches up with him on his wedding day. Kate Ommaney (cf. Ogilvy), Paul's former mistress and the mother of his illegitimate child, unexpectedly appears as he is being married to Margaret Fairbairn. During the ceremony Kate faints, thereby revealing her presence to Paul. The young bride has no suspicion of her husband's connection with the uninvited wedding guest, but the truth gradually emerges. Before the honeymoon, Paul and Margaret visit Mrs. Ommaney's house. Margaret at first believes the woman is deranged. She is unenlightened by her husband, for in his own interest Paul keeps the truth to himself. When the young bride learns that "Mrs." Ommaney is an unmarried mother, her former sympathies harden and she indulges in an outburst of moral revulsion.

But her aunt, Lady Janet Dunwoodie, discerns the true relationship between Paul and the strange Mrs. Ommaney. Now overwhelmed with self-recriminations, the repentant husband throws himself upon the mercies of his wife and father-in-law. Margaret's father, a platitudinizing latter-day Polonius, wants to hush the matter up by paying compensation to Mrs. Ommaney and by sending her and the baby to live in Australia. Margaret, on the other hand, is revolted by deception of any kind; she will only agree to live with Paul on condition that he adopt the baby and admit publicly to being the father. But she has not reckoned with Mrs. Ommaney: the baby's mother is prepared to accept the loss of Paul, but she has no desire to give up her child. Mrs. Ommaney decides to return home and bring up the baby in her father's house.

There seems no hope for Paul. Margaret remains obdurate, and her marriage appears doomed until Lady Janet intervenes to urge her to forgive and forget. Thirty years before, Lady Janet had refused to marry the man she loved because he had been unfaithful to her; as a result, she had grown old without being a wife or mother, a "heavier tragedy" than anything Margaret has to bear. Though Lady Janet prided herself on spurning such a man, and though the world had respected her for it, in her heart Lady Janet regretted the decision. Moved by her aunt's story, Margaret submits to a reconciliation with Paul. As the couple embrace, Paul humbly asks what he can do to atone. "Help unhappy women," replies his wife.

One of the few admirers of this play was William Archer. Archer, who had dismissed *The Professor's Love Story* as "a calculated disloyalty to art, a patch-work of extravagant farce, mawkish sentiment, irrelevant anecdote,"[7] acclaimed *The Wedding Guest* as Barrie's first significant play: "Hitherto, Mr. Barrie has only trifled with the stage, but now we can offer a very sincere welcome to our new dramatist."[8] The welcome was short-lived. *The Wedding Guest* proved to be a sort of emetic by which Barrie permanently rejected Ibsen from his system.

Nevertheless, the play is a strong indictment of its author. Paul, Barrie's persona, is as guilty of moral turpitude as Professor Goodwillie is innocent: now it is the ladies who are guiltless victims of duplicity. Lady Janet, the elderly spinster, probably represents Barrie's sister Jane Anne; but her tragedy is not the play's primary concern. The underlying story is that of a man who has deserted his mother and a baby (David) to marry a rival woman whom he has deceived about his past. Mrs. Ommaney is clearly the deserted mother, but the rival woman is named Margaret! In Margaret and Ommaney, Barrie has split the mother-figure into two characters: the deserted mother and the virgin-wife. These characters are variations on the Painted Lady and her daughter Grizel in *Sentimental Tommy.* Significantly, both Margaret Fairbairn and Mrs. Ommaney want to possess the baby. Barrie's real wife, Mary Ansell, has been obliterated in creating this new fantasy; yet the play preserves the writer's guilt feelings in marrying while he was in love with another woman—Margaret Ogilvy.

Thus Barrie tries to desert his mother, but he cannot—for the rival woman is the inviolable Margaret—not a Bell Golightly or a Lady Gilding. Mrs. Ommaney, the wronged mother, is the Margaret that Barrie knew as a child; the Margaret of the play is his mother as a girl, the fantasy-virgin with whom he was infatuated. In the last act, Margaret Fairbairn condemns her father for keeping her as a child instead of making a woman of her. The same condemnation applies to Barrie who had done precisely that to the memory of his mother.

II Quality Street, The Admirable Crichton, Little Mary

With *Quality Street* (1901), Barrie amply compensated for the box-office failure of *The Wedding Guest.* With Maude Adams playing the heroine, Phoebe Throssel, the new play opened in Toledo, Ohio, in October, 1901, and the next month was transferred to the Knickerbocker Theatre, New York, where it played to full houses for many months. The London production followed, in September, 1902, at the Vaudeville (459 performances). Here Phoebe was played by Elaine Terriss, and (Sir) Seymour Hicks scored one of the great successes of his career as the hero, Valentine Brown. In August, 1921, following the triumph of *Mary Rose, Quality Street* received a notable London revival, with Fay Compton (the original Mary Rose) playing Phoebe. There have been numerous other revivals and foreign-language productions, among these a German version, *Qualität Strasse,* which ran for many months in Berlin during World War I. The play has also been turned into a musical, *Phoebe of Quality Street,* with music by Walter Kells; in this form it was first presented at Wood's Theatre, Atlantic

City, in April, 1921; then at Schubert's, New York, in May of the same year. The musical was not a success and there is no record of its production anywhere in England.

The setting of the first, second, and fourth acts of *Quality Street* is the blue and white room in the house of the Misses Susan and Phoebe Throssel, genteel ladies who recall the spinster sisters, Miss Betty and Miss Kitty, in *Lob Lie-by-the-Fire or, The Luck of Lingborough* (1874) by Mrs. Gatty (Juliana Horatia Ewing) as well as similar characters in Mrs. Gaskell's *Cranford* (1851-53). The blue and white room is identical in appearance with the Hanky School of *Sentimental Tommy,* but the time is some seventy-five years earlier in the era of the Napoleonic Wars. Miss Susan is resigned to dying a spinster. Long ago she had fallen in love with a young man called William, but he had married someone else. However, as the play begins, her young sister Phoebe ("of the ringlets") is anticipating a proposal of marriage from dashing Valentine Brown, the local doctor's junior partner.

The curtain goes up on a spinsters' knitting party. In a scene adapted from an episode in *Sentimental Tommy,* the ladies are entertained by Miss Fanny reading aloud from a volume of love stories. Phoebe arrives, having encountered Valentine in the street; she is trembling with excitement but will not reveal her news until she has dealt with a Recruiting Sergeant who is being surreptitiously entertained by the maidservant. While the other ladies retire, Phoebe bravely tackles the soldier; and, before turning him out, she discovers that he has had a successful day, having recruited six men, including a gentleman of the town whose name he declines to mention. To her sister, Phoebe discloses that Valentine Brown has promised to call that afternoon to tell her something important. Both ladies assume that this news will be a proposal of marriage. Susan is as delighted as her sister; and the prospect of Phoebe's marriage seems opportune for both of them, for they have just learned that their precarious private income has been lost through bad investment—one actually arranged for them by the well-intentioned Valentine Brown. The sisters know that they can expect no financial assistance from their brother James. Phoebe's expectations are unexpectedly dashed, however, when Valentine arrives and announces that he is the gentleman who had enlisted that day. He has come to say farewell—not to propose marriage.

Ten years elapse. The sisters have managed to earn a meager living by turning their elegant house in Quality Street into a private school. Phoebe has become a prim "schoolmarm," her attractive ringlets hidden under a spinster's cap. She looks at least twenty years older. On this day Captain Valentine Brown returns unexpectedly from the wars. When he is ushered into the blue and white room (now transformed into a classroom), it is apparent that he has lost a hand. Valentine confesses to Susan that he had often dreamed of returning to the blue and white room, just as other soldiers dreamed of home. Then he confronts Phoebe. Time and change have marked both of them, but the confrontation is most painful to Phoebe, since she is aware of having lost her looks. Awkwardly, Valentine explains that he wishes to escort the sisters to a ball. Phoebe declines the invitation, believing that she has forever lost Valentine, as well as her beauty. She is further depressed at the visit of pretty young Charlotte Parratt and Ensign Blades. The latter, a former student of the Throssel sisters, treats Phoebe as a subject worthy of a young man's condescension.

Left alone with Susan, Phoebe grieves for her lost youth, until, suddenly inspired, she put on her hitherto unused wedding gown, takes off the spinster's cap, and starts to look young and pretty once again. She decides on impulse to go to the ball masquerading as her "niece" Miss Livvy, the daughter of James Throssel. When Valentine reappears, he is introduced to the young lady; and, as Phoebe has "retired with a headache," he offers to escort Livvy in her place. Before their departure the girl embarrasses Valentine by noticing his gray hairs and the disparity in their ages.

Miss Livvy's charms prove irresistible. Closely escorted by Valentine, the belle of the ball is besieged by handsome officers who whisper their infatuation and proclaim their eagerness to fight over her. But, though she flirts shamelessly with all men, Livvy is really interested in only one of her admirers: she is convinced that Valentine has fallen in love with her. He visits the house in Quality Street several times to ask after Phoebe, yet his interest in Livvy seems to indicate where his passions lie. Valentine is the girl's escort to every ball, and she now plans to entice him to the point at which he will propose marriage, then to reject him as too old. In this way he will experience some of the anguish that Phoebe has endured. She can be so cruel because Valentine has taken away her love, "the one great glory that is in a woman's life."

Livvy's plan proceeds smoothly when she catches sight of two spinsters from the knitting circle. They have come to the ball to confirm their suspicions that Livvy and Phoebe are one and the same person. The masquerade seems about to end ignominiously when, through a fortunate misunderstanding, the ladies' suspicions are allayed. Now two of Livvy's admirers begin to quarrel over her, and Phoebe suddenly realizes that she is wearying of the role she has created. But by now Valentine has appeared, and she must brace herself for the inevitable proposal. Once again, however, Valentine fails to live up to expectations: instead of offering protestations of love, Valentine reprimands the girl for her outrageous flirting. He tells her that men love the modest violet not the flaunting flower and that he is in love not with her but with Aunt Phoebe. Indeed, it was Livvy who had made him aware of his love for her aunt; for the latter's "ladylikeness" and propriety had shone by contrast with her niece's lack of these qualities. He is resolved to ask for Phoebe's hand. Livvy's attempts to break his resolution, to denigrate Phoebe, are of no avail. The infuriated Valentine repudiates the girl and walks out. Phoebe is now elated, for she knows beyond any doubt that Valentine loves her.

Back in Quality Street Phoebe resumes her old-fashioned spinster's dress and the cap that hides her ringlets. Miss Willoughby, a member of the knitting circle, visits the sisters to inquire after Livvy. The Throssel sisters explain that their niece is indisposed and confined to her room; but their visitor suspects Phoebe of jealously keeping the girl away from Valentine Brown. After Miss Willoughby has gone, Phoebe tells Susan that she cannot marry Valentine without revealing her deception, but such a disclosure is beyond her powers. To end the deception, she has written to Valentine requesting him never to come to the house. Her appeal is ignored; Valentine enters and proposes marriage. Phoebe, who promptly rejects him, is evidently touched by the description of a bachelor's lonely life.

Undeterred, Valentine is persisting with his proposal when two more ladies from the knitting circle put in an appearance. Acutely embarrassed, Phoebe rushes from the room. The two visitors, who share Miss Willoughby's suspicions of Phoebe, now mention their suspicions to Valentine Brown. As a physician, he decides that his duty is to inquire into Livvy's state of health. He disappears into the girl's bedroom and returns with an inscrutable expression on his face. The two ladies take his manner to mean that the patient is too ill to be disturbed. They depart, leaving Valentine alone with Patty, the maidservant, from whom he demands to know why Phoebe had deceived him. His anger is quickly dispelled when he learns first of Phoebe's grief and then of the other "deception" practiced on him: the sisters' refusal to inform him that they had lost all their savings in the investment he had arranged for them. Patty explains why Phoebe has been unable to dispose of Livvy: the other spinsters watch the house and would not believe the girl had gone unless they actually saw her depart.

Unaware that Valentine knows her secret, Phoebe reappears in the guise of Livvy. Acting as her doctor, Valentine says that Livvy is well enough to go home; and, going into the bedroom, he collects some wraps, pretends to put them on an imaginary invalid, and "conducts" the empty wraps into a waiting carriage. It is now plain to the two sisters that Valentine Brown knows everything. A moment later he returns to claim Phoebe as his wife.

The play's climaxes are built out of the unexpected actions or responses of Valentine: his enlistment in the army, his preference for Phoebe over Livvy, and his removal of Livvy by participating in Phoebe's deception. But, after the first act, the forward action is determined by the masquerade which in many respects anticipates the plot of *Rosalind* and that play's preoccupation with the idea that a young woman always remains inside the older one. And in *Quality Street* as in *Rosalind*, Barrie exploits the theatrical appeal of a dual role in performance. The other theme of *Rosalind*, that love is only possible when illusion prevails, is countered by Valentine's repudiation of the illusion in discovering his love for the real woman. The ball scenes are essentially a variation on the Cinderella story—in which the prying sisters take the place of the ugly sisters and the possibility of Livvy's being unmasked replaces the twelve o'clock deadline when Prince Charming's beautiful choice reverted to being an ill-kempt scullery maid. The immediate popularity of Barrie's play is thus as understandable as the perennial success of Shaw's *Pygmalion*, which, aside from the ending and the lack of sentimentality so characteristic of *Quality Street,* is basically another version of the same fairy tale.

It is difficult to believe that Barrie's play, with its delicate world of frills and lace reminiscent of Mrs. Gaskell's *Cranford,* is not the work of a female dramatist. *Quality Street* is a hymn to feminine modesty and decorum; the play is as quaint as an antique music box, and the characters of the ladies seem as delicate as pieces of old china. The filigree of Barrie's workmanship approaches the texture of Pope's *Rape of the Lock,* another work that it is difficult to credit to a male writer. But Pope's poem is unblemished by the sentimentality that was to destroy the popularity of *Quality Street* as soon as the age of Mary Pickford was over. This uncomfortably maudlin play illustrates the sentimentalist's refusal to admit to the harsh realities of life. Barrie's no longer youthful heroine can pass herself off as the belle of the ball, thus effortlessly realizing every woman's dream of recapturing her youth; and the hero, with a nobility that transcends belief, declares his preference for age and modesty rather than for youth, beauty, and vitality. This choice, as Barrie wickedly knew, is what every woman over thirty wants—even though it is a lie.

In fact, Valentine Brown's preference for Phoebe corresponds to Barrie's infatuation with Margaret Ogilvy. The narrator of *The Little White Bird,* published in the same year as the first production of *Quality Street,* expressed the same taste for older women. Valentine and the narrator are, of course, personae of Barrie. However, the author's type-figure is split in *Quality Street,* just as the type-figure of the mother was in *The Wedding Guest.* Barrie is represented in actuality by the uncharitable brother James and in fantasy by the lover Valentine. The hero's name emphasizes his idealization. Appropriately, James, the Mr. Hyde to Valentine's Dr. Jekyll, is never seen throughout the play; the absentee brother is a repetition of the unregenerate deserter. Valentine is also a "deserter," but he redeems himself by returning to claim Phoebe after repudiating Livvy, the rival woman. He returns symbolically castrated, his loss of a hand providing a parallel to the mutilation of Captain Hook and the burning of the glove that Jamie brings to his invalid mother who sits by the window in Thrums. The infatuation for Livvy has been short-lived; she bewitches him only because of her passing resemblance to Phoebe as a young girl.

Again, as in *The Wedding Guest,* the character of the rival woman obliterates Barrie's wife, Margaret Ogilvy's actual rival, because, like Margaret Fairbairn, she has been drawn in the image of Barrie's mother. But Livvy is not simply another aspect of Phoebe; she is a fantasy created by her to entice Valentine and to prove his true qualities. Valentine's response to the deception puts Phoebe in much the same position that tricking the Professor had put Lucy White: she acquires guilt feelings where she had none before. Valentine is now the innocent party. She must destroy the masquerade, put an end to her deception. But at the point where Phoebe must "absorb" Livvy or make her disappear forever, she can only contrive to turn her creation into an invalid. Phoebe and Livvy are thus fused into their prototype—the invalid Margaret Ogilvy who is to be "cured" by the one who deserted her. Valentine's treatment is to take control of the illusion and send it where it belongs, since Phoebe (Margaret) is all that he wants. He picks up the rival woman—a bundle of nothing—and packs her off in a carriage to brother James.

There have been few recent revivals of *Quality Street*, but after *Peter Pan, The Admirable Crichton* (1902) has remained popular with theater audiences. Charles Frohman produced the play in England and America, and this time the world premiere occurred in London, at the Duke of York's Theatre, November, 1902, with H. B. Irving playing Crichton (328 performances). In the United States, the play opened at the Lyceum Theatre, New York, in November, 1903, with William Gillette playing Crichton. *The Admirable Crichton* was the first play by Barrie to be seen in France. An English-language production was given in June, 1903 at the Renaissance Theatre, Paris, and in the fall of the same year, there was a successful French-language production, using the translation by Octave Uzanne. At least two motion-picture adaptations of *The Admirable Crichton* are known to have been made: a silent film called *Male and Female*, directed in 1919 by Cecil B. DeMille and starring Gloria Swanson and Thomas Meighan, and a 1957 British "talkie" version with Kenneth More as Crichton.

Barrie took the title of his play from an epithet bestowed by Sir Thomas Urquhart on James Crichton (1560-85?), a Scottish traveler, a scholar, and swordsman; his play's hero is Bill Crichton, a butler whose resourcefulness emulates the historical Crichton's. One of Barrie's notebook entries for 1899 indicates that the sources of the first act, in which Lord Loam and family entertain their servants, was a similar real-life occurrence in the household of Rosalind, Countess of Carlisle, an aristocrat with radical views.[9] The "basic idea" for the rest of the play was evidently derived from a remark made by Conan Doyle, while he was staying in 1893 with Barrie in Kirriemuir: "If a king and an able seaman were wrecked together on a desert island for the rest of their lives, the sailor would end as king and the monarch as his servant."[10]

The play as a whole embodies Barrie's only sustained social and political message, and it is expressed in the course of the comedy by the butler who declares that there must always be one to command and others to obey, that divisions into classes are the natural outcome of a civilized society. The true servant—such as Crichton—actually likes disdain from his superiors and shows disdain to his inferiors. The action of the play demonstrates that equality is unnatural. Circumstances may alter specific cases, but they do not alter the natural law that there must always be a master and servants to obey him.

The play falls into four acts: "At Loam House, Mayfair" (Act I), "The Island" (Act II), "The Happy Home" (Act III), and "The Other Island" (Act IV). When the curtain rises on the first act, the Honorable Ernest Woolley, a character who might have wandered from a Wilde comedy, is visiting his uncle, the Earl of Loam. Lord Loam is a radical peer, dedicated to the promotion of equality and to the breakdown of class barriers; once a month he applies his political philosophy at Loam House by compelling his servants to be his equals. Ernest has arrived on the day set aside for this function. It is likely to be the last such occasion for a considerable time, for Lord Loam—accompanied by his three daughters, Lady Mary, Lady Catherine, and Lady Agatha, and by Ernest and the Reverend Treherne—is shortly to embark on a yachting voyage to remote regions of the earth. Crichton is a born conservative convinced that class divisions and inequality are natural to civilized communities; but, as Lord Loam's butler, it is not for him to disapprove of the radical opinions of his master. The monthly ordeal is the dismal failure he expects it to be, though it is only through Crichton's intercession that Lord Loam manages to emerge from it with a minimal loss of dignity.

The butler is so comfortingly reliable that the gentlemen are delighted when he agrees to act as manservant during the voyage. The ladies, however, have to be content with the services of little Tweeny, the "*between* maid," so called because she is not anything in particular as a servant, though Crichton has deigned to cast a favorable eye on her. The butler's obvious anguish during the monthly ordeal intrigues Lord Loam's daughters, and they question him about his attitude to the class system. In reply, Crichton rejects his lordship's opinion that equality would prevail if man returned to a state of nature. If such a reversion occurred, Crichton is sure that the election of a head would be the first task undertaken: "Circumstances might alter the cases; the same person might not be master; the same persons might not be servants. . . . Nature would decide for us." The haughty Lady Mary is the most curious about Crichton's answer, but even she does not wonder very much—though Barrie tells us that she would have wondered a great deal more if she had known what was coming.

Lady Mary begins to find out two months later. The scene is now a desert island in the Pacific, on which the passengers of Lord Loam's yacht have been shipwrecked. Lord Loam himself had been lost overboard and evidently drowned. Except for Crichton and Tweeny, the survivors are ill-clad and even worse equipped for enduring the rigors of a desert island. But Ernest is hopefully stuffing an S.O.S. into a soda-water bottle which Crichton is assigned to cast into the sea. At the outset only the butler shows any inclination to undertake the necessary tasks for providing food and shelter. When Lady Mary points this out, Crichton casually remarks that the rule of no work—no dinner, the natural law of the island—will soon change the habits of the other men.

Lady Mary interprets Crichton's remarks as the expression of an attitude inconsistent with his stated disbelief in equality; yet the butler cryptically maintains that his opinions remain unchanged, that on an island, as at home, there must be one to command and others to obey. Clarification of his meaning is delayed by Ernest's sudden warning of the approach of a tiger. The "animal" turns out to be Lord Loam, bedraggled and exhausted, crawling on all fours through the bushes. He had been washed ashore, clinging to a hencoop,, and for two days after that had wandered over the island trying to catch fish, flesh, or fowl to satisfy his hunger. The starving peer is now drawn irresistibly toward Crichton's cooking pot, but Lady Mary intervenes to insist that he assert his position as chief person on the island before doing anything else. Ernest openly defies his uncle until Crichton puts his head in a bucket of cold water and threatens to repeat the treatment whenever the boy is inclined to witty instead of useful. Such behavior toward a peer's nephew incenses Lady Mary, and she urges her father to assert his authority over Crichton. Lord Loam thereupon confronts his manservant, only to be told that the question of leadership does not rest with master or man: it is to be settled by Nature.

Infuriated with the butler's reply, Lord Loam gives him a month's notice. Lady Mary explains that, in view of this situation, this means relegation to another part of the island. When Crichton insists on remaining, Lord Loam and company decide upon an alternative course of action which consists in leaving the butler to himself. Quickly regaining his usual composure, Crichton settles down beside his cooking pot. Treherne, the last of the party to desert the butler, learns the reasons for Crichton's equanimity: hunger will drive the others back to the cooking pot when the smell of dinner is borne in their direction. Food is one of nature's irresistible calls! As it grows dark, Crichton bends over the fire, stirring the pot. For a while he is alone; then Lord Loam and his entourage slowly creep out of the shadows, drawn by the warmth of the fire and the smell of food. Nature is at work—even on Lady Mary: she is the last to come, the most reluctant and the least submissive.

On the island, two years later, the course of nature and Crichton's position are no longer in any doubt. Crichton's special talents have naturally made him master. The others now call him "Gov" (Governor), while Lord Loam has been reduced to "Daddy." After abandoning all hope of rescue, the voyagers have turned their energies to making the island habitable. Under Crichton's direction they have succeeded remarkably well. They live in a sturdy log cabin fitted with modern conveniences constructed by Crichton from the wreckage of the yacht. Everyone is now usefully employed: Lady Mary and her sisters have become cooks and maidservants, vying with each other for the honor of waiting on "Gov." A now unwhimsical Ernest has set his heart on marrying Tweeny; as he ventures the hope that she will deign to consider his proposal, Tweeny remains unswervingly faithful to Crichton.

On this day, however, the "Gov" has decided to honor "Polly" (Lady Mary) by taking her as his consort. Immensely flattered by the "Gov's" choice, Lord Loam promptly gives his blessing.

Crichton and Lady Mary are preparing for their nuptials when the sound of a ship's cannon echoes across the island. The hour of rescue is at hand, but Lady Mary is unwilling to be rescued. She has a happy home and the prospect of a rosy future as "Gov's" wife. Crichton, on the other hand, is determined to play the game. As Lady Mary stretches out her arms, crying that she will never give up her "Gov," he reverts to the humble bearing of a servant in the presence of his mistress and addresses her as "My Lady." He is prepared to face the fact that their life on the island has ended.

Some months later, back in that "other island," Agatha and Catherine are at Loam House, surrounded by trophies of their adventure and reading aloud some glowing reviews of Ernest's book. He has just published an account of his heroic exploits on the desert island, describing how he had guided the others through the deadly perils of that savage environment. Crichton's assistance is generously acknowledged in a footnote. The butler's presence at Loam House is quite another matter. Ernest's book is the "official" version of what occurred on the island, but Crichton, of course, knows the truth, and Crichton never tells a lie. Lady Brocklehurst, a reincarnation of Wilde's Lady Bracknell and the mother of Lady Mary's fiancé, is a notoriously suspicious woman who usually "pumps" Crichton whenever she calls at Loam House. As a visit from Lady Brocklehurst is imminent, there is good reason for alarm.

But Lord Loam is even more disturbed at Lady Mary's attitude. She is determined to follow Crichton's example and play the game, which in this instance means breaking her engagement with Lord Brocklehurst unless her father tells that wealthy young peer about her connections with the butler. Lord Loam avoids this unpleasant task, and his daughter is on the point of telling Lord Brocklehurst herself, when he admits to an affair with one of her maidservants. There remains the problem of Lady Brocklehurst, from whose relentless pryings no family skeltons are said to be safe. On the threshold of uncovering the truth concealed by Ernest's book, the grim dowager advises her son to look out for explanations that begin with "The fact is . . ."; for such remarks are usually lies. Unaware that they are being tested by this method, Ernest and Lady Mary promptly expose themselves as liars. Lady Brocklehurst then concentrates her inquiry upon Crichton.

Fortunately, though the butler never lies, his replies to Lady

Brocklehurst's questions are so ambiguous as to be misinterpreted by her in a manner that removes all suspicion. There are no longer any obstacles to the marriage of Lady Mary and Lord Brocklehurst. Crichton is invited to enter Lord Brocklehurst's service, but refuses, declaring that he intends to leave service forever. Left alone with Crichton, Lady Mary admits that she is ashamed of deserting him; she assures him that he is the best man among all the people she knows. Crichton humbly maintains that this may be true on an island but not in England. Lady Mary thereupon objects that this must be one of England's shortcomings. Crichton, however, will not hear a word against his country. He is a perfect servant and an even more perfect Briton.

The premiere of *The Admirable Crichton* opened in London while Shaw was at work on *Man and Superman,* and in his "Epistle Dedicatory" to the play, Shaw mentions how "Mr. Barrie has . . . while I am correcting my proofs, delighted London with a servant who knows more than his masters." Shaw relates Crichton to his own Enry Straker, 'motor engineer and New Man . . . an intentional dramatic sketch of the contemporary embryo of Mr. H. G. Wells's anticipation of the efficient engineering class. . . ."[11] But the comparison with Straker misses the point of Barrie's creation: Crichton does indeed, like Straker, know more than his masters; but, unlike Straker, he knows when to appear not to know more. If Straker is the New Man, Crichton is the old one, accepting the status quo, never flaunting his talents as Straker flaunts his polytechnic education and his mastery of the internal combustion engine. Strakers may break class boundaries; Crichtons, never.

Barrie's critics have sometimes praised his play for its original view of social relationships; it has been commended on the one hand for its good-humored radicalism, and on the other for its entertaining treatment of the gospel of reaction. Neither of these estimates is justifiable. Barrie's message—and *ergo* Crichton's, his spokesman's—is simply "know your place." Insofar as it is possible, Barrie's position is strictly neutralist in dealing with the class system; the true arbiter, as he sees it, is nature, which determines that the Darwinian law of adapt or perish applies to the class system. A process akin to natural selection elevates Crichton to leadership on the island; the same process selects Lord Loam as a leader in civilized society. Crichton understands the Darwinian law and accedes to it.

A complete determinist, he will not lift a finger to alter any of the circumstances in which he finds himself. Accordingly, his insistence on "playing the game" is a philosophy of resignation; and his refusal to find anything wrong with England is a Panglossian acceptance of the status quo.

No serious analysis of *The Admirable Crichton* is likely to do justice to the play's brilliantly sustained satire. Wilde had mocked the British aristocracy by deflating its serious preoccupations to trivialities and inflating its trivialities to the scale of serious preoccupations; Barrie's mockery is accomplished by contrasting the inadequacy of the master with the perfection of the servant. Crichton's conservatism and unbending formality parodies the supposedly aristocratic norm, and his behavior is made all the funnier because of the failure of Lord Loam and his entourage to recognize this as a reflection on themselves. The slightest suggestion of sentimentality would have demolished the effect of Barrie's satire, but fortunately he had, for the time being, expended his sentimentality on *Quality Street*. In *The Admirable Crichton* lack of sentimentality is a concomitant of allowing the fantasy to work itself out without explaining or justifying the author in a prototypic situation.

But the prototypes are not absent from the play. Crichton, Tweeny, and Lady Mary are recognizably personae of Barrie, Margaret Ogilvy, and Mary Ansell; and the incompetent Lord Loam who walks over the island on all fours—like the dog-man William Paterson in *The Little White Bird* and like Mr. Darling in the dog kennel in *Peter Pan*—is a characterization of the "negligent" parent, David Barrie Senior. However, the core of the play is the island situation, the fantasy in which anything is possible, in contrast to the framing actuality consisting of the scenes in England. On the island, Crichton-Barrie dominates; and the women are his servants, eagerly accepting any favors he bestows on them. Tweeny and Lady Mary, rivals for Crichton, tolerate each other's existence; and "Lady" Mary is acceptable as a wife without being transformed into an image of Margaret Oglivy. Back in England, things are very different: Crichton-Barrie cannot marry Lady Mary; the social inhibitions away from the fantasy-island also reflect the psychological ones. His destiny is manifestly with Tweeny, and he humbly accepts it. With the confrontation of Crichton and Lady Mary in the last act, Barrie brings the play to an end on the verge of a sentimental scene; but his restraint at this point is an impeccable judgment. Unique among his plays, *The Admirable Crichton* endures, relevant and sparkling as the day it was written. It is Barrie's comedic masterpiece.

Little Mary, first produced in September, 1903, at the Wyndham's Theatre, London, was a less profitable venture than Barrie's two previous plays, though it assembled a notable cast, including Gerald du Maurier, John Hare, and Nina Boucicault.

As we shall see, the significance of *Little Mary* is expressed in a joke represented in the play's title, but not explained until the end of the final act. The germ of the play, however, was evident as early as *Walker, London,* in which the following dialogue occurs:

> ANDREW. Take a stomach: remove the—
> NANNY. Disgusting!

Act I of *Little Mary* is hardly more than the induction to what follows. While he is having a prescription made up, the elegant widower, Lord David Carlton, is invited to wait in the parlor of old Mr. Reilly's chemist shop. It is an unusual room cluttered with chemical apparatus and children's playthings, but the most exceptional features are three boxes fastened to the brick wall. They serve as cribs for babies, children who are "mothered" by twelve-year-old Moira Loney, the old chemist's granddaughter. Moira is instantly attracted by Lord Carlton, but she also pities him for, as she explains, he suffers from a sickness common to the rich, an ailment that doctors cannot cure. Her grandpa has diagnosed this illness and is writing a book about it; one day he will touch a spring that will set all the rich people going again. Moira is sure that she is to help him, but she does not know how; soon after Lord Carlton has departed, Grandpa tells her. He has finished his book, and Moira is to read it until she is eighteen, at which time she must give up her babies and go out to make converts among the great ones. Those she cures must not be told the nature of the remedy since it would startle them too much. They must be saved without their knowledge or understanding. Moira first objects to such deception, but Grandpa assures her that it is for the greatest good of the wealthy; whereupon she settles down to read volume one of his book, *The Medium, or how to cure our best people.*

Six years pass. The scene is now the courtyard of Lady Georgy's country cottage. Lady Georgy, Lord Carlton's sister, is the mother of Lord Plumleigh, a teenager with the reputation of being the idlest boy in the school, and Lady Millicent, a nineteen-year-old invalid who is confined to a wheelchair. Two years before, Millicent had been engaged to Sir Frank Cosham when his sudden death gave her a shock from which she had never recovered. Today Millicent is due to receive medical attention from two professional humbugs, Sir Jennings Pyke, an eminent specialist, and Dr. Topping, the local physician. Unknown to these gentlemen, Lady Georgy has also invited the celebrated lay-healer Moira Loney (known professionally as the Stormy Petrel) and her medium, Little Mary. The Stormy Petrel has been setting society ablaze with her extraordinary cures, but her name is anathema to the medical profession.

Residing with his aunt is Lord Carlton's son Cecil, who is making a fool of himself over an actress. Lord Carlton has enlisted his sister's aid in breaking up the romance, and the method she has decided on is similar to that to be used by Maggie in Barrie's *What Every Woman Knows.* She has brought the young couple together and gained their confidence while quietly employing a detective to keep an eye on them. Lord Carlton is far from satisfied with the results. Eleanor, the actress, whom he suspected of being a gold-digger, has turned out to be a perfectly nice girl, and Cecil is determined to marry her. An awkward interview between father and son, comparable to the scene between Mr. Torrance and Roger in *The New Word,* serves only to deepen Cecil's resolution. After meeting Eleanor, Lord Carlton is equally unshaken in his determination to oppose a marriage between his son and an actress.

Moria Loney arrives. Now eighteen, she is as serious and as irrepressibly maternal as ever. Lord Carlton has forgotten her, but Moira recognizes him and loses no time in refreshing his memory of the girl in the chemist's shop. Carlton is delighted to see her again. Her babies, he learns, have been taken from her; and Grandpa is dead. He does not suspect that Moira is the Stormy Petrel. Meanwhile, Lady Millicent has been brought in to be examined by Sir Jennings and Dr. Topping. The two doctors, furious to discover that the Stormy Petrel is also in attendance on their patient, warn Lady Georgy of the consequences of Moira's cures. When Moira had finished her work on a certain Colonel Frisby that gentleman had tried to blow his brains out. After Moira admits that her presence is likely to have a strange influence on everyone in Lady Georgy's household, she advises those who wish to remain unchanged to leave as soon as possible. The incredulous doctors are informed that she will cure Millicent within a month. Appalled at this apparent charlatanism, Lord Carlton accuses Moira of being a common cheat and declares that he will make it his business to observe her methods; if he detects any fraud, he will expose her publicly. The Stormy Petrel's reply is to warn him that, if he remains, he himself may change—even though he has no faith in Moira's cures.

A month later, Lord Carlton is again visiting Lady Georgy's cottage. According to the butler, everything is just as usual; but his lordship has a very diffierent impression. The family now breakfasts at eight instead of after ten. Lord Plumleigh gets up even earlier—to work at push-ups and at a strict timetable of academic studies. Cecil has fallen out of love with Eleanor; and, with the aid of his father, he contrives to extricate himself from an undesirable engagement. Despite these changes, none of the family is aware that Moira Loney has changed anything. Lady Georgy believes that the Stormy Petrel has failed with Millicent—apart from bringing some color to the girl's cheeks. But Lord Carlton detects the work of Moira in everything he sees. His old affection for her returns when he finds her weeping because she is lonely and unloved and has no one to mother.

But the Stormy Petrel's hour of triumph is at hand. Sir Jennings and Dr. Topping have declared that Moira's treatment of the patient is pernicious. Moira is urging them to take a closer look, when Millicent skips down the staircase and announces that she is cured. Retaining his composure, Sir Jennings pockets his consultation fee and departs in the company of Dr. Topping. The family, now conscious of Moira's responsibility for all the changes that have occurred, begs her to reveal her secret. She refuses until asked by Lord Carlton. Then she instructs the butler to bring down "Grandpa"—the three volumes of his book. Her secret is here. Grandpa, she explains, had discovered the amazing truth that what we are depends mainly on what we eat, that "we are good or bad, stupid or entertaining, cynics or in love, mainly as the result of diet. . . . *Love* is mostly phosphate of lime."

Grandpa's book contains recipes for whatever a human being wishes to be. Grandpa came to the conclusion that the wealthy eat too much, though they refuse to face the fact that this is what is wrong with them. To overcome their sensitivity on this point, he had advised Moira to invent a euphemism for the object of the cure. Hence the so-called medium "Little Mary," her mild name for the stomach, and the nature of the cure—taking the weight off Little Mary by insisting on only one dinner a day. As Moira has anticipated, the family is disgusted by her revelations—all, that is, except Lord Carlton, who claims that he is the only person she has not helped. He wants to be twenty-five again, though Moira says that this change is beyond her powers. She is easily proved wrong, for Lord Carlton insists on marrying her. Moira needs someone to mother, and he needs a young wife who will dedicate herself to making a man out of an idle aristocrat.

Barrie's critics and most of his admirers are in agreement in being unable to "stomach" *Little Mary*, Roy regards it as a play of no permanent value; and Moult, who deplores it as "cynically barren," accuses Barrie, in this play, of using the drama as a kind of garbage heap for ephemeral or trivial ideas, just as some years before he had, rather more appropriately, used journalism.[12] Darton is one of the few *aficionados* of this comedy, which he compares favorably with Shaw's *The Doctor's Dilemma*, a gratuitously flattering and quite unsupportable comparison.

After *The Admirable Crichton*, *Little Mary* is a great disappointment. Having sorted out the relationship of master and servant, Barrie now turned his attention to solving the problems of the rich. He shows himself, like Shaw, to be an advocate of the simple solution; but Shaw at his crankiest would never have perpetrated anything so ridiculous as Grandpa's panacea. What still makes Barrie's play readable is the gentle mockery of what the author patently believed in. Grandpa's theory is shown to be sound when applied to Millicent, but Barrie prevents us from taking it too seriously by satirizing it through Moira's explanation. The view that what we are depends chiefly on what we eat may not be too difficult to accept until we are told that love is mainly phosphate of lime.

In contrast to *The Little White Bird* (1902), *Little Mary* concerns a girl who gives up her babies for a book. It is not inappropriate that Barrie considered his writings his most important gifts to his mother. Grandpa, like Barrie, spends most of his time writing, neglecting his wife and family. Eventually, he regards the book as the significant and immortal part of himself. When he finishes it, he is ready to die. Then Moira inherits it; and, while she is engrossed in its pages, her babies are taken away. The book makes Moira the lonely (Loney) one; however, its pages are not without hope, for they teach her the fantasy that people can be made or remade just as they want to be. Grandpa's panacea can be recognized as an expression of Barrie's belief in the possibility of change, the fantasy that an individual can be transformed into an entirely different person. The ultimate source of this fantasy is Barrie's childhood impersonation of his brother, his attempt to usurp David's identity. Moira's identification with Margaret Ogilvy is clear from the outset: Lord Carlton first meets her as a "virgin-mother" tending babies in boxes which may symbolize coffins as well as wombs. As coffins, they anticipate the underground home of the lost boys in *Peter Pan* (1904).

If Moira can no longer mother babies, she can find consolation in nursing adults. Not unexpectedly, the heroine gives the stomach, which she regards as the source of all trouble, the same name as Barrie's wife. The book had merely specified the stomach; Moira identifies it as Little Mary. Little Mary is the medium of change, the cause of the transformation of David's usurper into an aging notability. The latter can only become young again by "taking the weight off" Little Mary and by marrying Moira Loney.

Mary Ansell as Little Mary is plainly a devouring woman. And, significantly, one of the evils caused by Little Mary is shown to be confinement to a wheelchair (Margaret Ogilvy's affliction). However, Millicent who had lost her fiancé in a tragic accident is representative of Barrie's sister Maggie rather than his invalid mother. The invalid is cured in the same way as Lord Carlton: by clearing out Little Mary. Barrie's getting rid of his wife was, at least in fantasy, a way for him to take the place of David and become united with Margaret.

III *Illusion, Disillusion, and Pantomime*

Alice Sit-by-the-Fire (1905) was written for Ellen Terry, but she was uneasy in the role of Alice; and this fact may have accounted in part for the comparatively short London run of 115 performances. The London production opened at the Duke of York's in April, 1905. In December of the same year, Charles

Frohman presented the play at the Criterion, New York, and gave Ethel Barrymore her first "star" role as Alice.

The play belongs with *Quality Street* and *Rosalind* in its nostalgia for lost girlhood, a nostalgia intensified for the original production by the widely known fact that the aging Ellen Terry had, as a young woman, acted Shakespeare's Rosalind and other romantic roles comparable to those which Alice Grey comes to realize that she has outgrown. In this play, Amy, aged seventeen, Cosmo a naval cadet of thirteen, and baby Molly have little or no recollection of their parents. The children were born in India and shipped back to England for their upbringing and education. Their parents, Colonel and Mrs. Grey, remained in India. But Amy has just received a telegram informing her of the imminent return of her father and mother. The children are far from enthusiastic at the news. Molly has got used to a nurse; Cosmo is embarrassed at the thought of a father who might try to kiss him; and Amy, who has been mothering the family and running the household, expects her parents to disapprove of the results. Fortunately, Amy's friend Ginevra is more encouraging. The two girls have been doing the rounds of all the London theaters that present serious, thought-provoking drama; and they are now sure they know what life is really like. Ginevra observes that Mrs. Grey (Alice) has been in India for so long that she cannot be expected to know anything about life; therefore, Amy's duty will be to enlighten her.

The children are not in the living room when the Colonel and Alice arrive, and their absence gives the couple a brief opportunity to speculate on the kind of welcome to expect. Alice, who is full of doubts, wants her children to love her at sight; but she suspects gloomily that none of them will. The Colonel tries to assure her that children are bound to love their mother. Alice is also overanxious because she has not yet settled down to middle age and motherhood—though in India she had mothered all her husband's soldiers; and they, to reciprocate, had fallen in love with her. The Colonel did not expect his wife to settle down until a year after their return to England—an allowance he made for marrying a woman many years younger than himself. Alice, for her part, looked forward to "coming of age" at the same time as her daughter.

When the nurse enters, one of Alice's worst fears is realized. She is urged not to touch Molly as the child does not take to "strangers." Nurse proves correct: baby screams as soon as

Alice picks her up. Cosmo creeps in cautiously and manages to evade a kiss from his father; but his mother's display of affection is not to be denied. The boy is prepared to make allowances for adults—particularly when they happen to be parents; however, he does not count on having a mother like Alice, a middle-aged woman who actually likes fun. He makes the mistake of reflecting indelicately on her age, and Alice responds by "flipping" his face with her hand. Cosmo takes this gesutre as a smack, and thus Alice's relations with her son are strained from the outset.

The meeting with Amy is even more disappointing. Mother and daughter are awkward and restrained, and a series of misunderstandings between them develops when Amy begins to talk mysteriously of knowing more of the world than her mother can ever hope to know. Alice instantly assumes that the girl has been having a secret love affair. Later, Amy starts to entertain similar suspicions of her mother when she catches a glimpse of Alice being kissed by handsome, young Stephen Rollo, and arranging what appears to be an assignation with him. However, the kiss is simply the innocent greeting of an old acquaintance. Stephen is a soldier who had been befriended by the Greys while they were in the Punjab. Unaware of the truth, the stage-struck Amy resolves to rescue her depraved mother in accordance with methods she has seen depicted in the theater: she will make the supreme sacrifice of going to Stephen Rollo and of offering herself in place of Alice.

Stephen lives in bachelor apartments, tended by Richardson, a young female servant or "slavey." Shortly after dinner, Richardson admits a strange young woman wearing evening dress and an opera cloak. It is, of course, Amy, steeled to endure a "fate worse than death" and dressed in the appropriate stage costume. Her encounter with Stephen creates more misunderstandings. As he has never seen the girl before and has no knowledge of her connection with Alice, Rollo is perplexed at her demand that he return her mother's love letters and end his sordid affair with a married woman. When Richardson suddenly announces the arrival of Colonel Grey, Amy, in consternation, darts into a cupboard. Alice, who arrives a few moments later, notices the hem of a woman's dress caught in the cupboard door.

Amused at detecting Stephen in a secret affair, she works her way over to the cupboard and finds an excuse for looking inside.

Her discovery comes as a great shock, but with remarkable presence of mind, she shuts the cupboard door without disclosing to the Colonel that she has found their daughter hiding in a man's apartment. Alice now concludes that Amy's dark references to her knowledge of life had alluded to an intrigue with Stephen Rollo. She must hasten to rescue the girl from depravity without letting the Colonel know that his daughter is a "fallen woman." Contriving to dance with her husband, she whirls him around until he falls, giddy and exhausted, into a chair, at which point she grabs Amy's hand, pulls her out of the cupboard, and seems to greet her at the door as an unexpected arrival.

However, Colonel Grey is not as unobservant as his wife imagines. Amy has to be "introduced" to Stephen (and the latter is genuinely surprised to learn that the mysterious girl is the daughter of his friends, the Greys), yet the Colonel notices that she puts on a glove that he had found on the floor of the apartment when he arrived. Questioned by her father, Amy confesses that she is Stephen Rollo's fiancée, in the hope of concealing her mother's adultery. Alice confirms Amy's story in order to withhold her daughter's shame. But, by this time, Colonel Grey has no doubts that Amy was hidden in the apartment when he arrived. Alice, who has to intercede to prevent a confrontation of the two men, asks to be left alone with her daughter. Prepared to hear the worst, she is first astonished, then amused to learn of Amy's efforts to shield her "guilty" mother's reputation. Everything is clear to her when the girl explains how the theater had taught her about life. Alice realizes that, if she explains immediately the truth to her daughter, the girl will feel ridiculous. Accordingly, she makes no attempt to disillusion her.

When mother and daughter return home, the girl urges Alice to throw herself upon her husband's mercy. Alice pretends to put herself in Amy's hands; complying meekly, she goes in to speak to the Colonel. Amy, now left alone with Ginevra, discusses further strategy in the light of their theatrical knowledge. It seems inevitable to the girls that the Colonel will follow the rules and order his wife to leave his presence forever. This situation is customarily resolved in the theater with the aid of a child who, appearing at the opportune moment, clasps the hands of both parents, draws them together, and asks what is to become of their helpless infant if they are separated. Difficulties confront the girls because Molly is too young a baby to undertake the necessary reconciliation. When Stephen's unexpected entrance breaks up this discussion, Ginevra impulsively seizes the opportunity to offer herself to him as a sacrifice in place of Amy. Although by this time it is clear to him that he has a part to play in sustaining Amy's illusion, only the timely appearance of Alice prevents Stephen from making a quick escape from such confusion. With bowed head, Alice informs him that all is over between them; her husband knows all. Amy promptly adds that her commitment to marry Stephen is also at an end. The apparently grief-stricken young man replies that Alice does not seem to be the same woman. She is not. Alice says that she can now see only through Amy's eyes.

The girl is directing the farewell scene of Alice and Stephen when the Colonel enters, evidently furious at his wife's confession and resolved on a showdown with her lover. Amy is ordered up to bed. With the girl out of earshot, the trio suddenly snap out of melodrama and rock with laughter. Alice has to explain to Stephen the cause of Amy's confusion; she admits that sustaining the misunderstanding had been irresistible, particularly when she saw how Amy began to love her mother only when she became her mother's protectress. Alice considers that the game has now gone far enough. Amy must be told the truth before she falls asleep.

The breaking of illusions is one way of growing up, and henceforth Alice, as well as her daughter, will have come of age. This little escapade has been Alice's last fling—for the reality of her life in India, where she was the innocent sweetheart of all the young soldiers, has been reduced to a child's fantasy. From now on the Colonel's lady will be a very different person, a mother dedicated to the care of her children. As Alice puts it, "My girl and I are like the little figures in the weather-house; when Amy comes out, Alice goes in. Alice Sit-by-the-Fire henceforth." When she bids her husband make way for the "old lady," the Colonel responds with mock-severity in the manner of a villainous husband of melodrama. Amy, misunderstanding her father's stern voice, peeps anxiously into the room. She is dressed in her nightgown and looks more like Peter Pan's Wendy than a girl of seventeen. Timidly, she clasps her parents' hands; and, drawing the couple together, she asks the poignant question that will settle her fate.

Where *Walker, London,* was indebted to Congreve, *Alice*

Sit-by-the-Fire owes one of its most entertaining episodes to Sheridan. Barrie's second act, containing the game of hide-and-seek in Stephen's apartment, is inspired by the famous "screen scene" in *The School for Scandal.* But most of *Alice Sit-by-the-Fire* is a clever manipulation of melodramatic intrigue which Barrie parodies as a play within a play. Alice's disillusionment in the course of sustaining her daughter's illusions provides a commentary and framework for the parody. Significantly, Barrie the dramatist equates theatrical illusion with the fantasies of adolescence. Alice's desire for this vanishing experience gives the play its nostalgia and also its sentimentality, which emerges toward the end of the last act only to be effectively blocked by the parody and counterparody that bring down the curtain.

At this point it is necessary to state categorically that Alice Grey is not, as some of Barrie's commentators have maintained, a character comparable to Shaw's Candida, and symbolic, like her, of Goethe's "Eternal Feminine that leads Man forward and upward." Neither is Alice the Great Earth Mother, though it is possible that Ellen Terry invested her with a profundity that is nowhere discernible in Barrie's text. Braybrooke gets very close to the truth when he argues that *Alice Sit-by-the-Fire* is "about one thing only and that thing is the mind of a woman."[13] A woman—not *Woman*; and we have encountered her many times since *Margaret Ogilvy.*

In his old bachelor's reverie, "Dream Children," James Elia (Charles Lamb) confronts the children of his fantasy marriage to Alice W——n, the girl he had loved and lost. Recalling the end of the dream, he described how "suddenly, turning to Alice [one of the dream children] the soul of the first Alice [the dream mother] looked out at her eyes with such a reality of re-presentment, that I became in doubt which of them stood there before me. . . ." As his dream children vanish, Elia seems to hear their voices saying, "We are not of Alice, nor of thee, nor are we children at all. . . . We are only what might have been. . . . "[14] Barrie's play strikingly resembles the conclusion of Lamb's reverie; for Alice and Amy are his dream wife and child, both modeled on Margaret Ogilvy, the soul of the mother looking out at the eyes of the daughter.

Where *Quality Street* and *Rosalind* split their heroines into character and masquerade, the mother and daughter of *Alice Sit-by-the-Fire* are two distinct characters. And, instead of a masquerade to deceive the hero, there is self-deception by the heroines: Alice is a middle-aged mother who imagines she is still a young girl; her daughter is a young girl who believes that she is an experienced woman of the world. Barrie's contrast of Alice and Amy shows the latter's identification with romance and illusion as the means by which the former, recognizing her own past in her daughter's present, grows out of the last vestiges of girlhood and becomes reconciled to the "autumn" of life. The play as a whole, like Elia's reverie, is a vision of what might have been.

The brothers' prototypes appear as Stephen (David) and Colonel Grey (Barrie); in the fantasy Amy (the virgin Margaret) and Alice (the mother Margaret), each in her own way, "rejects" the young lover, though Barrie makes it clear that there is never any serious amorous involvement to be repudiated. Relationships with Stephen are shown to be the outcome either of misunderstandings that impel Amy's willingness to sacrifice her honor or of a desire on the part of Alice to mother lonely young men, when, like Moira Loney, she is separated from her children. The Colonel, an ideal husband, is never jealous or even remotely suspicious of his wife's behavior. He indulgently dismisses Alice's interest in Stephen as the vestiges of her adolescence, suggesting in fantasy that Margaret Ogilvy would outgrow her preference for David.

Barrie wrote *What Every Woman Knows* (1908) for Maude Adams, who was to appear as the heroine, Maggie, in the American premiere of the play. But the first production was actually given in London, at the Duke of York's Theatre, in September, 1908, when Maggie was played by Hilda Trevelyan (384 performances). The play was, however, far more successful in America than in England. Charles Frohman took over $80,000 in ticket sales before the play opened at the Empire Theatre, New York, in December, 1908. Later, there were two film versions: a Paramount picture of 1921, directed by William DeMille, and starring Lois Wilson as Maggie, and an MGM "talkie" of 1935, directed by Gregory La Cava, with Helen Hayes as Maggie and Brian Aherne as John Shand.

Frohman's association with Barrie was to end with the American production of *What Every Woman Knows.* In 1915, the year before Barrie's next play was ready for staging, Frohman died in the *Lusitania* disaster. One of the survivors, who had seen Frohman a few moments before he was drowned, claimed that the impresario's last words were those of Peter Pan: "To die will be an awfully big adventure. . . ."

In *Alice Sit-by-the-Fire* Barrie had depicted the ideal husband, a model of indulgence toward his wife. However, the wife's indulgence toward the husband may be even more admirable and necessary. Barrie considered that every woman started out with a secret advantage over every man. *What Every Woman Knows* shows that behind every successful man there is a determined woman. Maggie Wylie, the determined woman of Barrie's play, is a spinster with two bachelor brothers, David and James, and elderly father, Alick. These are, of course, the Barrie family names and the original relationships, except for Alick (Alexander) who was J. M. Barrie's elder brother. Barrie also had a grandfather named Alexander who worked as a stonemason, and we are informed in the introduction to Act I that Wylie and Sons own the local granite quarry as a result of David's enterprise.

Maggie's happiness is the primary concern of her menfolk. She has set her heart upon marriage, but at twenty-seven her chances of securing a husband seem slim. What counts against her even more than her age and her plainness is, she believes, her lack of charm. Charm would have made up for her other deficiencies. David and James shower gifts upon their sister in the hope of consoling her, but to no avail. Maggie, facing the truth about herself, expects to die a spinster.

It is ten o'clock, the Wylie's usual bedtime, but on this particular evening the brothers have no intention of retiring. A prowler has been reported in the neighborhood, and on one occasion a local police officer has seen the man climbing out of a window in the Wylie house. Oddly enough, nothing—not even the silver plate—appears to be missing. David and James have reason to suspect a return visit by the prowler. Standing in the doorway, James catches a glimpse of someone hiding in the bushes. He withdraws into the livingroom, and according to a prearranged plan, the house lights are extinguished. A few minutes later, the burglar climbs through the window into the darkened living room. He is closely watched by the Wylies.

Instead of proceeding to plunder the house, the burglar piles more coal on the fire, selects a few books, takes out pen, ink, and paper, and settles down to study. He is caught in the act as the brothers emerge from their hiding place. The Wylies recognize the intruder as John Shand, a young man from the village who doubles a career as railroad porter and college student. Asked to account for his housebreaking activities, Shand explains that he is too poor to afford books; the Wylies, on the other hand, have over six hundred books which they never bother to read. Shand had entered the house to use the facilities of this neglected library. The brothers are at first disposed to hand the intruder over to the police, but David suddenly sees Shand as a possible answer to Maggie's problem. A proposition is offered the young man: the Wylies will pay for his education on condition that five years hence Maggie can marry him, if she so wishes. After some show of reluctance from Maggie as well as John, the proposition is accepted. Maggie thereupon makes it clear that her interest in all matters is now identical with John's. She takes his side in settling the financial arrangements. And, when she retires to bed that night, she has two books under her arm; for she does not want the man who may one day be her husband to know anything she does not.

Six years have passed. It is election night in Glasgow, and John Shand is one of the candidates. So far, the results have not been declared; and the Wylies are waiting anxiously in the Shand Committee Rooms. Maggie, ready for the worst, is prepared to give John her support for another campaign if this one fails. She has deferred her legal right to marry him until the election is over, and is willing, if necessary, to go on waiting until he wins a seat in Parliament. Fortunately, she has very little waiting to do. The roar of a crowd heralds Shand's arrival. Dazed and disheveled, he announces the result: he has been elected an M.P., with a majority of 244. Maggie openly defers to his opinion that the victory is the outcome of his own unaided efforts. Secretly, she knows that it is Maggie Wylie who has provided most of the inspiration.

John remains insensitive to the remarkable attainments of the woman he has agreed to marry, indifferent to Maggie's efforts to educate herself in his interest; but his election triumph puts her achievements to the test almost immediately. Three notabilities who call on the new M.P. are received by Maggie while John is acknowledging the acclaim of the electorate. The Hon. Mr. Tenterden is a party whip, escorting his sister, the beautiful and haughty Lady Sybil, and his aunt, the Comtesse de la Brière. These celebrities must be treated tactfully as people likely to advance John's career. Unfortunately, Maggie fumbles the encounter; and her plainnness and lack of savoir-faire contrast unfavorably with the dazzling Lady Sybil.

Between themselves, the visitors discuss their conviction that marriage to someone as humble as Maggie would be a disadvantage to an aspiring politician. This hardly matters in Shand's case: he is not expected to have any political future. He had made his reputation as a mob orator, but demagoguery is not tolerated in the House of Commons. Shand might survive the arena if he could be induced to learn finesse from Lady Sybil. In spite of her fastidiousness, Lady Sybil is attracted by him. She extends an invitation to Shand to call on her when he visits London. Maggie gloomily interprets this invitation as the offer of a rival. John, obviously interested in Lady Sybil, is nevertheless resolved to stand by his contract: he tells Maggie that a bargain is a bargain. All that he knows of her has earned his respect, and respect is enough for him, a humorless Scot without any pretensions to romance. He brushes aside as an irrelevancy her promise to act differently from other wives if he should ever fall in love with a woman who has charm. About Maggie he has no doubts, for he is certain, with the self-assurance of most men, that he knows her far better than she can ever know him. Maggie, in a gesture of magnanimity, tears up the contract and offers him freedom. But John is too conscious of his obligations to accept the opportunity of escape. As the excited electorate burst into the Committee Rooms, he introduces her as the future Mrs. Shand—and Maggie proves equal to the occasion. Hoisted aloft on her brothers' shoulders and urged to make a speech, she complies by throwing out her arms as if in a vast embrace, and crying, "My constituents."

In the next act, the Comtesse de la Brière, visiting the London house of the Shands, is pleasantly surprised by its elegance; but the wife of the rising young politician seems as stupid as ever. While Shand is addressing his ladies' committee, Maggie is preoccupied with knitting. Meanwhile, Lady Sybil has very cunningly moved into John's life by heading the committee in which he is most interested. Maggie's reception of a government minister, Mr. Venables, gives the Comtesse an entirely different opinion of Shand's wife; for Venables believes that the young politician's speeches are "doctored" by a woman, probably his wife. Impressed by John's wit, he cannot understand why it colors his speeches and never his conversation. Actually, Shand cannot even recognize a joke when it is pointed out to him.

The witty remarks are surreptitiously inserted by Maggie when she types out his speeches. John is blind to this, just as he is unaware of Maggie's skillful political maneuvering in his name and on his behalf. She explains to the Comtesse that her husband, like all successful men, cherishes the belief that his success is selfmade. She contrives to remove Venables' suspicions and even to turn the minister's visit to her husband's advantage. The Comtesse now recognizes the real Maggie; and, admiring what she sees, she warns her to beware of Lady Sybil.

A few days later, Maggie inadvertently finds John embracing Lady Sybil. It is the Shand's second wedding anniversary and the Wylies have journeyed down from Scotland with a gift. In the midst of his love affair, John has overlooked the occasion; but Maggie surprises him by helping herself to the pendant he had bought for Lady Sybil. Through her action the guilty lovers realize that their secret has been detected. John who now openly admits to his passion for Lady Sybil, declares that he is willing to give up his career in order to live with her. The Wylies are furious; but, as their altercation with him achieves nothing, Maggie urges them to leave the matter in her hands. Then, calmly, to the amazement of her husband and Lady Sybil, she accepts the situation as a *fait accompli,* and suggests that it might even be possible to arrange matters so that John's career is unharmed. He has declared that Lady Sybil is the inspiration of his political work; in that case, before his separation from Maggie is publicized—to the detriment of his reputation—he is to spend a month with his mistress writing the greatest speech of his career, a speech that will make him indispensable to his party. Maggie arranges for the couple to spend the month at the cottage of the Comtesse de la Brière. Before parting from her husband, she hands him a letter that he is not to open until the month ends.

The days pass painfully for John and Lady Sybil. The "great speech" has been rejected by Venables, for Shand has somehow lost his touch. At the same time, Lady Sybil has started to grow tired of his company. Maggie opportunely arrives at the cottage with a second speech garnished with the "Shandisms" that have made her husband famous. It is passed on to Venables without John's knowledge. Having reached the end of her tether like Lady Lilian in *Half an Hour,* Lady Sybil abruptly terminates her affair with Shand. When she has gone, the Comtesse reads aloud from Maggie's letter, and John learns that everything that had happened was predicted by his wife. As Maggie had anticipated, after a few weeks of Lady Sybil he had grown sick to death of her. John is momentarily horrified to discover that a speech reworked by Maggie has fallen into Venables' hands; but, when the minister enters full of praise for the wit and sprightly intelligence of the new speech, Shand suddenly sees his wife in a new light. The truth is a humiliating experience. But Maggie reassures him: "Every man who is high up loves to think that he has done it all himself. . . . Every woman knows that." As John is not amused, Maggie proceeds to teach him how to laugh—the best cure for a man who has found himself out.

The wiliness of the Wylies is recompense for Barrie's patronizing treatment of the Auld Lichts in the Thrums stories: *What Every Woman Knows* is a tribute to Scots canniness. Maggie and her brothers may be fit subjects for comedy, but this fact did not preclude the dramatist from respecting the qualities that make them the salt of the earth. The brothers are shrewd where anything material is concerned, but their sister's shrewdness extends the family range to perspicacity in dealing with human beings. Maggie knows not only what every woman knows, but like Crichton, she also understands when to suppress her knowledge. Yet for all of her insights into others, the person she knows least is herself; for her assumption that she lacks charm is utterly without foundation. Lady Sybil's charm is merely the superficial glamor of a pretty girl; but Maggie's is the subtle allurement of an intelligent woman who knows when to flatter, when to hold her tongue, and how to make herself indispensable, while always retaining an air of disarming naïveté. If Maggie knew only what every woman knows she would be no match for Lady Sybil. But, as a canny Scot, she knows much more; she triumphs by wielding the iron hand in a velvet glove.

Though Barrie is again concerned with disillusionment, it is not his heroine who has to be disillusioned; for Maggie has none of Alice Grey's fantasies. During most of the play she shows a level-headed understanding or businesslike control of every situation. But the hero, the dour Scotman, is confronted with reality; he has to be taught the final disillusionment of how to laugh at himself. John Shand's disillusionment is all the more shattering because Maggie has carefully nurtured his self-deception. She contrives to give the impression that every challenge to her is one to John instead. It is John who thinks up "Shandisms," who manipulates his fellow politicians, who understands himself and the sources of his inspiration. Yet each act, except the third, reaches its curtain-climax in a show of mastery by Maggie. Shand fails to discern this mastery in the first and second acts, and at the turning point in the third act he mistakes her scheme for a sportsman-like gesture of capitulation. But, even though he goes away with Lady Sybil, John has swallowed Maggie's bait. He has once again misjudged his wife; and, though her activities in the third act had not appeared at first sight to be another triumph for Maggie, in retrospect, as the fourth act unfolds, she emerges as masterly as ever.

The reversal of action can thus be seen as the first move in a game that leads to the checkmating of Lady Sybil and the exposure of John's weaknesses. Of course, Barrie stacks the cards against Shand and in favor of Maggie from the outset. Even at the denouement, when Shand discovers what every woman knows, he gains no future advantage over Maggie. She remains his sole inspiration, the brain behind his political maneuvers, and the "onlie begetter" of the Shandisms that have made his reputation as a public speaker. Barrie never tells us how a Maggie Shand would have coped with a man whose share of original genius was greater than his wife's. His own career persuaded him that this was an irrelevant consideration. There had to be a determined woman behind every successful man—even a successful man who had no wife must have had a mother.

Much critical discussion of this play has been concerned with determining precisely what it is that every woman knows. According to Darton, "it is, in the long run, everything, but chiefly that men are children, and every wise woman can manage a child."[15] For Braybrooke, the play exposes the instinctive awareness of the female that "men are always fools and women are always wise, at least women like Maggie."[16] As for Roy, Barrie is asserting that every woman knows that she has "in her hands the making or the marring of a man, and that man is terribly dependent on women, no matter how strong and independent he thinks he is."[17] These views present not conflicting interpretations but merely differences of emphasis; they are all valid "messages" for those who seek them in this play. But, as Roy recognizes without, unfortunately discussing his view, there is something deeper in this play than its "message." "Some smart London critic once said that *What Every Woman Knows* was a play about a man who had really married his mother. There is," he notes, "more truth than fiction in this statement."[18] He might have added that anyone familiar with *Margaret Ogilvy* would have no need to ask "Which man?" or "Whose mother?"

Though written in the year prior to his divorce and at a time when Barrie was already aware of his wife's adultery with Gilbert Cannan, *What Every Woman Knows* belongs "autobiographically" to 1892-94 and earlier, not to 1908. The play embodies a familiar transposition of roles. Shand's wife represents the prototypic Margaret Ogilvy; the mistress, Lady Sybil, is an equivalent for Barrie's wife, Mary Ansell. The characters are involved in a triangular situation that parallels the relationships of Grizel, Tommy Sandys, and Lady Pippinworth (*Tommy and Grizel*), and of Lucy White, Professor Goodwillie, and Lady Gilding (*The Professor's Love Story*). Maggie is a more vital, more plausible re-creation of Lucy White. Where Lucy's quick-witted opportunism is a "given factor," Maggie's native shrewdness emerges convincingly against the background of Wylie materialism, and she is an unsentimentalized Margaret Ogilvy.

Shand is one of two personae for Barrie. The other, James Wylie, is from the outset cut down to the level to which Shand is later reduced. Described as a commoner fellow than David, he is at first, like his brother, a bachelor whose only fear is women. In Act II Maggie speaks of him as having acquired a wife, Elizabeth. James is a vision of Barrie as a failure, uninspired by Margaret Ogilvy. John, on the other hand, is a counterpart of the successful Barrie who is often neglectful of his mother but always inspired by her. Significantly, his thirst for literature leads Shand into the situation by which he becomes irrevocably tied to her. Later, oblivious to all that Maggie has done for him, he tries to desert her for a younger, attractive woman who can give him no inspiration whatever.

Maggie Shand was Barrie's ugly duckling. His next heroine, like Phoebe Throssel, was to be another Cinderella. The wartime pantomime, *A Kiss for Cinderella* (1916), with Hilda Trevelyan as Miss Thing and Gerald du Maurier as Robert the Policeman, opened at the Wyndham's Theatre, London, in March, 1916 (156 performances); it was revived with great success at the Kingsway Theatre, London, at Christmas of the same year. The American premiere was given at the Academy Theatre, Baltimore, in December, 1916, and the production was transferred in the same month to the Empire Theatre, New York. In 1926, Herbert Brenon, who had directed the first film version of *Peter Pan,* also directed a Paramount film of *A Kiss for Cinderella,* with Betty Bronson (the movie Peter Pan) as Miss Thing and with Tom Moore as Robert the Policeman.

A Kiss for Cinderella is closer in manner and spirit to *Little Mary* than to *Peter Pan.* It is not a "full dress" pantomime, for the familiar Cinderella story occurs only as a dream sequence in Act II. However, Jane Thing, the heroine, is called Cinderella during most of the play; and the Policeman who kisses her before she dies is intended as a modern-dress version of Prince Charming.

Even Barrie's ardent admirers have not showered unqualified praise upon *A Kiss for Cinderella.* Braybrooke, who finds something "really Holy" in the title of the play and who describes the first two acts as "charming" and "promising," considers the rest of the work as a sudden fall "into cheap and amateurish satire . . . the play has lost its golden light."[19] Darton, whose enthusiasm for the Scots "Genius" usually outrivals Hammerton and Braybrooke, admits that Barrie's play "is certainly very sentimental, and has a distinct thinness of plot and characterization."[20] Significantly, most of Barrie's admirers were enthusiastic about *A Kiss for Cinderella* when it was first produced and played to packed houses—to wartime audiences intolerant of "serious" drama and hungry for escapist fantasies and pantomimes. These same audiences made *Chu Chin Chow,* a trite "oriental" musical based on the story of Ali Baba and the Forty Thieves, the record-breaking production in London during the years when the flower of England's manhood was dying at the Marne, the Somme, and at a thousand other places between the North Sea and the Alps. Postwar reactions to *A Kiss for Cinderella* betray the uneasy awareness of Barrie's admirers that the "Master" had reacted to the war by writing a sentimental pantomime and, perhaps even more disturbingly, that this was just what Londoners had wanted to help them forget the truth.

The first act of *A Kiss for Cinderella* takes place in Mr. Bodie's London studio during World War I. Mr. Bodie (Barrie), the "least distinguished person in *Who's Who,*" is an elderly unmarried artist—though he has the habit of referring to an armless statue of Venus de Milo as his wife. It is evening, and Mr. Bodie is resting in a corner of the studio when his reveries are interrupted by an unexpected visitor, a policeman—David, the play's hero. He is investigating an infringement of the blackout regulations, and Mr. Bodie is apparently the culprit. But the case is not quite as straightforward as it appears. According to Mr. Bodie, the windows had been boarded up; someone must have removed the boards.

The real culprit, Bodie suggests, is a certain Miss Thing, known familiarly as Cinderella, who is a drudge or "slavey" (like Tweeny in *The Admirable Crichton* and Richardson in *Alice Sit-by-the-Fire*) employed by the housekeeper to do all the menial work. Cinderella collects boards and makes them into boxes. Mr. Bodie cannot explain their purpose, but he knows that they are connected in some way with Germany. The suspicious policeman is also informed that Cinderella knows a number of German words. She has been trying to find out how to send a letter to Germany without Lord Haig's knowing about it, and plying Mr. Bodie with questions about punishments meted out to people who are caught harboring enemy aliens. Determined to track down what is probably a dangerous case of espionage, the policeman takes down Cinderella's address and then slips into the pantry to overhear her conversation with Mr. Bodie. When the young "slavey" appears in response to Mr. Bodie's ringing of the servant bell, they are soon discussing Cinderella's expectations for an invitation to a ball at which she hopes to meet the Prince of Wales. In due course the Policeman emerges and proceeds to interrogate the suspect. Dissatisfied with her cryptic remarks about a ball, princes, and the importance of having pretty feet, he decides to pursue his investigations incognito at the "slavey's" house.

On the evening of the same day, the policeman has found his way to a street in a poor district of London. While he is prowling about outside one of the houses, the "fourth wall" of the building dissolves so that the audience can see the interior of Cinderella's home. One feature of her room resembles the parlor of the chemist's shop in *Little Mary*: nailed to the wall are four boxes used as cribs for the children "mothered" by Cinderella. The heroine is at home dealing with various clients, for she ekes out a living by doing odd jobs at a penny per customer. She gives an elderly gentleman a fitting for a new coat, hands over a stiffly starched shirt front to another man, gives advice to old Mrs. Maloney on how to ease her husband's pains, and offers much-needed pity to unlovable Marion who is being turned out of her home in consequence of a domestic scandal similar to that in *The Wedding Guest.* A bearded man dressed as a sailor comes in and asks for a shave—the policeman in disguise. When Cinderella attempts to shave him, the false beard comes off in her hand—at which point the policeman steps out of his disguise.

Unobserved, the children in their boxes have been watching the girl at work. At the sight of the policeman's uniform, they start to scream. Cinderella's shocking secret now stands exposed she has been taking care of neighbors' children; and, while most of them are allies, one of the babies turns out to be a German. Cinderella's wish to communicate with the German baby's parents is the motive behind her interest in sending letters to Germany. Children mean more to her than patriotism. Her love for them is so intense that she wishes she had been the Old Woman who lived in a shoe. However many children Cinderella had had, she would have known what to do with them. The policeman's suspicions are dispelled, but he now has grave doubts about Cinderella's expectations of a ball and marriage to Prince Charming. He has the notion that it is all make-believe; but Cinderella, is convinced that a magic coach will be coming for her that very evening. Though it is a cold night, she goes into the street and sits on the doorstep to wait for the sound of horses' hoofs. Before leaving her, the policeman takes off his scarf and wraps it round her neck; but Cinderella promptly removes it and winds it around her precious feet which must be preserved in readiness for a certain pair of glass slippers. Then she falls asleep.

A dream sequence follows. Cinderella's Fairy Godmother suddenly materializes. As it is wartime she is dressed in a Red Cross nurse's uniform. Offered three wishes, Cinderella asks her Fairy Godmother for a ball, a chance to nurse the wounded, and the experience of being loved by a man of her choice. All three wishes are granted: the first in the dream; the second and last in Act III, when Cinderella is no longer asleep. Cinderella's ball is a fantasy created in part out of details from earlier sections of the play. The proceedings are observed throughout by the children, clad in their nightdresses and sitting in an elegant private box. A procession appears, headed by the Lord Mayor and continuing with Lord Times (an imaginary creation suggested by Mr. Bodie's description of the power of the press), the Censor (complete with executioner's ax), the King, the Queen, Prince Hard-to-Please, and the courtiers. The King turns out to be a cockney who strap-hangs, as if traveling in a crowded subway, while addressing his subjects. The Prince looks exactly like the policeman, and in the background flit the shadows of Mr. Bodie and unlovable Marion. Now the traditional Cinderella story unfolds until the clock strikes twelve and the dream dissolves. As the scene draws to a close, Cinderella is seen huddled motionless on the doorstep. Snow silently covers the deserted street.

Two months later, Mr. Bodie is at the seaside visiting his spinster sister, Dr. Nellie Bodie, who runs a private infirmary and assists at a nearby convalescent home for wounded soldiers. Cinderella is now a patient in the care of Dr. Bodie, for her friend the policeman, who had found the girl frozen and unconscious, had taken her to a London hospital where she had been nursed through pneumonia. After being discharged from the hospital, she had been sent by Mr. Bodie to his sister's infirmary. Though technically convalescent, there is little chance of the girl's recovery. Dr. Bodie remarks how Cinderella, who had a genius for showering affection on others, has been starved of food and affection all her life. Cinderella's genius is displayed as she rests on her army-style hospital bed, surrounded by the worshiping British Tommies she has "mothered." She is surprised to see Mr. Bodie; for she had expected her regular caller, the policeman she now calls David.

Through her long illness the girl has come to realize that she is not the real Cinderella. When Bodie asks how she has found this out, the girl's reply counters the gospel of Moira Loney: the more she eats, the more she understands. Inquiring after the children, she learns that Mr. Bodie is taking care of them until Cinderella is well enough to resume her mothering. Stranger things are happening than Mr. Bodie's relinquishing of art to become a children's nursemaid. One of the wounded Tommies, Danny, a former plumber, is being tended by a probationer-nurse who is none other than the beautiful and erstwhile sophisticated debutante, Lady Charlotte. As Cinderella observes, "It's just the war has mixed things up till we forget how different we are." (This episode is reminiscent of *The Admirable Crichton* as well as the playlet *Barbara's Wedding* which Barrie wrote at approximately the same time as *A Kiss for Cinderella.*)

But the girl's mind is soon on other matters, for David's arrival is imminent. Cinderella is uncertain about his feelings toward her, although a letter she has recently received from him looks remarkably like a billet-doux. David enters with a small parcel and comes to her bedside. To him she is no longer Cinderella but Jane, the girl for whom he has brought an engagement ring of a very unusual kind. To Jane, though he is not exactly Prince Hard-to-Please, he is nevertheless the man of her choice, and to her delight his policeman's idea of an engagement ring turns out to be a pair of glass slippers. David puts them on her feet and embraces her. Whereupon Barrie mercifully rings down the curtain before the dying Cinderella has time to discover that David's first kiss is to be her last.

This conclusion is an unfortunate blemish on what might have been as delightful and popular a children's play as *Peter Pan.* The second act, and in particular the bizarre dream sequence, shows Barrie the fantasy-maker at his most imaginative. But Act III is out of harmony with the rest of the pantomime. Where it may have succeeded in moving sentimental adults, it erred in destroying the illusion of pantomime for children who delight in the spectacle of a scullery maid transformed into a princess, but are unlikely to be impressed with the spectacle of a Cinderella turning into a Little Nell.

Anyone familiar with the fairy tales of Hans Christian Andersen will have no difficulty in recognizing Act II as the Cinderella story embedded in a variation on the pathetic tale of "The Little Match Girl." On a cold winter's night, Andersen's heroine huddles in a doorway and strikes her matches in a futile effort to stay warm. She sees wonderful fantasies in the leaping flames: a warm fire, a feast, a Christmas tree, and the spirit of her grandmother, the only person who had ever been kind to her. Next morning, New Year's Day, passers-by find the girl's body; she has been frozen to death. But her face is resplendent with a smile of delight at the fantasies that brought her joy in the moment of death. "She must have tried to warm herself," say the passers-by. But Andersen, as if pitying their superficial understanding, explains: "Nobody knew what beautiful visions she had seen, nor in what a halo she had entered with her grandmother upon the glories of the New Year."[21]

Barrie's pantomime, though as painful in its conclusion as

the Andersen story, lacks at least the false note of triumph that is supposed to mitigate the Match Girl's end. The sentimental finale of *A Kiss for Cinderella* does not counterbalance the play's major theme: the destructive power of fantasy. Cinderella's illusions lure her to her death. Before she dies, she tells Mr. Bodie that she no longer believes in her fantasies; yet she identifies her dream prince with David, and the obliging policeman helps to re-create her fantasies by proposing to her when he knows she is on her deathbed and by giving her the glass slippers that belong in the dream-world and not in the reality that Cinderella claims to have accepted. In death, like the Little Match Girl, Cinderella is resplendent with the joy of her fantasy. She destroys herself by reverting to self-deception even though she says she has seen through her illusions.

Ironically, underlying the theme of the destructiveness of illusion, Barrie preserves his own fantasy. Although the play is set in wartime, the real conflict is still between Barrie and his dead brother. David is represented as a righteous figure, a prince, a keeper of law, and the guardian of Cinderella-Margaret. The first act centers on the question of whether Cinderella-Margaret is a traitor, or, in terms of the prototypic story, whether Margaret Ogilvy loved one of her sons at the expense of the other. In the second act, not only is the heroine exonerated, she is even condoned for loving an "enemy" child—obviously Barrie. In the character of Mr. Bodie, Barrie helps in spinning Cinderella-Margaret's dreams. But, although he admits the union of the heroine and David in the dream sequence, he separates the couple in the awakening by allowing Cinderella-Margaret to die. With his first full-length play, *Walker, London,* written before his marriage and his mother's death, Barrie had laughed at illusions and had suggested, with the masquerade of Jasper Phipps, that they could be discarded once they had served their turn. But nearly a quarter of a century later, *A Kiss for Cinderella* accepts the inescapability of illusions. Fantasy has now become equated with death. We can almost hear the ghostly voice of Mary Rose as the curtain falls on the dying Cinderella.

CHAPTER 6

Major Plays: Last Phase

I Dear Brutus

SHAW once said that for him the tragedy and comedy of life lay in the consequences of our "persistent attempts to found our institutions on the ideals suggested to our imaginations by our half-satisfied passions. . . ."[1] In the absence of a comparable statement from Barrie, we can indicate his view by replacing Shaw's "found our institutions" with the words "mold ourselves." The pathetic and tragic figures in Barrie's plays are usually those characters who make a total retreat into fantasy or who endeavor to adjust their lives to conform to their illusions. On the other hand, Barrie tends to make tragicomedy out of situations in which a character's growing awareness of his or her illusions first conflicts with and then reaches harmony with an accepted reality. The attainment of this kind of harmony becomes a kind of "comedic catharsis" through which the individual discovers fundamental truths about himself. Where characters in social drama are in search of solutions, they are in search of themselves in the psychological tragicomedy of Barrie. Any one of Barrie's plays is only slanted toward comedy or tragedy to the extent to which his characters do or do not achieve self-discovery.

Dear Brutus (1917) and *Mary Rose* (1920) are complementary allegories of the discovery and loss of the soul: one proceeding through awareness of illusions and repressed desires to a new apprehension of life; the other retreating by way of fantasy into a limbo of half-forgotten dreams. Barrie saw illusions as the masks of repressed wishes. With *Dear Brutus* he became one of the first writers to dramatize a modern psychological view of the dream-state as a condition in which repressions come to the fore; in the second act of his play, he presents a dream in which the repressed desires of his characters are acted out as experiences of "what might have been."

Dear Brutus, produced by Gerald du Maurier, opened at the Wyndham's Theatre, London, in October, 1917. Du Maurier himself played Mr. Dearth (365 performances). There were, subsequently, three successful London revivals of the play as well as many touring and repertory productions. In the United States, the play opened at the Apollo Theatre, Atlantic City, in December, 1917, and was transferred toward the end of the same month to the Empire Theatre, New York City. This production was most notable for the outstanding performance of Faith Celli as Margaret Dearth.

Dear Brutus takes its title from lines in Shakespeare's *Julius Caesar* which express Barrie's leading theme: "The fault, dear Brutus, is not in our stars,/But in ourselves, that we are underlings."[2] However, a more striking Shakespearean influence on Barrie's play is *A Midsummer Night's Dream.* Though *Dear Brutus* begins in anticipation of *Shall We Join the Ladies?* (written some three years later) with a group of visitors being entertained in the country house of a mysterious, diminutive host, the action soon shifts to an enchanted wood on Midsummer Eve where modern equivalents of Hermia, Demetrius, and Helena play out a love comedy under the magical influence of the host (Lob), who now begins to look very much like a latter-day Puck.

Barrie was probably familiar with the traditions of Lob described in *Lob Lie-by-the-Fire or, The Luck of Lingborough* (1874) by Mrs. Gatty (Juliana Horatia Ewing):

> Lob Lie-by-the-Fire—the Lubber-fiend, as Milton calls him—is a rough kind of Brownie or House Elf, supposed to haunt some north-country homesteads, where he does the work of the farm labourers, for no grander wages than
>
> "—to earn his cream-bowl duly set."
>
> . . . His history is less known than that of any other sprite. It may be embodied in some oral tradition that shall one day be found; but as yet the mists of forgetfulness hide it from the story-teller of today. . . .

Little or none of this is discernible in the Lob of *Dear Brutus,* but Barrie may have derived from Mrs. Gatty his character's love of flowers and some elements of his childish spirit of mischief. Barrie's later transformation of Lob into Sam Smith, the avenger of *Shall We Join the Ladies?* is the reverse of Shakespeare's transformation of the evil demon Puck into the mischievous, merry sprite of *A Midsummer Night's Dream.* If Barrie's Lob is a relative of Puck, he also reminds us of Mr. Punch and Old King Cole; and, in one stage direction where Lob is described as a dwarf with a domed head and little feet, we are told that "probably no one has ever looked so old except some newborn child."

Nevertheless, if Lob is the oddest character in the play, he is by no means the most important. In his directions to Act I, Barrie informs us that his two chief characters are Darkness and Light, arch-enemies who will come to grips in the course of the play. The darkness of *Dear Brutus* is the darkness of illusion or self-deception. Until their arrival at Lob's house, Barrie's characters had obscured the truth about themselves. But later, in Lob's enchanted wood, the darkness lifts; and what had previously been repressed or concealed stands vividly exposed.

Lob's guests include three couples: the Coades, the Dearths, and the Purdies, ranging from the elderly to the youthful, and representing a variety of marital relationships. The Coades have arrived at the tranquility that sometimes comes with old age. Mr. Coade is a benign, sweet-tempered old man who has forgotten his long-deceased first wife in the course of years of devotion to his second, familiarly called "Coady." The Dearths, by contrast, are an incompatible younger couple whose marriage is rapidly breaking up. Dearth is still in love with his beautiful wife, Alice; but she—a moody, egocentric woman—is contemptuous of her husband and incapable of expressing the selfless love of a mother or a wife. The Purdies, who are even younger, are a trivial couple whose superficial relationship is also disintegrating. A helpless, pleading sort of woman, Mabel Purdie recalls the Painted Lady in *Sentimental Tommy;* and she is destined to suffer in the same way as that unfortunate character, from the infidelity of her "magerful" man. Purdie, whose exalted view of his own intellectual capacities is tempered only by the belief that marrying Mabel was the one serious mistake in his life, is in love only with the pursuit of love. He had tired of his wife as soon as he had married her.

Lob's other guests are two single ladies. Joanna Trout, who has replaced Mabel in Purdie's inconstant affections, once possessed a natural gaiety and attractiveness which have been effaced by the seriousness with which she regards her involvement with a married man. There is also the haughty Lady Caroline Laney, an incarnation of all the haughty aristocratic women in Barrie from Lady Pippinworth onward. Lady Caroline is the product of a select finishing school where she had learned to pronounce her *r*'s as *w*'s and where her snobbery had been refined to a level of aloofness and disdain attainable only among the British upper classes.

The eight guests are attended by the butler Matey. In no respect a second Crichton, Matey is a wily character, a somewhat eccentric blend of Sam Weller, Uriah Heep, and Bill Sikes. Before the play opens, he has been helping himself to the ladies' jewelry. As the lights go up on the first act, the ladies have come together after dinner to unmask the butler and to coerce him into admitting all that he knows about their mysterious host. But we are to learn more about the ladies than about Lob, who remains for the most part an enigma. Matey evidently tells all that he knows about his master, and the ladies supply other details from their observation. Lob, who appears to be ageless, has claimed to be all that is left of Merry England. Mrs. Coade and Joanna Trout identify him with Robin Goodfellow.

The interrogation of Matey is interrupted by Lob's arrival. Mrs. Coade immediately responds in a motherly way to his childish impulses to mischief; but, when the other ladies are more suspicious of his impish behavior, Lob counters their suspicions with a disarming air of innocence which he sustains even when Mr. Purdie and Mr. Coade arrive to announce that they are proposing to take the ladies on an adventure to find a mysterious wood that is said to appear only once a year, on Midsummer Eve. At first, Lob artfully discourages his guests from their expedition in the hope that his discouragement will actually increase their curiosity. But, when Mrs. Dearth maliciously tests his sincerity by proposing to give up the idea, Lob bursts into tears and admits that he really wanted them to go in search of the wood and that it is not good for him not to get what he wants. He crawls under the table and sulkily declares that nobody loves him. Lady Caroline urges the others to ignore Lob's tantrums, but some of guests go on their knees to plead with him. They agree to go look for the wood as this is the only thing that will placate their eccentric host. While they are collecting their hats and cloaks, Lob climbs out triumphantly. His satisfaction at getting what he had wanted is clouded only by the damage done to the flowers he had knocked from their bowl when he had crawled under the table. He picks them up and lavishes upon them the love that he had tearfully demanded from his guests. When Joanna appears, she asks Lob what he has been saying to the flowers; but he evades a reply, hinting instead that he is aware of her intrigue with Purdie. Then he departs, leaving the lovers together.

Purdie is deluding himself that his shabby little affair with

Joanna is an ennobling higher love, superior to any relationship possible with his wife. However, Mabel, who catches her husband in the act of kissing Joanna, takes an unsympathetic view of the higher love. When she confronts the lovers, Purdie strikes an heroic pose and defends Joanna's virtue from Mabel's sarcastic imputations, while Joanna asserts that Mabel is the one really at fault in having such an unpleasant habit of putting people in the wrong. Purdie, undisturbed by any qualms of conscience, regrets only that he had met Mabel before Joanna, his real soul-mate. Destiny had dealt harshly with him. If only he could begin again, things would be very different. His wish, expressed aloud, stirs Joanna's memory of the recent interrogation of Matey; for he too had expressed the desire for a second chance. And, before the first act has concluded, most of Lob's guests will utter the same wish. This desire that they have in common has brought them together on Midsummer Eve.

Evidently a second chance is the only way for the Dearths to save themselves. Their childless marriage is foundering. Alice Dearth despises her husband; and he, who had once been a talented artist, has degenerated into an alcoholic. Through liquor, he has vainly tried to obliterate his awareness of Alice's unconcealed loathing for him. Dearth is a pitiful creature; his wife is pitiless. Indeed, Alice is the most unpleasant creation in Barrie's gallery of women characters. Her maliciousness, unrelieved by the slightest hint of generosity or compassion, makes her virtually a stock villainess of melodrama.

Freddy Finch-Fallowe, the admirer who followed Alice before she married Dearth, has begun to follow her again. Like Purdie, Alice is convinced that she had made the mistake of marrying the wrong person; and she is now on the brink of deserting her husband for Freddy. Dearth, on the other hand, believes that the lack of a child has made his marriage a failure, and he has no dreams of a second chance. For a long time his only dreams have been those he gets out of bottles. The prospect of an adventure in search of the mysterious wood holds no excitement for him. When the other guests return with Lob, Dearth tells them he will not be joining their little expedition. On their return they will find him in the garden. He goes over to the French windows and begins to draw the curtains—only to recoil at the shock of what he momentarily glimpses.

Turning upon Lob, Dearth demands to know what people receive when they venture into the mysterious wood; and now

Lob discloses to his guests that the wood will give them what most of them desire—a second chance. Mrs. Coade is the only person repelled by this prospect, and she alone does not venture into the wood. But the other guests are excited by the opportunity of living their lives anew. They are about to rush out by the door when Dearth stops them and asks why they do not go through the French windows. So saying, he opens the curtains. Lob's guests are stunned with fear and amazement at what they see: the garden has vanished, and in its place is a gloomy wood illuminated here and there by faint beams of moonlight.

One by one the guests muster sufficient courage to pass through the windows. As they enter the wood, their hands rise to their foreheads as if a hammer blow had struck each of them there. Then they wander on out of sight. The last to disappear is Matey. The unsuspecting butler comes into the room to prepare his master for bed. Lob shows him the wood; and, when the terrified servant peers out at the dark trees, his master gives him a sudden shove that sends him spinning after the others. As the curtain falls on Act I, Lob is standing alone, staring into the wood and quivering with terror and delight at the unknown.

Lob's wood is the setting for the whole of Act II. In a series of episodes enacted among enchanting moonlit glades echoing to the song of a nightingale, the characters who have entered the wood participate in the experience of what might have been. We first come upon Matey and Lady Caroline reclining luxuriously under the trees. The vision of what might have been has transformed them into an affectionate married couple. Matey, no longer a thieving butler, is now a wealthy business tycoon; and Lady Caroline fawns ingratiatingly upon him. The former snob has become as "Matey" as her husband; and the erstwhile butler, now a self-made man, assures her that he had been born to rise to the top no matter how he had begun. Though this episode is bound to recall the third act of *The Admirable Crichton*, its hero displays none of the enterprise shown by his illustrious predecessor on the desert island. Nevertheless, Lob's wood readjusts class differences as effectively as Crichton's island. In marrying Matey, Lady Caroline has dropped into the social niche to which she naturally belongs; her disdain and unbending haughtiness had been the veneer that had concealed her inherent servility. Matey, on other hand, had suppressed his natural assertiveness beneath the servile status of a butler.

The loving couple are about to return to their Rolls-Royce when they notice the mournful figure of Joanna. In her "second chance" the former Miss Trout has become Mrs. Purdie; but, in taking Mabel's place, Joanna has received all her misery too. She skulks through the woods in search of her unfaithful husband who is enjoying the higher love with Mabel. Clearly, Joanna was far happier as a single woman than in the dream-world married to the man she loves. The second chance has allowed Purdie to exchange his wife and mistress, but there has been no transformation of his character. However, Joanna is still in love with him; in her misery she asks the people she meets in the wood whether they have seen her lost "husband."

Mr. Coade suddenly dances out of the trees. He is gaily dressed and playing a whistle he has cut from a twig. Joanna's troubles are of little interest to him; for he is preoccupied with his music and dancing, with savoring the sheer joy of existence. In another moment he dances off into the woods while Lady Caroline and Matey gambol after him, like children following the Pied Piper. Now Purdie and Mabel flit in and out among the trees. Purdie, at first hesitant, looks furtively into the shadows to see whether Joanna is watching him. His suspicions are justified, for Joanna has hidden herself behind a tree to observe all that unfolds between her "husband" and Mabel. But Purdie, confident that he is unobserved, proceeds to unburden his soul to the only woman who "understands" him. After telling Mabel that he would not make the mistake of marrying Joanna if he had a second chance, Purdie vanishes among the trees with his soulmate, while the wretched Joanna trails surreptitiously behind them.

The nightingale again bursts into song as two other forms come into view. Mr. Dearth, a hale and hearty figure accompanied by his adolescent daughter, Margaret, has made his way into the wood in order to paint by moonlight. While Dearth sets up his easel, Margaret gaily frisks about, exchanging small talk with her father. She is interrupted by the reappearance of Mr. Coade who, playing his whistle, dances round them and then jigs away into the shadows. With Coade's departure, Margaret's mood suddenly changes: she clings in terror to her father; a nameless dread has overtaken her. She senses that unknown powers are trying to take her away from her father. Without knowing why, she guesses that in some way she is only a might-have-been. Dearth tries to console her; he tells the girl that might-have-beens are merely ghosts. He too might have been a great painter instead of a happy nonentity; he might even have been a miserable waster without a lovely young daughter like Margaret.

Gradually, the girl's gaiety returns. Now she puts her hair up and gives Dearth a glimpse of the Margaret that will be. Father and daughter discuss Margaret the child and speculate about Margaret the woman who may one day leave her father to get married and rear children of her own. Dearth is saddened by the thought that the years that turn the child into the woman will inevitably deprive him of his daughter. These reveries of past and future are disturbed by the intrusion of a strange woman. It is Alice, the Mrs. Dearth of Act I, but now, in the vision of what-might-have-been, the wife of the Honorable Freddy Finch-Fallowe.

The same deep passions burn within Alice, but a disastrously unsuccessful marriage to Freddy has left her destitute; and, in order to stay alive, she is reduced to begging, which obliges her to conceal her sullenness and resentment beneath a mask of humility. She is wandering through the woods in search of scraps of food that may have been left by tourists. Her physical hunger is, of course, a reflection of the spiritual starvation that had, in real life, devoured her compassion. With Dearth and Margaret, however, generosity and pity are instinctive. Though they have no food for the vagrant woman, they provide her with all the money they can spare. Alice takes what they have to offer and then expresses her resentment at such charity by sneering at them and flaunting her social superiority. Finally, warning Dearth to take care of his daughter as such treasurers are "easily lost," she wanders away and is soon lost to sight among the trees.

Dearth and Margaret cannot get the strange woman out of their minds. In particular, Alice's parting words have reawakened the girl's old fear of being lost. As she begs her father to take her out of the wood, Dearth notices the light of a distant house, which Margaret is certain had not been there previously. Again she implores her father to take her out of the wood, but he resolves on impulse to go to the house to get some food for the strange woman. Without knowing why, Margaret is terrified of the house. Dearth scolds her mildly for her fears, then sets off alone in the direction of the light. When he has disappeared from sight, the wood begins to grow dark. Margaret, terror-stricken, runs through the trees calling after her father; and, as she is lost to view in the blackness, we hear her plaintive cry, "Daddy, come back; I don't want to be a might-have-been."

When the curtain rises on the third and final act, darkness still prevails. But the darkness has carried us back from the wood into Lob's house, the very house whose light had drawn Dearth away from the daughter of his dreams. Human forms grope their way into the room and turn on the light. The first of Lob's guests to return from the enchanted wood are Purdie and Mabel, who, still caught in the delusion of their dream, are rejoicing in their relief at escaping from Joanna. The room seems unfamiliar, and they fail to recognize Lob when they discover his little body hunched up in a chair beside the fire. He is apparently asleep, but there is an enigmatic leer on his face. Joanna makes her way into the room. Held by the dream, she begins an altercation with the "lovers" that recalls Mabel's argument with Purdie and Joanna in Act I.

But this little triangle is never to be played out. Suddenly their hands rise to their foreheads. The illusion fades, and the three young people come to their senses and remember their former relationships. Yet the memory of the dream remains as clear as the reality to which they have returned. Purdie now knows the truth about himself: he is not a passionate lover tragically married to the wrong woman; he is a mere philanderer. Humiliated by this sudden exposure of his true nature, he is further humbled by the thought that, if human character is incorrigible, his philandering with Joanna is bound to occur again. But Joanna thinks otherwise; she admits that her own philandering may continue, but her experience in Lob's wood has turned her against any further intrigues with Mabel's husband. Purdie now announces that he has discovered something far greater than himself in Lob's wood; he has found the truth about human nature. He has learned that men's lives are not shaped by fate or destiny; men are simply the victims of their own weaknesses. In brief, the fault is not in the stars, but in men. There is a debasing force within us that most people have the strength to control, though they usually allow it to master them and to drive them into pettiness or selfish indifference toward those for whom they are most responsible.

Mabel, Joanna, and Purdie now have the fun of watching the other guests return from the wood. As they wait, there is a sound of footfalls on the stairs. It is Mrs. Coade, who enters clad in a bathrobe and carrying a scarf for her husband. At this moment Matey also appears, still under the delusion that he is a business tycoon. Then Lady Caroline arrives; and, to the intense amusement of others, he introduces her as his wife. She continues to act out the role of Matey's devoted spouse even when the butler suddenly recovers and reverts to his former servile manner. When Lady Caroline emerges from her dream-state, she is horrified at her humiliation and furious with Lob. The wood seems to have taught her nothing.

The sound of Mr. Coade's pipe heralds his arrival. He prances into the room as jauntily as he had gamboled through the trees. Under the influence of the dream, he fails to recognize his wife; but her face enchants him and he tells her that he has seen it in his dreams, the dreams of a bachelor who had never until that moment found the woman he wanted to marry. Thereupon he proposes to her. The vision of Lob's wood has confirmed the original impression of everyone that the Coades are ideally married. But it has also shown Mr. Coade the truth about himself. For years he had cherished the delusion that it was his competency and not his character that prevented him from writing a great book, but the dream experience had shown otherwise. He had been a poor man in Lob's wood, but all his time there had been frittered away just as in real life where he was too wealthy to strive for anything.

Alice Dearth enters and introduces herself as the Honorable Mrs. Finch-Fallowe. She tells the assembled company that she is hungry because she had given her sandwiches to a starving girl and her father. Then she tries to impress the others with her sophistication and high breeding; but they are more interested in her description of the man she had seen in the wood. Could it have been Dearth? The man in question comes into view cheerfully singing a French song and looking as hale and handsome as Alice had described him. He has come to ask for food for the starving woman he had met in the wood. But suddenly he catches sight of Alice, who is now dressed not in rags but in an evening gown. Instantly he suspects her of tricking him, while Alice is terrified that he has come to demand his money back.

At this moment Dearth notices that his own clothing is different from the attire he had been wearing in the wood. The couple are thrown into confusion, but out of this confusion comes gradual enlightenment. Alice is the first to recover. When she realizes that Dearth is actually her husband, it dawns upon her with painful clarity that, although she is more fortunate than if she had been Mrs. Finch-Fallowe, Dearth is not. It is she who has turned him into a waster and an alcoholic. Dearth comes to, his head in his hands, torn with grief at the irrevocable loss of his dream-child and at the misery of his real existence with Alice. Then he looks up to thank Lob for the experience of an hour with Margaret.

One by one the guests depart until only Joanna and Matey remain to discuss their adventure in Lob's wood. Joanna is curious to know whether such an adventure can have a permanent effect. All that Matey can tell her is that it does once in a while. But Barrie, in his concluding stage directions, assures us that there is hope for those who, like the Dearths, have the courage to find a new way. As the curtain falls, we catch a glimpse of Lob coaxing the flowers to grow in the morning radiance of his summer garden. Darkness and the shadows of Midsummer Eve have vanished. Light is triumphant.

Mention must be made of two plays by other dramatists dealing with the theme of the "second chance." Lord Dunsany's *If* (1922) concerns a man who is given a second chance and finds his life utterly changed—for the worst. J. B. Priestley's *Dangerous Corner* (1932), directly influenced by P. D. Ouspensky's theories of time, contrasts a hypothetical unpleasant situation (what might have been) with an actual pleasant one. However, Priestley's purpose, like Dunsany's, is to reveal the infinite possibilities pregnant within any given moment of time; his characters are mere creatures of time and circumstance. But Lob's guests are victims of their own illusions; they practice self-deception in order to conceal the truth about themselves and what they have done to others. The lesson of the enchanted wood is pointed in the Shakespeare passage from which the title, *Dear Brutus,* is taken: we are what we make ourselves; but we make ourselves blindly and then blame Fate for the unfortunate consequences. The conclusion of Barrie's play affirms that people who understand what might have been may find the resolution to shape what will be and to make it better than the past.

For all its semblance of wider implication, this "message" is fundamentally personal. In *Dear Brutus* Barrie shows a clearer understanding of the nature of his own problems than in any other play. For the first time he recognizes most of his fantasies for what they are and places them where they belong: in the dream-state or in the unconscious. Accepting that what-might-have-been will never come to pass, he nevertheless considers dreams to be of "therapeutic" consequence if they are fully recollected when the dreamer returns to consciousness.

Unfortunately, a number of critics in pursuit of "wider implications" have been misdirected by a curious "red herring" released by Barrie for the exclusive consumption of his American public. In a letter from the dramatist to William Gillette, read aloud to the audience at the New York premiere of *Dear Brutus* in December, 1917, Barrie proffered the following "explication" of his play: "Dear Brutus is an allegory about a gentleman called John Bull, who years and years ago missed the opportunity of his life. The 'Mr. Dearth' of the play is really John Bull. The play shows how on the fields of France father and daughter get a second opportunity. Are now the two to make it up permanently or for ever to drift apart? . . . Future mankinds are listening for our decision. . . ."[3] We presume, we hope, out of kindness to Barrie that this "explication" was written with his tongue in his cheek. It makes nonsense of the play, but was written, perhaps, in a puckish mood, to recompense the public for being unable to hunt-the-slipper in *A Kiss for Cinderella* by providing a game of hunt-the-meaning in *Dear Brutus.*

Not unexpectedly, with Barrie's assistance as "explicator," *Dear Brutus* was promptly overrated by its earliest critics. Braybrooke observed, "It would be indeed hard to find a play that would have a greater influence on our present outlook than Dear Brutus."[4] However, we may look in vain for the influence—except where it is to be expected: on Barrie's next play. Braybrooke is, on the other hand, rather more perceptive in discussing the "meaning" of the play: "With gentle irony Barrie shows us that we are as we were made, once and for all, that the second chance, if it came to us, would be no better used than the first chance."[5] Some fourteen years later, Roy amplifies this view: "Perhaps the gist of the philosophy of *Dear Brutus* is that chance matters comparatively little in this life, and that character is everything. . . . If we wish to change, we must mould and develop character."[6] Moult, more interested in Barrie's dramaturgy than his "message," comments soundly, "Technically the play is convincing; the bridge between the actual and the true is built superbly."[7]

Dear Brutus is virtually auto-analysis. Lob's enchanted wood, like the islands on which anything is possible, is a symbol for Barrie's own unconscious; and the dreams that it holds are fantasies that express Barrie's own repressed wishes. Mr. Coade, playing his pipe as he dances merrily through the trees, is an adult Peter Pan: David grown old—and without Margaret Ogilvy.

By turning Mr. Coade into a bachelor, the fantasy has separated him from the mother-wife, Mrs. Coade. The other male characters in the wood are all personae of Barrie. Purdie, repeating the performance of Tommy Sandys by pursuing one woman while he is pursued by another, is Barrie in the familiar role of "magerful" lover. Matey, idolized by Lady Caroline, repeats the fantasy of Crichton being worshiped by Lady Mary on the desert island. Both "Ladies" represent Barrie's wife, Mary Ansell, who, in fantasy, humbly acknowledges her husband as lord and master. In contrast to Matey, Dearth shows Barrie happily dissociated from his wife. In the world of what-might-have-been he is an artist and the father of the young girl named Margaret.

Dearth's dream-daughter is, of course, Margaret Ogilvy, reduced to a fantasy-creation that lives only in the memory of the artist. Barrie, as Dearth, has represented himself as Margaret's father because he had come to regard himself as her literary creator. Barrie's mother had been dead for many years, But Margaret Ogilvy lived on as a character in her son's books. In the third act, Barrie, accepting his marriage to Mary Ansell as the cause of his mother's death, shows the evil wife, Alice, as the reason why the dream-Margaret has no real existence. Unfortunately, some of Barrie's fantasy endures even where the dreams are supposed to have disappeared. By holding the wife responsible for Margaret's "death," Barrie absolves himself, along with Dearth, although exoneration of this kind can in no way be reconciled with the play's leading theme.

Lob, whose magic produces the fantasies of the unconscious, has puzzled many of Barrie's critics. But we should not be in haste to follow the usual practice of writing him off as nothing more than an eccentric Master of the Revels. Our earlier association of Lob with Sam Smith, the hero of *Shall We Join the Ladies?*, suggests that Lob is yet another persona of Barrie, but a very curious one. Lob is an old man who looks and acts like a baby. And is it not entirely appropriate that Barrie should represent himself in the character of an adult fantasy-maker who gives expression to infantile fantasies? For the adults of the play, like the adult Barrie, are controlled by the fantasies of a child. From this standpoint the whole play may be understood as an image of the dramatist's psyche.

In giving theatrical expression of the fantasy of *Dear Brutus,* Barrie was to show himself to be an accomplished master of mood and atmosphere. His audience was left with a lasting impression of the emotional spectrum of character reflected in a subtle interplay of light, shadow, and color. There is nothing in his other plays to compare with the shock of Dearth is pulling aside the curtain to expose the sombre darkness of Lob's wood, or the eerie loveliness of fading moonlight in the enchanted glade where Margaret loses her father forever, or that bizarre final glimpse of Lob talking to the flowers in the radiant morning sunlight. To find anything comparable to the magic and charm of *Dear Brutus* we have to turn to *A Midsummer Night's Dream. Mary Rose,* Barrie's next play, has a different kind of enchantment: in place of the forest of dreams, we find a magic island like Prospero's in *The Tempest.*

II Mary Rose

Mary Rose received its premiere in London, at the Haymarket Theatre, April, 1920, when Fay Compton in the title role gave the performance of her career. The American premiere followed in December of the same year, with Ruth Chatterton playing the part of Mary Rose.

In *Mary Rose,* as in *The Tempest,* the island is a place of enchantment, full of noises that have the power to enthrall the human spirit. Each island seems a haven or place of concealment for those who come to it willingly. The island hides Mary Rose who had desired to return to it; it conceals Prospero and Miranda who make it their refuge from oppression and exile. But here the similarities cease. Mary Rose's Island that Likes to be Visited has no Prospero, no Ariel, and no Caliban. It is not the inspiration for another Gonzalo, nor even a trysting place for lovers; it is a magic land of enticement, luring the heroine from her parents, husband, and child, from the world in which she had almost grown up.

Roy, who shows more sensitivity to the play than most of Barrie's other commentators, sees it as a conflict of the dual existence that every human being experiences: the passage through "the present" from birth to death; and, at rare moments within "the present," the awareness of that part of one's being that is unchanging, fundamental, timeless, and eternal; in short, the confrontation of self and soul.[8]

Several commentators have plausibly argued that the story of *Mary Rose* was derived from "Kilmeny," a fairy-tale poem by James Hogg, the Ettrick Shepherd (1770-1835). But Barrie's tale of the girl who vanishes and returns long afterward, still as youthful as when she had departed, may also owe something to the Greek myths of Endymion and Persephone. There is an earlier suggestion of his use of the Persephone myth in the "eternal recurrence" of the heroine at the conclusion of *Peter and Wendy*. But, where the conclusion of his children's story conveys some of the joy and hope expressed in the myth of spring's awakening, the "adult drama" of *Mary Rose* is concerned with irrevocable loss: loss of identity and loss of daughter, wife, child, and mother. Barrie's heroine loses intelligible contact with the world and ultimately drives herself out of it. Her incommunicability, emerging as a motif in the final act, gives the play a peculiarly contemporary interest—one reflected recently in the similar plot of Michelangelo Antonioni's film *L'Avventura,* which deals with the isolation of the individual and the impossibility of communication between the sexes.

The main plot of *Mary Rose* is set within an enclosing narrative, just as the island itself is framed by the inscrutable sea. As the play opens, the silent gloom of an old manor house in Sussex is being disturbed by the intrusion of the housekeeper, Mrs. Otery, and of a young Australian soldier Harry. Mrs. Otery soon realizes that there is no need to show Harry over the manor: the place is familiar to him. He had lived there as a boy, and childhood memories crowd upon him as he passes through the cobwebbed, shadowy rooms. A pathetic ghost lingers in this shell of the past. The house is haunted by a spirit who has sought so long and so hopelessly that she has almost forgotten the object of her search.

Mrs. Otery is reluctant to talk about the ghost, and she also discourages Harry from pursuing his memories into the room where he had slept as a child. Strangely, the door to this room locks of its own accord, as if to exclude all would-be intruders. Harry understands from this situation that he cannot rediscover his lost childhood by consciously seeking the past. When the hidden memories become too oppressive, the door of recollection will swing open by itself. When Mrs. Otery leaves him, he settles into a chair to wait. Dusk gradually conceals his form, and he stirs apprehensively as the bedroom door opens and closes very slowly. Then he disappears into the darkness.

When the light returns, the room in which Harry was sitting looks as it had thirty years before, prior to Harry's birth. The manor is the home of the Morlands whose only child is Mary Rose. The Morlands are a middle-aged couple who have achieved tranquility in marriage by taking the line of least resistance. In their side-stepping of life's complexities, they have tried to keep Mary Rose perpetually immature; but at the age of eighteen the girl has fallen unwittingly in love with her childhood playmate, Simon Blake. When it is clear that the young man reciprocates the girl's love for him, the Morlands are reluctantly prepared to speak with him even if it means losing their daughter. Their prospective son-in-law is amiable enough, but the Morlands have a secret to reveal to him which, they think, may cause him to reconsider the idea of marriage to Mary Rose. And so they unfold their strange story of an incident that had occurred when Mary Rose was eleven, an incident of which the girl can recall nothing. They have never discussed it in her presence and only speak of it to Simon when Mary Rose is out of the room.

Mr. Morland had been on a fishing holiday in the Outer Hebrides. One day he had hired a boat to fish for trout in the loch while Mary Rose was left to do some sketching on a nearby island. Toward dusk it was time for father and daughter to return to the mainland. Morland waved to Mary Rose and then rowed toward the island with his back toward her. When he landed, she had disappeared; and the most thorough search of the island revealed no trace of her. Twenty days after his daughter's disappearance Morland suddenly caught sight of her while he was wandering, grief-stricken, along the shoreline. She was on the same little island, sketching unconcernedly in the position he had last seen her. This time he kept her in sight as he rowed to the island.

When he reached Mary Rose, he could tell by her attitude that she was unaware that anything strange had occurred. Certainly she had no idea that twenty days had elapsed since her father had waved from the fishing boat. The uncanny experience appeared to have had no serious effect on Mary Rose, but the Morlands had sometimes had the impression that the girl had fleeting but incomprehensible visions of her lost days, and she had been observed talking to herself and listening for sounds that never came. As she grew older, she seemed, fortunately, to have outgrown these habits. But Mrs. Morland is inclined to associate her daughter's exceptional immaturity at least in part with the strange incident. It is as if the island had drawn off the girl's potentiality for any development beyond adolescence.

Simon is too much in love with Mary Rose to be repelled by Morland's story. It is agreed that the young couple are to be married, and they are left alone to discuss their plans. Mary Rose now discloses her idea for the honeymoon: she wants to go to the Outer Hebrides—to see the island she had visited as a child. Inadvertently, she mentions that an old woman had just reminded her of the island; but there is no person of this description in the manor house. At this point Simon notices that Mary Rose is listening intently for some inaudible sound. Disturbed at her suggestion, he reluctantly offers to take her, one day, to the island in the Outer Hebrides—but not during their honeymoon.

Four years elapse, and Mary Rose has her way; she brings Simon, now her husband, to explore the little island. Cameron, a young Highlander, has rowed them across from the mainland. Like John Shand and Rob Angus, the heroes of *What Every Woman Knows* and *When a Man's Single,* Cameron seems little more than a dour Scots gillie until a turn in the conversation reveals him to be a man of education, a brilliant student from Aberdeen University who is working his way through college. Captivated by the beauty and innocence of Mary Rose, he later feels himself personally involved in her tragedy. Soon after they have landed, Cameron shows an extensive knowledge of the island's reputation for mystery; and he suspects that it is called the Island that Likes to be Visited because an island that had visitors in the natural way would not need to have such an unnatural desire. He mentions the story of a baby boy who had disappeared on the island, never to be found; but the local villagers believe that in some mysterious manner the child is still there. And he speaks of the island's uncanny presences whose call can be heard only by those for whom it is intended.

While Cameron and Simon are involved with preparations for the return to the mainland, Mary Rose hears the call of the island. Mysterious whispers, uttering her name, rise to a crescendo. Her arms go out to Simon, but he is too busy to notice anything unusual. Then, as the enchantment proves irresistible, Mary Rose, unobserved by Simon and Cameron, passes from view. When they look for her, it is already too late. They realize to their horror that the island has once again claimed its own.

Cameron's remarks about the lost child on the island provide a clue to the reason for Mary Rose's second disappearance. Before setting out for the island, she had left her own infant son in the care of a nurse. The voices that entice her into twenty-five years of oblivion evidently lure her to the lost child Cameron had mentioned. Simon had earlier warned his wife that her own baby would one day cease to be a child. Except in dreams, all mothers eventually lose their babies, for time turns infants into men and women. Mary Rose responds to this prospect with an eager anticipation of the day when her son will be a man and can take his mother on his knee, instead of vice versa. She can think of the future only in terms of the image of mother and child, regardless of who is occupying the roles. And, when she disappears out of time, it is to become the unaging mother of an unaging baby: in effect, she is deserting her real son to nurse a fantasy.

Twenty-five years later, the tragedy of Mary Rose's second disappearance has become a bearable memory. The Morlands are resigned to the fact that everything about their daughter belongs to the past. Nothing has been heard of her since she vanished inexplicably so long ago. Yet she is never far from the thoughts of her husband and parents. Simon has not remarried. Trying to forget his grief in the pursuit of a naval career, he has risen to command his own ship. He visits the Morlands whenever he is on leave.

This time a startling telegram is awaiting him. Cameron, now minister of a parish in the Outer Hebrides, has cabled the news that Mary Rose has reappeared and is being brought back to her husband. Cameron's telegram is already a day or two old, and Simon suddenly realizes that a young lady he had seen getting off the train at the local station must have been his wife. When Mary Rose arrives, she looks exactly as she had looked twenty-five years before on the island. Cameron, who escorts her, explains the circumstances of her reappearance. Two fishermen had discovered her sleeping peacefully, and there was such a look of joy on her face that they were reluctant to awaken her. But joy had given way to bewilderment when Mary Rose awoke imagining that her husband had deserted her and assuming that she had slept only for an hour or two.

Confronted by the changed appearances of her parents and Simon, the shocking truth is forced upon her. Then, with a sudden surge of panic, she thinks of her baby. Mrs. Morland discloses to Cameron that Mary Rose's son, Harry, had run away to sea when he was twelve. He had written several times from Australia; then his letters had ceased. Mary Rose is told none of this history; but she passes into her son's bedroom to learn for herself that she has lost him as irrevocably as he had lost her. The discovery kills her.

The lights dim into darkness, then return again to reveal the room as we saw it when the play began. Harry is slumped in a chair. Mrs. Ottery enters carrying a candle in one hand and a cup of tea in the other. Dazed by his dreams of the story of Mary Rose, and in a far more serious spirit than when he had entered the manor house, Harry questions the housekeeper again. He learns that the Morlands and Simon are dead, and that the dilapidated manor is haunted by the ghost of Mary Rose who wanders restlessly from room to room in search of her lost baby. Harry now believes that he can bring peace to his mother by revealing his identity to her ghost. But, when the pale and weary wraith appears, suspecting somehow that Harry is not her son but the person who had stolen him from her, she has a momentary impulse to kill him. By this time she no longer remembers clearly what she is seeking. She sits upon her son's knee just as she had once wished, but has no understanding that what she is doing is the fulfillment of an old desire. The mother, bereft of her child, has become childlike herself, confiding to this "stranger" that she wishes to return to her island to play. It is not clear to Harry why Mary Rose had ever left her island, and why all her memories—even of the place she longs for—are slipping away. He concludes, despairingly, that God has forgotten her; Mary Rose must be unwanted by Heaven and earth. But, although almost everything is now beyond her comprehension, her sufferings are at an end; the son she has forgotten has returned to her. "Celestial music" calls to Mary Rose; and, with her arms outstretched, "she walks out through the window into the empyrean."

Superficially, *Mary Rose* appears to have a structure as complex as that of *Dear Brutus,* which is sometimes mentioned as the outstanding example of Barrie's skill at preserving clarity along with structural complexity. In *Dear Brutus,* Act I provides background; Act II, counterpoint to Act III. Characters are contrasted in the successive acts by being shown first as they seem to be, then as they might have been, and finally as they are. Barrie intensifies this contrast by including in each act episodes that are paralleled in the other two. The apparent complexity of *Mary Rose* arises from Barrie's simple device of splitting what should have been the final act or epilogue—Harry's return and his encounter with the ghost of Mary Rose—into two scenes which are used to frame the rest of the action. This device gives the scenes enclosed by the frame the effect of a flashback and, at the same time, serves to create an aura of mystery; for the connection between the opening part of the frame and all that follows does not become apparent until Act III. Aside from the frame device, the play's action follows a straightforward chronological sequence.

The true similarity between *Dear Brutus* and *Mary Rose* lies not in structure but in atmosphere. Both plays are essentially supernatural tales in which the usual horrific element has been replaced by wistfulness and pathos. That eerieness tempered with sadness, so evident in Barrie's treatment of the ghost of what-can-never-be and the dreams of what-might-have-been, arises out of a yearning after the fantasy rather than the recoil from it that is so much more characteristic of the ghost story. Pathos is not out of place in presenting fantasies that are more attractive than actuality to their author. But Barrie's bitter-sweet nostalgia does not make him oblivious to the dangers inherent in the seductions of illusion and fantasy.

Mary Rose is in part a variation on the Peter Pan story, with an unaging mother replacing the unaging boy; but caught up in the plot is a motif that appears in numerous other works from Washington Irving's "Rip Van Winkle" to James Hilton's *Lost Horizon*: the idea that absence from the world results in exemption from time. In *Mary Rose* this theme is merely one aspect of Barrie's larger concern with the disastrous consequences of trying to withstand time and change. The Morlands, who want their daughter to remain a young girl, have the misfortune of seeing their wish fulfilled. For, though Mary Rose becomes a mother, she is destined never to develop beyond a young girl's emotional and physical state; and this arrested development helps to kill her. As a mother, Mary Rose deserts her own baby for a child who, like Peter Pan, can never grow older. The consequences destroy her and wreck the lives of her husband and parents. Hence, if there is a "message" in *Mary Rose,* it can be expressed not as "Except ye . . . become as little children, ye shall not enter into the kingdom of heaven" (as one critic has suggested),[9] but as the conviction that to attempt to hold back the clock, to deny the future for the sake of the past, is the pursuit of a fantasy that ultimately destroys the pursuer.

This "message" is pointedly self-critical, for it applies directly to Barrie's own preoccupation with the prototypic story. *Mary Rose* recalls Barrie's childhood belief that he had been deserted by Margaret Ogilvy in favor of David. In the play, Barrie and his brother are represented by Harry and the lost child on the island. Margaret Ogilvy, in the character of Mary Rose, leaves Barrie/Harry for the fantasy-baby. Mary Rose wants an unaging child; her parents want an unaging daughter; but the only way to prevent a young person from growing into an adult is to kill him. The mother who wishes to keep her child eternally young is thus unconsciously desiring its death. Barrie translates the Morlands' love for Mary Rose and Margaret's love for David as unwitting expressions of the death-wish. Mary Rose's disappearance represents Barrie's feelings that Margaret Ogilvy had ceased to be his mother when she became preoccupied with the dead David.

Appropriately, in the play, the son avenges himself on the mother by disappearing at approximately the age David had reached when he was killed. He makes his way across the world to another island (Australia) at the very antipodes to that on which he has lost his mother to a rival child. Years later, Mary Rose reappears on the Island that Likes to be Visited. The significance of her return in an unchanged state is that she is unable to develop beyond the point at which she had ceased to be a mother to Harry. What she might have become had been suggested years before in her vision of the old lady who had reminded her of the Island that Likes to be Visited.

Mary Rose's frantic search for her son, like her response to the call of the lost child, drives her out of the world of the living. As a ghost, she encounters Harry; and she impulsively thinks of killing him: for something tells her that he is the person who had stolen her son, as in several senses he is. Patently, Harry the man has absorbed Harry the child; but he has also usurped the place of the lost child on the island. Or, perhaps more precisely, Harry's "desertion" has made him one with the lost child. But this "fusion" of man and lost child is beyond Mary Rose's understanding. The ghost's lack of comprehension approximates to Margaret Ogilvy's relapse into childishness shortly before her death. But more significant than her lack of understanding is her lapsed memory. In her search for Harry she has forgotten the island and presumably the lost child she had found on it. The last act thus implies that the neglected son's "revenge" had at last effaced his mother's memory of the rival.

III The Boy David

After *Mary Rose* sixteen years elapsed before Barrie completed another full-length play. In the interim he gave to the London stage only the two playlets, *Shall We Join the Ladies?* (1921) and *Barbara's Wedding* (1927). It was generally assumed by the 1930's that he was content to rest upon his laurels. But just a few months before his death, he broke his silence in the theater with a new play based on the biblical story of David in the first book of *Samuel.*

The Boy David (1936), which proved to be Barrie's swan-song, was previewed in Edinburgh, at the King's Theatre in November, 1936, and then moved, in the following month, to His Majesty's Theatre, London, where it ran for only fifty-five performances. Despite the talented acting of Elisabeth Bergner as David and an outstanding supporting cast, including Godfrey Tearle as King Saul and Sir John Martin-Harvey as the prophet Samuel, the London critics were harsh to the play and the production. It was Barrie's worst failure, surpassing even that of *The Wedding Guest* nearly forty years earlier. R. L. Green in his study of Barrie offers several explanations for the fiasco: Barrie was too ill to supervise the production; the play was too lavishly produced and presented in too large a theater; and public attention had been diverted from the theater by the spectacle of Edward VIII's abdication. But there are two other, more convincing explanations that Green does not mention. In the first place, Barrie had become "old-fashioned." The cynical, sophisticated comedies of Somerset Maugham and Noel Coward, followed by the new political extravaganzas of Shaw and the powerful upsurge of dramatic work by O'Casey and O'Neill, had remorselessly eclipsed the theater of whimsy, fantasy, and sentiment over which Barrie had reigned. And, in the second place, Barrie's grip had faltered. *The Boy David* was less a play than a bravura piece for the actress who took the role of David. The finest things in it, from David's first swaggering words, "Mother, I have killed a lion!" to the beautiful concluding scene in which he confirms his eternal friendship with Jonathan, turned out to be memorable episodes in an uneven chronicle rather than the highlights of an integrated dramatic work.

The stanchest admirer of *The Boy David* was James A. Roy, who discerned in it a profound tragedy and the supreme expression of Barrie's mystic exaltation, of his communion with the intangible and the eternal.[10] None of these glorious qualities are evident to me—or to the numerous theater critics of the first production who wrote off *The Boy David* as a sort of ineffectual Peter Pan for Bible lovers. Regrettably, Mr. Roy withholds enlightenment from those of us who are insensitive to the sublimity of Barrie's last play. His assessment of *The Boy David* is evidently based on revelation rather than interpretation, and those who lack the prophetic gift must decide for themselves whether to take it or leave it. Mr. Roy did, however, notice rather more helpfully that Barrie himself defended *The Boy David* against the charge that it was merely another and feebler *Peter Pan.* The dramatist insisted (cryptically for the critics) that, when he wrote the play, he was thinking less about the biblical David than about another David who was younger and closer to him. Mr. Roy, having taken us thus far, thereupon concludes, erroneously we think, that the Boy David was James Barrie as a boy.[11] Of this matter we shall have more to say in due course. But, if Mr. Roy is in error on this point, he also shows indifference on another: the uneven quality of the play.

The play's unevenness was mainly the outcome of its unnecessary complexity. It was supposed to be about the *boy* David, but Barrie felt constrained to carry the story through to the death of Saul while at the same time preserving his original intention. He tackled this problem by following Shakespeare's method in *Macbeth,* depicting later events as a series of visions experienced by the hero. The main action of the play concerns David's boyhood, beginning with his first meeting with Samuel and continuing through his encounter with Goliath. This straightforward chronological sequence is interrupted in Act III, Scene 1, by six dream episodes in which David glimpses visions of the future, ending with the deaths of Saul and Jonathan.

The play then returns to the main action in a final scene, showing David and Jonathan as boys, affirming their covenant of eternal friendship. Thus, aside from the "dream scene," the play is substantially a dramatic treatment of 1 Samuel 16-18. The dream episodes, on the other hand, are based on events described in the concluding chapters of the first book of Samuel; they are brought to a climax with David's song of lamentation over the deaths of Saul and Jonathan, which Barrie quotes almost in its entirety from 2 Samuel 1. The play leaves the reader with an impression that the dramatist had endeavored to leave nothing out. Even Chalmers, who worshiped Barrie, implies that *The Boy David* belongs in the library rather than in the theater. The best thing he can say about the play is that it is "a delight" to read.[12] The breathless succession of dream episodes actually adds nothing but confusion to the main action. They create a false diversion in which Saul, who is really the play's antihero, appears as the tragic hero of a secondary plot whose relationship with the David story is inadequately developed.

However, the play's structural deficiencies do not obscure Barrie's real interest in writing it. Significantly, aside from his earliest efforts as a playwright, this work was his first dramatic one whose character and plot were derived from an external source. Even more significantly, when at last Barrie turned to an external source, he chose to dramatize the story of David. His purpose is discernible from the outset—in the play's variations from the biblical narrative. Barrie follows his source in placing David's home in Bethlehem, but he emphasizes that the town was chiefly important for its wool, thereby representing it as a biblical equivalent of Thrums. Where the text of Samuel indicates that David's first meeting with the prophet was in a place of sacrifice, Barrie relocated the scene in the home of David's father, Jesse, suggesting therewith a biblical correspondence to the house in Kirriemuir where David Barrie was born.

The Bible specifies the names of three of David's seven brothers, and Barrie represented them as characters in his play; but he also included a brother named Amnon who is nowhere mentioned in Samuel as one of the sons of Jesse. Amnon was, in fact, the name of David's firstborn who committed incest and was subsequently slain by command of his brother, Absalom. In Barrie's play Amnon is characterized as David's most vindictive brother. The biblical narrative makes no mention at all of David's mother, but Barrie had, perforce, to include her in the play so that he might depict her twofold tragedy: first, as a woman who mistakenly believes her boastful son to be a coward; and, second, as a mother destined to "lose" the child she loves best. At the end of the first act, Samuel, speaking of David, warns her that, if her son is chosen by God, he will be famous and mighty; but she will lose him and will never share in his triumphs. David's mother, reconciled to her future loss, bravely replies that she would have her son great and terrible regardless of the consequences.

These consequences are not, however, depicted in Barrie's play. His real concern is with how the boy David became a man. In terms of the prototypic situation, the play is a fantasy in which David Barrie is reconciled with his brother James

(Jonathan) and allowed to grow up. Saul's role in the fantasy is clear from Act II, Scene 1, in which he recognizes David as an alter ego of his youth. Saul represents David the father, to whom Barrie had frequently ascribed the responsibility for the younger David's death. In the play, as in the biblical story, Saul's attempts to kill David are frustrated; and the boy lives to attain manhood.

As Barrie portrays David, he has, like Sentimental Tommy Sandys, the courage not of his convictions but of his illusions. According to the biblical text, the boy impressed Saul by describing how he had killed singlehanded a lion and a bear. Barrie transforms this tale to make it look like a fantasy invented by David to impress his family; for among his brothers, the boy has the reputation of being a coward and a boaster. But, far worse than this invention, is his own self-deception; for he believes that what he has done in fantasy makes him a man. But he is destined not to grow up until the end of the play when he has acquired the strength of his real adversary, instead of some imaginary potency. Even his killing of Goliath does not put an end to his fantasies; for, like Peter Pan exulting over the death of Captain Hook, David follows his victory by impersonating Goliath, as if to usurp the giant's strength by assuming his identity.

These details point to the nature of Barrie's fantasy "reconciliation" with his brother. First, though David and his mother are destined to be separated, the latter is ready to accept his future greatness as recompense for her loss. A legendary hero is to be born out of the fantasy-maker. Second, and arising out of the preceding observations, Barrie is reconciled with David by identifying himself with the wonderful boy as his "creator": the fantasy-maker who "created" the legendary hero. As in his fantasy the mother is prepared to give up her David, Barrie is at last able to accept him as a brother instead of a rival. Hence, in the final scene, David makes his covenant with Jonathan. As the play comes to an end, David, able to take up the symbol of potency (Goliath's javelin which is like a "weaver's beam"), has become a man.

IV *The Literary Position of James Barrie*

"Probably," writes Henry Bett concerning Barrie, "there is no modern writer with regard to whom there has been so wide a disparity of judgment, as between the critical opinion of the nineties and that of today. Stevenson, and most other people forty years ago, unhesitatingly regarded Barrie as a writer of genius. Many critics today would think the word is scarcely to be applied to him, except in some very qualified sense, and then with a reference rather to his plays than to his novels. . . ."[13] The extent of the reaction against Barrie may be seen in recent criticism by David Daiches. Daiches, in a BBC radio talk, later published in *The Listener,* denounced Barrie as a writer who had perversely exploited "his public's emotional concern with human relationships," and who had created a "cruelly sentimental world" in which "he takes a positively masochistic pleasure in frustrating all normal expectations about the proper satisfaction of adult human relationships. . . . Time and again Barrie builds up all his sentimental resources to picture a relationship on which the whole emotional centre of the play or story rests and then he destroys it before our faces. . . . At the bottom of all this lies a fierce resistance to the implications of any mature human relationship."[14] Elizabeth Bowen avoids direct condemnation of Barrie, but her sensitivity to the man and his work is nonetheless deprecatory: "Barrie was spared the final ironic tragedy: he never ceased to believe in the worth of his own work. . . . With people he seems to have avoided any relationship that his imagination, under the rule of symbols could not in its turn rule, mould and inform. The failure of his marriage . . . went in deep: this was something worse than death. I am convinced there was not a trick in his art: not only did technical hard work go to the output of it, but he was innocent of, at least, the *wish* to exploit."[15] Most guarded of recent assessments is, perhaps, Allardyce Nicoll's: "To assess correctly the position of Sir James Barrie assuredly is a difficult task: it is very easy to dismiss him as a mere sentimentalist without worth; it is as easy to allow his charm to persuade us into believing him an author far greater than he actually was." As Nicoll then observes, Barrie's plays "have nothing to say to us about the iniquities of the social world; in such iniquities Barrie was not interested. . . . In a civilization highly conscious of economic conditions and dominated by behavioristic psychology his is a lonely figure. . . ."[16]

The foregoing chapters suggest that Barrie's isolation was the inevitable consequence of his intense and exclusive self-interest. *The Boy David* shows him, even in his last play, still preoccupied with fantasies involving the prototypic situation. His work seldom rises above his own psychological problems to say something of wider significance. In play after play he had seemed about to transcend the limitations of the prototypic story in order to deal with matters of greater consequence. But, when he raised serious issues, he usually reduced them to charming essays in whimsy or sentiment.

As A. C. Ward observes, "There are no standards of literary judgment applicable to Barrie. It is possible to write either that his world is more delightful than the real world, or that it is unpleasantly sweet and sickly. His plots are preposterous . . . his characters incredible . . . his dialogue sometimes as creaky as a rusty machine. . . . The illusion of life-likeness given by Barrie to his characters comes not from their conformity to the human model but from the fact that they are consistent with Barrie's own imaginative world. . . ."[17]

Nevertheless, Barrie could and did develop great skill in handling dramatic structure, and he has been justly praised as "a master in the projection of character by such choice of expressive detail. . . ."[18] But his fundamental subject matter shows no development from *When a Man's Single* to *The Boy David.* And—not surprisingly—at least one critic has come forward to put Barrie's reputation as a dramatic craftsman in its place. H. H. Child remarks, "Barrie's love of theatrical detail and process was rather like Kipling's love of tools and ships and motor-cars and machinery. This boyishness in Kipling led him on to venerate good craftsmanship and to abhor slick and sloppy work. . . . Barrie's boyishness, his love of playing with the theatre, is, perhaps, the cardinal fact. . . . How large and exciting and infinitely various a toy for a boy to play with!! It was a thousand pities that he could not play with the theatre without having to grapple with what the theatre is there to reflect, or expound, or, in its own way, to play with—obstinate stuff called reality, which often refuses to obey and sometimes makes the playing boy look silly. . . ."[19]

There can be no doubt that the bulk of Barrie's work is destined for oblivion. The novels are deservedly forgotten, though a tolerant reader could still be entertained by *The Little Minister* and *Sentimental Tommy.* Stevenson was too eager to find genius in Barrie the novelist, and even Shaw overrated Barrie in describing him as "a born storyteller"; but Shaw hastened to qualify this judgment by noticing that the author of *The Little Minister* "sees no further than his stories—conceives any discrepancy between them and the world as a shortcoming on the world's part, and is only too happy to be able to rearrange matters in a pleasanter way." As for Barrie's plays, Shaw found them to be pure romance in which all the inconsistencies of character are "corrected by replacing human nature by conventional assortments of qualities."[20] A. S. Collins provides an enlightening comparison between the two dramatists. "While Shaw whetted the intellectual appetite of his audience, Barrie played on the sentiments of his and gave little more than a hint of social criticism. . . . Barrie in general sought neither to criticise nor to penetrate below the surface of life . . . [he] turned his back on the disagreeable in life and set about pleasing an audience which, like himself, wanted its heart moved, but without pain, and its fancy lit up with rosy lights."[21] In short, Barrie gave the theatergoing public what it thought it really wanted—a drama of sentiment for those who sought an alternative to the contemporary intellectual drama of Shaw and Granville Barker, for those who sought rich dramatic experience without having to think or feel too deeply for it. But, as Shaw observes, people are led to the theater by an appetite for drama "which is no more to be satisfied by sweetmeats than our appetite for dinner is to be satisfied with meringues and raspberry vinegar."

The theatergoing public has not lost its taste for sweetmeats—merely its taste for Barrie's particular brand. Hence it is unlikely that we shall see many revivals of even his finest work: *The Admirable Crichton, What Every Woman Knows,* the one-act plays, and the late fantasies; though it is persistently rumored that Alfred Hitchcock, doyen director of movie-thrillers, is planning a film of *Mary Rose.* Only *Peter Pan* brings Barrie's name perenially before the public—though among recent critics, Brigid Brophy has attacked it for ruthlessly exploiting the emotions of children and A. C. Ward maintains that its "hearty juvenilism" has worn thin. As a play, however, *Peter Pan* is still an obligatory dramatic experience for every child; while as a story, it has achieved the distinction of being ranked popularly with *Alice in Wonderland* as an established children's classic. It is not inappropriate that Barrie's fantasies should find their only enduring audience in the nursery, but is regrettable that a dramatist so technically gifted should never have widened his scope beyond his own childhood illusions.

Shaw, in a more generous mood, once praised Barrie for having relegated the banalities of the well-made play to the dustbin. It was, perhaps, no great triumph to have replaced the well-made play with a corpus of well-made fantasies; but it is as a master of fantasy, or not at all, that Barrie will be remembered.

Notes and References

Chapter One

1. On Thrums and the Kirriemuir background to Barrie's early fiction, see further John Kennedy, *Thrums and the Barrie Country* (London, 1930) and J. A. Hammerton, *Barrieland: A Thrums Pilgrimage* (London, [1929].) Kennedy's book is particularly helpful on the Auld Lichts.
2. P. R. Chalmers, *The Barrie Inspiration* (London 1938), p. 200.
3. Thomas Moult, *Barrie,* (London, 1928), p. 62.
4. Sir John Hammerton, *Barrie: The Story of a Genius,* (London, 1929), p. 185.
5. George Blake, *Barrie and the Kailyard School,* (London, 1951), p. 64.
6. There is no adequate bibliography of Barrie's journalism, but the interested reader will find useful listings of articles by Barrie in the Barrie bibliographies of Herbert Garland and B. D. Cutler.
7. F. J. H. Darton, *J. M. Barrie,* (London, 1929), p. 34.
8. George Blake's *Barrie and the Kailyard School* is the most illuminating study of the whole movement.
9. Hammerton, p. 181.
10. Moult, p. 57.

Chapter Two

1. George Blake, pp. 56, 72-73.
2. See Denis Mackail, *Barrie: The Story of J. M. B.,* (London, 1941), pp. 22-23; Sir John Hammerton, *Barrie: The Story of a Genius,* (London, 1929), pp. 21-24; A. E. W. Mason's article on Barrie in *The Dictionary of National Biography,* 5th Supplement (1931-1940), pp. 46-47.
3. *Margaret Ogilvy,* (New York, 1927), pp. 5-17 (excerpts).
4. Sigmund Freud, *The Interpretation of Dreams,* (New York, 1950), p. 152.
5. Freud, p. 149.
6. See Mackail, pp. 181, 197, 212-13; Hammerton, pp. 244-46. (Note Barrie's letter on James Winter's death.) Hammerton pp. 336-37 reveals Margaret (Ogilvy) Barrie's attitude to William as a "replacement" for James.
7. Mary Ansell, an actress, was the daughter of an affluent licensed

victualler. A year younger than Barrie, she first met the writer through Jerome K. Jerome (see Hammerton, p. 256). On her relationship with Barrie, see Mackail pp. 185 ff. As an actress, one of Mary's most important roles was that of Nanny O'Brien in the first English production of *Walker, London.* On Barrie's apprehension of his mother's objection to Mary as a daughter-in-law, see Mackail, p. 217. On Barrie's marriage, honeymoon in Switzerland, and his mother's death in 1895, see Mackail, pp. 221-33; Hammerton, pp. 255-56, 266. On the affair between Gilbert Cannan and Mary, and Barrie's divorce, see Mackail, pp. 414-17. Note that Mrs. Barrie's affair was first detected by a gardener at Black Lake in Surrey, where much of *Peter Pan* was conceived.

8. On Barrie's fondness for islands, see further his article, "Wrecked on an Island," *National Observer,* Feb. 17, 1894, which Hammerton maintains, "was the last of his contributions to miscellaneous journalism. For that reason alone it should be noted, and still more on account of its subject and the great affection he was to show for islands in works of his later years. Up to 1894 the island had not been too conspicuous in his scenic effects . . ." (Hammerton, p. 259, and see also p. 131).

9. Freud, p. 149.

10. Hammerton, p. 189.

11. Thomas Moult, *Barrie* (London, 1928), pp. 71-73.

12. Hammerton, p. 208.

13. RLS to Henry James, December 5, 1892. See *Letters of R. L. Stevenson,* ed. Sidney Colvin (New York, 1899), II, 331.

14. Blake, p. 72.

15. RLS to Barrie, December, 1892. See *Letters of R. L. Stevenson,* ed. Sidney Colvin, II, 332.

16. Blake (p. 72) comments accurately on Jess and Leeby: "Barrie presents them as an intolerable couple of gossips and peeping Thomasinas." He adds, less convincingly I think, "On the whole . . . we must take it that Barrie was consciously guying his own people. He was incapable of pity for his fictional victims."

17. Moult, p. 92.

18. Hammerton, p. 203.

19. RLS to Barrie, December, 1892, in Stevenson, *Letters,* II, 332.

20. Moult, p. 108.

21. Hammerton, pp. 234-35.

22. Patrick Chalmers, *The Barrie Inspiration* (London, 1938), pp. 153-54.

23. Hammerton, p. 322.

24. F. J. Harvey Darton, *J. M. Barrie* (London, 1929), p. 54.

25. Moult, p. 154.

26. See first section of this chapter, on the prototypic story.

Chapter Three

1. There are many authorized and unauthorized versions of the "Peter Pan" story by other hands. Among these are the retelling (1930) by May Byron of *Peter Pan in Kensington Gardens;* Daniel O'Connor's *The Story of Peter Pan* (1912), a version of *Peter and Wendy;* and G. D. Brennan's edition (1909) of a retelling of the play in story form. Most of the retellings antedate the publication of Barrie's dramatic text.
2. First night of the original production: Duke of York's Theatre, London, December 27, 1904.
3. The many changes are recorded in Roger Lancelyn Green's *Fifty Years of Peter Pan* (London, 1954).
4. Weston La Barre, quoted by H. R. Hays in *The Dangerous Sex* (New York, 1964), p. 22.
5. See also the early chapters of R. L. Green's *Fifty Years of Peter Pan* and Denis Mackail's *Barrie*: *The Story of J. M. B.*, pp. 309-18.
6. Notable minor differences—apart from Hook's soliloquy—are "new" songs for the pirates and the indication that the pirate captain's concern for "good form" was a consequence of his Etonian education. *Peter and Wendy* excludes any references to Eton.
7. Hesketh Pearson, *G. B. S. A Postscript* (London, 1951), p. 75.

Chapter Four

1. *The Plays of J. M. Barrie* ed. A. E. Wilson (London, 1947), p. x.
2. Darton, p. 94.
3. Roy, p. 211.
4. Moult, p. 213.
5. Darton, p. 91.
6. Braybrooke, p. 37.
7. Moult, p. 198.
8. Braybrooke, p. 41.
9. Roy, p. 204.
10. Moult, pp. 198-99.

Chapter Five

1. Roy, p. 146.
2. Darton, p. 29.
3. Moult, p. 112.
4. Moult, p. 123.
5. Roy, p. 148.
6. Moult, p. 122.
7. As quoted by Roy, p. 148.

8. As quoted by Moult, p. 159.
9. See further D. Mackail, p. 288.
10. As quoted in R. L. Green, *J. M. Barrie* (New York, 1961), pp. 32-33.
11. Bernard Shaw, *Man and Superman*, Standard Edition (London, 1947), p. xxvii.
12. Moult, p. 172.
13. Braybrooke, p. 73.
14. Charles Lamb, *Essays of Elia*, ed. Geoffrey Tillotson, Everyman's Library edition (London, 1962), p. 121.
15. Darton, p. 57.
16. Braybrooke, p. 18.
17. Roy, p. 199.
18. Roy, p. 200.
19. Braybrooke, p. 93.
20. Darton, p. 86.
21. Hans Andersen, *Fairy Tales*, translated by Mrs. E. V. Lucas and Mrs. H. B. Paull, Grosset & Dunlap Illustrated Junior Library edition (New York, 1945), p. 198.

Chapter Six

1. Bernard Shaw, *Plays Pleasant*, Standard Edition (London, 1947), pp. xvi-xvii.
2. Shakespeare, *Julius Caesar*, I. ii. 141-42.
3. P. Chalmers, *The Barrie Inspiration*, pp. 211-12.
4. Braybrooke, p. 69.
5. Braybrooke, p. 69.
6. Roy, p. 212.
7. Moult, p. 213.
8. See Roy, pp. 219-20.
9. Braybrooke, pp. 110-11.
10. Roy, p. 248.
11. Roy, p. 248.
12. Chalmers, p. 215.
13. Henry Bett, quoted from *The London Quarterly Review* (October, 1937), pp. 477, 481.
14. *The Listener* (May 13, 1960), p. 843.
15. Elizabeth Bowen, *Collected Impressions* (New York, 1950), p. 150.
16. Allardyce Nicoll, *World Drama* (London, 1964), pp. 698-99.
17. A. C. Ward, *Twentieth Century English Literature 1901-1960* (New York, 1964 ed.), pp. 123-25.

18. E. B. Watson and B. Pressey, *Contemporary Drama* (New York, 1961), p. 769. [Editors' introduction to *Dear Brutus.]*
19. H. H. Child, *Essays and Reflections* (Cambridge, 1948), pp. 117-18.
20. Bernard Shaw, *Our Theatres in the Nineties,* Standard Edition (London, 1948), Vol. III, pp. 244-46.
21. A. S. Collins, *English Literature of the Twentieth Century* (London, 1960), pp. 285-86.

Selected Bibliography

PRIMARY SOURCES

A. *Collected Editions*

All the significant fiction and miscellaneous prose writings prior to 1912 may be found in any one of the following: the Thistle Edition, 12 vols. (New York: Charles Scribner's Sons, 1896); the Kirriemuir Edition, 10 vols. (London: Hodder and Stoughton, 1913); vols. I-VIII of the uniform green cloth edition (New York: Charles Scribner's Sons, 1918); and vols. I-IX of the Peter Pan Edition (New York: Charles Scribner's Sons, 1929).

All the plays Barrie wished to preserve are available in the one-volume "Definitive Edition" published as *The Plays of J. M. Barrie,* ed. A. E. Wilson (London: Hodder and Stoughton, 1947). On p. 1271 Wilson indicates which plays were excluded from this edition.

B. *Individual Works: Fiction and Miscellaneous Prose*

Better Dead, London: Swan Sonnenschein, 1888. [Actually published in 1887, but post-dated to 1888.]

Auld Licht Idylls, London: Hodder and Stoughton, 1888.

When a Man's Single, London: Hodder and Stoughton, 1888.

An Edinburgh Eleven, London: Office of the "British Weekly," 1889.

A Window in Thrums, London: Hodder and Stoughton, 1889.

My Lady Nicotine, London: Hodder and Stoughton, 1890.

The Little Minister. London: Cassell and Company, 1891.

Sentimental Tommy. London: Cassell and Company, 1896.

Margaret Ogilvy. New York: Charles Scribner's Sons, 1896. [The American edition preceded the British edition by one month.]

Tommy and Grizel. London: Cassell and Company, 1900.

The Little White Bird. London: Hodder and Stoughton, 1902.

Peter Pan in Kensington Gardens. London: Hodder and Stoughton, 1906. [Illustrations by Arthur Rackham.]

Peter and Wendy. London: Hodder and Stoughton, 1911. [Illustrations by F. D. Bedford.]

Farewell, Miss Julie Logan. London: Hodder and Stoughton, 1932. First published in a Christmas supplement to *The Times*, London, December 24, 1931.

The Greenwood Hat. London: Peter Davies, 1938. Preface by the Earl Baldwin of Bewdley. A collection of early journalistic writings interspersed with Barrie's later reminiscences.

M'Connachie & J. M. B. New York: Scribner's, 1939. Preface by Hugh Walpole. A collection of Barrie's speeches.

Letters edited by Viola Meynell. New York: Scribner's, 1947.

When Wendy Grew Up: An Afterthought, Foreword by Sydney Blow. New York: Dutton, 1957.

C. *Plays*

Richard Savage. 1891. [Privately printed.] Written in collaboration with H. B. Marriott Watson.

The Wedding Guest. New York. Charles Scribner's Sons, 1900.

Walker, London. London: Samuel French, 1907.

Quality Street. London: Hodder and Stoughton, 1913.

Half Hours. New York: Charles Scribner's Sons, 1914. [Contains *Pantaloon, The Twelve-Pound Look, Rosalind*, and *The Will*.]

The Admirable Crichton. London: Hodder and Stoughton, 1914.

Der Tag. London: Hodder and Stoughton, 1914. A topical playlet directed against the Kaiser.

Echoes of the War. London: Hodder and Stoughton, 1918. [Contains *The Old Lady Shows Her Medals, The New Word, Barbara's Wedding*, and *A Well-Remembered Voice*.]

Note: the Uniform Edition of the Plays (London: Hodder and Stoughton, 1918-38), contains first editions of the following plays not separately published before 1938: *What Every Woman Knows, Alice Sit-by-the-Fire, A Kiss for Cinderella, Dear Brutus, Mary Rose, Peter Pan*, and *The Boy David*.

D. *Unauthorized Collections of Fiction and Miscellaneous Prose*

Jess. Boston: Dana Estes, 1898.

A Holiday in Bed and Other Sketches. New York: New York Publishing Company, 1892.

An Auld Licht Manse. New York: John Knox, 1893.

A Tillyloss Scandal. New York: Lovell, Coryell Company, 1893.

Two of Them. New York: Lovell, Coryell Company, 1893.

A Powerful Drug. New York: J. S. Ogilvie, 1893.

Life in a Country Manse. New York: J. S. Ogilvie, 1894.

SECONDARY SOURCES

A. *Bibliographies*

BLOCK, ANDREW. *Sir James Barrie: His First Editions; Points and Values.* London: W. & G. Foyle Ltd., 1933. Of little bibliographical value. Lists first editions of the major works and gives sale prices current during 1932-33. Block's introduction notices that the Depression had not significantly affected the price of first editions of Barrie and concludes therefrom that this "stability in price . . . might be claimed by the enthusiast as an indication of the intrinsic value of . . . [Barrie's] writing."

CUTLER, B. D. *Sir James M. Barrie: A Bibliography.* New York: Greenberg, 1931. Useful but not definitive; generally inferior to Garland in coverage of periodical material.

GARLAND, HERBERT. *A Bibliography of the Writings of Sir James Matthew Barrie Bart., O. M.* London: The Bookman's Journal, 1928. Authoritative to 1927, but not definitive. Gives details of Barrie's "editiones princeps," and a substantial listing of contributions to books and periodicals; also contains a short and quite inadequate list of secondary sources.

B. *Biographies and Literary Studies*

ASQUITH, LADY CYNTHIA. *Portrait of Barrie.* London: Barrie, 1954. Mainly of biographical interest; an affectionate study by a close friend and fervent admirer.

BLAKE, GEORGE. *Barrie and the Kailyard School.* London: A. Barker, 1951. Indispensable reading for anyone seriously concerned with Barrie and his Kailyard contemporaries. Blake makes no attempt at a full-length study of Barrie, but nevertheless succeeds in a few brief pages in writing more perceptively about J. M. B. than any other critic. The book is concise and enlivened by some delightful irony.

BRAYBROOKE, PATRICK. *J. M. Barrie: A Study in Fairies and Mortals.* London: Drane's, 1924. A superficial, poorly written book that frequently parades blind admiration in the guise of literary criticism. Typical of many "studies" of Barrie by his first generation of "critics."

CHALMERS, P. R. *The Barrie Inspiration.* London: Peter Davies, 1938. The "Inspiration" did not find its way to this book, which is even worse than Braybrooke's: a "masterpiece" of disorganized trivia. About two-thirds of the book is rambling, undocumented biographical gossip, utilizing lengthy quotations from Barrie. The rest is a superficial commentary on some haphazardly chosen novels and plays. Chapter VI provides a sketchy discussion of Barrie's use of Scots dialect, and Chapter

VIII argues unconvincingly that Barrie wrote Daisy Ashford's *The Young Visiters.*

DARTON, F. J. H. *J. M. Barrie.* London: Nisbet & Co., 1929. Another study by a fervent admirer whose admiration often impedes the exercise of his critical faculties. However, it is a better-written and far more concise treatment that the other panegyrics; and it also manages to survey most of Barrie's works.

GREEN, ROGER LANCELYN. *Fifty Years of Peter Pan.* London: Peter Davies, 1954. A very useful survey of the theatrical history of Barrie's most popular play, with some enlightening chapters on the sources and genesis of Peter Pan.

———. *J. M. Barrie.* New York: H. Z. Walck, 1961. The best short study of Barrie. A well-informed and lucid monograph with a useful bibliography. Green helpfully provides a listing of all of Barrie's unpublished and uncollected plays.

HAMMERTON, SIR JOHN A. *J. M. Barrie and his Books.* London: Horace Marshall & Son, 1900. An early admirer's study of the man and his novels. Of little critical significance, the book remains useful for its factual information on Barrie's career in journalism.

———. *Barrie: the Story of a Genius.* London: Sampson Low & Co., 1929. An attempt at a definitive biography that provides generally reliable factual information, but is superficial in all other respects. Mackail's biography supersedes this one.

———. *Barrieland: A Thrums Pilgrimage.* London: Sampson Low & Co., [1929]. A discursive, "nostalgic" account of Hammerton's tour of the Kirriemuir and Forfar area. Contains sixteen photographs of the district. This book is evidently written for "literary tourists"—for people who prefer tours to literature but like to believe that they are acquiring culture en route.

KENNEDY, JOHN. *Thrums and the Barrie Country.* London: Heath Cranton, 1930. Traces Barrie's connection with Forfar and the Kirriemuir district. Serves much the same purpose as the preceding book by Hammerton. It is, however, somewhat more useful to the student of Barrie because it provides some historical background to the Auld Lichts. Contains also seventeen photographs of the Thrums country and a sketch map of the area.

MACKAIL, DENIS. *The Story of J. M. B.* London: Peter Davies, 1941. The "standard biography" of Barrie. Rich in factual material, but perversely written and lacking documentation and an adequate index.

MOULT, THOMAS. *Barrie.* London: Jonathan Cape, 1928. Uneven critical study. Moult saw Barrie as the leader of a reaction to

Ibsenism, but his commentary, which encompasses most of Barrie's work, does not effectively substantiate this idea.

ROY, JAMES A. *James Matthew Barrie.* London: Jarrolds, 1937. Among the most readable of biographical and critical studies. Not, however, very original in its use of biographical material nor very perceptive in its overdefensive "appreciation" of Barrie in the face of widespread reaction against or indifference to his work.

WALBROOK, H. M. *J. M. Barrie and the Theatre.* London: F. V. White & Co., 1922. Yet another study by an early admirer of Barrie's theatrical fantasies. Now of interest primarily as a record of contemporary reactions to the original productions of the plays.

C. *Articles*

BAILHACHE, J. "Le Sentimentalisme de Barrie," *Etudes Anglaises,* II (1938), 113-19. A perceptive reaction to British critical assessments of Barrie. The writer observes: "Considerée dans son ensemble, l'oeuvre de Barrie nous révèle que sa personnalité est celle d'un être inquiet à l'âme déchirée par les lois du réel, même s'il n'ose ou n'aime l'avouer, même si ses critiques anglo-saxons . . . se plaisent à imaginer un Barrie réaliste et énergique auquel ils puissent accorder les sympathies que l'auteur de *Peter Pan* avait inquiétées."

BEERBOHM, MAX. "Child Barrie," *Theatre Arts,* xxxviii (November, 1954), 18-20. This article was originally published in the London *Saturday Review,* January 7, 1905; and it reappears as a section of Beerbohm's *Around Theatres* (London: 1930). The reprint in *Theatre Arts* celebrated the success of the Broadway musical of *Peter Pan* with Mary Martin as Peter and Cyril Ritchard as Hook. Beerbohm's article discusses some of the ways in which Barrie's mind worked like a child's: "Mr. Barrie is not that rare creature, a man of genius. He is something even more rare–a child who, by some divine grace, can express through an artistic medium the childishness that is in him."

CHILD, H. H. "Barrie as a dramatist," *Saturday Review of Literature,* XXXII (January 29, 1949), 34-37. Mainly a review of the so-called Definitive Edition of Barrie's plays, edited by A. E. Wilson. Child regrets the omission of many one-acts. He also discusses certain "fixed ideas" that Barrie "played with"–the brave woman idea, father and son awkwardness, and baby worship.

DALE, A. "Peter Pan's Pater," *Cosmopolitan,* LII (May, 1912). 793-96. Unsubtle but interesting interview with Barrie in which the dramatist reveals that he wrote *The Twelve-Pound Look* in one day, that his favorites among his works were *Peter Pan, The Admirable Crichton,* and *The Twelve-Pound Look;* that he disliked writing *Alice Sit-by-the-Fire* and *Quality Street;* and that Act I of *What Every Woman Knows* is the only part of the play that has any "significance."

JELIFFE, S. E. and BRINK, L. "The Healing Function of the Dream." *Psychoanalysis and the Drama.* Nervous and Mental Diseases Monograph Series No. 34 (1922), 130-48. A discussion of the idea that the dream episode in *Dear Brutus* has a function analogous to that of dream analysis in psychoanalytic therapy.

MCGRAW, WILLIAM R. "J. M. Barrie's Concept of Dramatic Action," *Modern Drama,* V, 2 (September, 1962), 133-41. Acute study of some of the reasons for the critical reaction against Barrie. McGraw observes that Barrie "was a practitioner of deception and trickery par excellence. His plays are replete with devices to restrict one's attention to the immediate action. . . . Barrie's habit was to utilize the physical stage in a manner that might visualize . . . action as literally as possible." The article illustrates with examples from the plays how the dramatist moved toward elimination of dialogue for static, pantomimic effects, and how humor and idea in Barrie are conveyed principally through physical action.

MORTON, E. "Mr. J. M. Barrie as a Dramatist," *Bookman,* XXXII (October, 1910), p. 308. Discussion of Barrie's first dramatic work–his co-authorship with H. B. Marriott-Watson of the play *Richard Savage.* Morton endeavors, with the wisdom of hindsight, to distinguish Barrie's incipient dramatic genius from Marriott-Watson's mediocrity.

PEARSON, HESKETH. "Pinero and Barrie," *Theatre Arts,* XLII (July, 1958), 56-59. Hesketh Pearson's personal recollections of two dramatists. He first met Barrie in 1920, during a revival of *The Admirable Crichton.* Interesting primarily for its quoted remark of Shaw on Barrie: He "had a frightfully gloomy mind which he unfortunately could not afford to express in his plays . . ."; and also for Barrie's comment on *Better Dead*: "I think it awful. I should like to destroy every copy in existence."

PHELPS, W. L. "Plays of J. M. Barrie," *North American Review,* CCXII (December, 1920), 829-43. Brief survey of Barrie's dramatic output through *Dear Brutus.* Phelps suggests "unconditional surrender" is the only "intelligent attitude" to take to Barrie's plays. Contains a lengthy, valuable analysis of *The Admirable Crichton,* which, Phelps maintains, is "the greatest English drama of modern times. I doubt if we shall ever penetrate to the last significance, to the final essence of this play." Typical of many early articles overrating Barrie's importance.

STEVENSON, LIONEL. "A Source for Barrie's *Peter Pan,*" *Philological Quarterly,* VII (1929), 210-14. Argues convincingly that the structural framework and some of the narrative elements of *Peter and Wendy* and *Peter Pan* are derived from *Lilith* (1895), an horrific allegory for adults by George MacDonald, one of the founders of the Kailyard school and the author of a once-popular children's fantasy called *At the Back of the North Wind,* (1871).

WILKINSON, LOUIS. "Sir James Barrie, Confectioner and Parlour-Magician," *Dial,* LXXV (August, 1923), 167-69. A pioneer article in the reaction against Barrie who is described as a purveyor of "easy pretty illusions, and . . . agreeable fantasies" and a writer of "middle-class drawing-room humour . . . always safe." Barrie's treatment of love and sex is "a sort of obscene decency," and he takes refuge in sentimentalism because he is ashamed of passion and therefore lies about it.

Index

(The works of Barrie are listed under his name.)